While your body res_____ ___ ___ ___ __sy sending messages that can help you in your waking hours—messages that you can't afford to ignore. By deciphering your dreams, you can begin to learn more about your true self.

- HORSE—if a man dreams of horses, he probably is giving voice to an unconscious desire to be more attractive to women or to an unconscious fear that he is losing his virility.

- CAR—a person who dreams that he is driving a car may be expressing the feeling that he should be moving toward a certain goal.

- DRINKING—to dream of drinking might be to voice feelings of dissatisfaction about the dreamer's perceived lack of will power, self-control, etc.

- ELEVATOR—if you dream that you are in an ascending elevator, you may be expressing your belief or hope that your fortunes are rising, or your desire to go up in the world.

- SOAP—soap is a symbol of cleanliness. To dream of soap is generally to express feelings of guilt (hence, the desire to be cleansed), or the desire to perform some act which violates your moral code (after the performance of which you will feel the need to be cleansed).

- FIRE—fire symbolizes both death and sexual intercourse. To dream of fire is to reveal death wishes, or sexual desire.

What Your Dreams Mean

By Alan Davis

BANTAM BOOKS

TORONTO · NEW YORK · LONDON · SYDNEY · AUCKLAND

WHAT YOUR DREAMS MEAN

*A Bantam Book / published by arrangement with
Workman Publishing Company*

Bantam edition / June 1969

2nd printing . . . October 1969	8th printing . . January 1977
3rd printing . . . . March 1971	9th printing . . . . . July 1978
4th printing . . . . . June 1972	10th printing . September 1979
5th printing . . . . . . June 1973	11th printing . . January 1981
6th printing . . . August 1974	12th printing . November 1981
7th printing . . . . . April 1976	13th printing . . . August 1982
14th printing . . . September 1984	

ISBN 0-553-24843-X

Published simultaneously in the United States and Canada

PRINTED IN THE UNITED STATES OF AMERICA

H   23 22 21 20 19 18 17 16 15

CONTENTS

INTRODUCTION
    by Dr. Paul J. Gillette   1

PART I: HOW TO USE YOUR DREAM DICTIONARY   7
    1. What Science Knows About Dreams
       and Dreaming   10
    2. How to Keep a Dream Log   13
    3. What to Look for When Interpreting
       a Dream   17
    4. Sample Dreams and Interpretations   20
    5. Lucky Dream Numbers   29
    6. Interpreting Your Own Dreams   33

PART II: DREAM DICTIONARY   37

PART III: YOUR DREAM LOG   139

What
Your
Dreams
Mean

INTRODUCTION

Do our dreams have meaning?

Are these nightly visions actually scenarios which we ourselves invent to hint at powerful motivations, feelings and desires which are deeply repressed in our waking lives?

Or, are dreams no more than fleeting impressions, reflecting only inconsequential events, momentary physical discomforts, or random thoughts left over from the day?

There is strong disagreement among psychologists, psychiatrists and other experts in this field. Some schools of thought believe that dreams may not have any particular significance—or that it is impossible to interpret dreams with any scientific accuracy. Others, equally competent, are convinced that dreams do mean something—and that they symbolize thoughts which we suppress because they are too painful for us to express and face consciously.

What school of thought, then, are we to believe?

Under the framework of logic we call "the scientific method"—a reasoning process which dates back to Aristotle—the burden of proof lies with the proposer. This means that before I can validly state that a proposition is true I must prove that it is true. No one has yet proved the proposition that dreams are meaningful.

But the fact that no one has proved that dreams *are* meaningful cannot be taken as proof that they are *not* meaningful. This latter proposition must be proved also, and—so far, anyway—it hasn't been. Thus, until further evidence is forthcoming, the only valid statement which can be made on the subject is that *maybe* dreams are meaningful and maybe they aren't.

Scientists, of course, are notoriously intolerant of the word, "maybe." It challenges their sense of discovery. It affronts their desire for orderliness. In short, it makes them nervous. And so, when a maybe-situation arises, they search feverishly for data which might lead to its resolution.

Their search generally takes the form of an intellectual game which might be called, "Let's pretend." With respect to the meaningfulness of dreams, the process works something like this:

I realize that dreams may and then again may not be meaningful. So, for the purposes of investigation, I pretend (or, in the term which scientists prefer, I hypothesize) that they are meaningful, and I study them as if they were. I record numerous dreams, and I attempt to apply their content to phenomena in the waking lives of the dreamers. Then, when I've found parallels, I seek to explain the waking-life phenomena in terms of the dream content and/or to explain the dream content in terms of the waking-life phenomena. If my explanations are plausible, I've succeeded in constructing a theory of dream interpretation.

A theory, of course, is only a theory—not a universally-acceptable law. But it provides other scientists with a point of departure from which to launch their own investigations. And it enables students of the subject to form tentative conclusions about their own dreams and the dreams of others—conclusions which will be valid if my theory is valid. An element of doubt is always present, for the initial "maybe" remains unresolved. But tentative conclusions are better than no conclusions at all, so the enterprise is not entirely without merit.

The theory of dream interpretation which enjoys the widest acceptance among scientists today is that of Sigmund Freud (1856-1939). It is this theory, as built upon by behavioral scientists Carl Jung, Wilhelm Stekel, Louis S. London, Emil Gutheil and others, which serves as the basis for Alan Davis' *What Your Dreams Mean.*

Let's talk a little about the theory. Freud's primary hypothesis—the hypothesis which is at the basis of all psychodynamic thinking—is that humans have two mental levels, a "conscious" level and an "unconscious" level. Thoughts which we ourselves are aware of (the thought, for example, that today is a lovely day, or that I'd better get busy if I want to finish a certain job on time, or that

I'd like to date a certain girl) are said to exist on a "conscious" level. Thoughts of which we are unaware—if, indeed, there are such thoughts—are said to exist on the "unconscious" level. (Examples of such thoughts: I wish that my best friend would die; I want to have sexual relations with my mother.) Because such thoughts are too horrible for us to accept, Freud reasoned, we "suppress" them—that is, we shut our "conscious" minds to them, whereupon they take up dwelling in our "unconscious" minds.

Having thus established hypothetically a second, subsurface (or "unconscious") mental level, Freud proceeded to find examples of human behavior which appeared to be motivated by thoughts existing at this level. He reasoned, for example, that certain feelings of faintness and nausea which overcame him every time he approached the cemetery where his father was buried meant that he unconsciously hated his father. He further reasoned that the inability of one of his patients to experience sensation in her legs was the result of the patient's "unconscious" belief that she should be punished for certain sins of which she believed herself guilty. And, in both his own dreams and the dreams of his patients, he found certain actions, objects, characters and settings which appeared to be symbolic expressions of similar "unconscious" sentiments, beliefs, fears, anxieties and desires.

By the time that Jung, Stekel, London, Gutheil and other dream analysts had added their contributions to the subject, the list of dream actions, objects, characters and settings which appeared to symbolize "unconscious" thoughts was formidable. Indeed, some analysts maintained that *every* dream action, object, character and setting was symbolic of something, and that failure of an analyst to find symbolic meaning for the action, object, character or setting in question meant that the analyst had to search more diligently for a meaning, not that the action, object, character or setting in question was without meaning. Most dream analysts, however, took the position that some actions, objects, characters and settings are significant and others are not, the determining factor being what the analyst has learned about the waking life of the person being analyzed.

It is this position which is most generally accepted by

dream analysts today, and it is this position which Alan Davis' *What Your Dreams Mean* takes. *What Your Dreams Mean* lists actions, objects, characters and settings which seem most often to be significant when they appear in dreams, and it supplies the classical interpretations which most commonly seem to apply. The author points out: "Most definitions in *What Your Dreams Mean* offer a variety of possible interpretations—some of which may even seem contradictory. What you, [the reader], must now do is decide, based on your own knowledge of yourself, which of these interpretations apply to your dream."

All well and good. But, in using *What Your Dreams Mean* you must be careful not to lose sight of the fact that any conclusions you may form are only tentative conclusions. Freud's fundamental hypothesis is still only a hypothesis, not a law—and the possibility always exists that your dreams may not mean anything at all.

This doesn't mean that use of *What Your Dreams Mean* is an exercise in futility. Anything which forces you to think about yourself will help you gain insights into what it is that motivates you, what it is that makes you tick. If you inquire into the possibility that you might "unconsciously" hate your mother, you'll be examining your feelings toward her—even if there is no such thing as "unconscious" thought. And, by examining your feelings toward her, you'll be learning something about the way you operate. Also, you'll be paving the way for more harmonious relations with her, and for more harmonious relations with everyone else you have dealings with. Polonius' advice to Hamlet, "Know thyself," was sound when it was offered, and it remains sound today. Attempting to analyze your dreams is one way to contribute to your self-knowledge, and self-knowledge is a quality not to be despised.

Also, remember that while Freud's fundamental hypothesis has not been proved, neither has it been disproved. If dreams do in fact reveal symbolically the sentiments, beliefs, fears, anxieties and desires which in waking life we "consciously" do not acknowledge, your dreams may tell you a great deal about yourself. The operative word here is "maybe." Scientists may hate it, but, in dream analysis, it's a necessary evil. If you say to yourself,

"This dream means such-and-such," you'll be flirting with self-delusion. If you say, "This dream *may* mean such-and-such," you'll be following a path at the end of which might lie a great deal of self-knowledge. Polonius would love you for it.

One last point. While *What Your Dreams Mean* is not exactly comprehensive, it does contain the standard interpretations for most maybe-significant dream actions, objects, characters and settings. If you use it per instructions, you won't necessarily become as proficient a dream analyst as the behavioral scientists who specialize in dream analysis. But you'll be pretty proficient. When you reach that state, don't let your zeal for the subject entice you to go around analyzing other peoples' dreams. The key to dream analysis is knowledge of the person being analyzed, and, while you have that knowledge about yourself, you don't have it about other people—nor are you trained to elicit it, as psychologists, psychiatrists and other behavioral scientists are.

Okay, so much for this writer's thoughts on dream analysis. *What Your Dreams Mean* is yours. Use it. Good night, and pleasant dreams.

Paul J. Gillette, Ph.D.
Carbondale, Pennsylvania
June, 1968

PART I

HOW TO USE YOUR DREAM DICTIONARY

Everybody dreams—even people who claim that they don't. In fact, experiments conducted by scientists over the past two decades have proved conclusively that there is no person who does not have several dreams every single night of his life. *What Your Dreams Mean* will show you how to interpret your dreams. But, before consulting individual listings in the dictionary section, read carefully all the material in this first section—for only by becoming thoroughly familiar with the theoretical aspects of dream interpretation can you hope to use the dictionary profitably.

Part I is divided into five subsections: (1) *What Science Knows About Dreams and Dreaming;* (2) *How to Keep a Dream Log;* (3) *What to Look for When Interpreting a Dream;* (4) *Sample Dreams and their Interpretations;* (5) *Lucky Dream Numbers.* Read all five subsections in the order in which they are presented. Do not go on to another subsection until you are certain that you understand completely all the material in the earlier subsections. Then, when you have mastered all five subsections, you will be ready to start keeping your own dream log—and to begin interpreting your own dreams.

1 // What Science Knows About Dreams and Dreaming

The first scientific studies of the physiology of the human activity known as dreaming were begun in 1953 by a research assistant at the University of Chicago, Dr. Eugene Aserinsky. While studying the sleep habits of newborn babies, Dr. Aserinsky noticed that at regular intervals the eyes of sleeping babies would move very rapidly behind the babies' closed eyelids. Sometimes these periods of rapid eye movement would be as brief as ten minutes; at other times they would last for as long as half an hour.

Dr. Aserinsky then attached electroencephalographs— machines which measure brain-wave patterns—to the infants' heads. The brain-wave patterns recorded during the infants' periods of rapid eye movement bore a marked similarity to the brain-wave patterns of infants who were awake. Theorizing that the rapid eye movements meant that the infants were dreaming, Dr. Aserinsky assembled a test group of adult volunteers who agreed to allow him to observe them while they slept. As he had expected, every one of the sleepers exhibited the same rapid eye movements as the infants. And, when awakened during the rapid-eye-movement (or R.E.M.) state, every one of the sleepers reported that he had just been dreaming.

Other researchers took up where Dr. Aserinsky left off, and today it is commonly accepted that the R.E.M. and dream states are synonymous. Further, scientists have proved that dreaming is not only an experience common to all men but also is a vitally necessary activity. Persons who have been deprived of dream-time by being awakened every time an R.E.M. period began, automatically began having more and more R.E.M. periods, as if they were trying to make up for lost dream-time. And those who continued to undergo dream deprivation soon became restless and irritable in their waking lives. Some even began to display the symptoms of serious mental disturbance. Dreaming, the scientists were able to conclude, is necessary to maintain a normal mental balance.

Having thus ascertained that dreaming is both a universal and an essential function among humans, researchers sought to discover why we dream. So far a number of interesting and highly complex hypotheses have been advanced. But no scientist can yet say for sure that he knows why we dream. All that science knows for certain is that everyone does dream and that everyone must dream if he is to remain psychologically healthy. Some people may think that they do not dream; but, in these cases, what really happens is that the individual forgets his dreams—perhaps because it is emotionally too painful for him to remember them.

In any case, the average dreamer is far less interested in knowing why he dreams than in knowing what his dreams mean. And, on this count, science has a great many answers for him. Indeed, long before the discovery of R.E.M. states and of the universality of dreaming, psychologists and psychiatrists were inquiring deeply into the meaning of dreams.

The first scientist to do so was Dr. Sigmund Freud, the Viennese father of psychoanalysis, who theorized that man uses dreams to portray symbolically his innermost fears, hopes, tensions and hostilities. In other words, according to Freud, each object, each character, each setting and each action which appears in a dream may be symbolic of a hidden—or, to use Freud's word, unconscious—fear, hope or desire.

Freud's theories are by no means universally accepted. However, a vast majority of modern psychologists and psychiatrists do agree that dreams are symbolically meaningful. Among these psychologists and psychiatrists are the famed Drs. Carl Jung, Wilhelm Stekel, Louis S. London and Emil Guthiel. The interpretations which appear in this Dream Dictionary are, in effect, a translation into layman's language of the concepts advanced by these distinguished scientists. When you use the Dream Dictionary to interpret your dreams, you will thus be applying the principles of dream analysis pioneered by Freud and advanced by his colleagues and disciples.

2 / How to Keep a Dream Log

The first step in analyzing your dreams will be to begin keeping a dream log. A dream log is a nightly record of every dream you have and of every character, object, setting and action which appears in each dream.

This log is extremely important, because dreams are meaningful only in relation to other dreams and in relation to what you know about yourself as a person. If you attempt to analyze individual dream symbols or fragments of dreams without relating them to your other dreams and to what you know about yourself as a person, you will accomplish nothing. In order to understand fully what your dreams mean you must study *all* your dreams, *as a whole* and seek recurrent themes and patterns of symbolism.

Here is how to keep a dream log:

First, keep a pad and pencil at your bedside at all times. Then, every time you wake up after a dream, immediately write down everything you can remember about that dream. These are the key points to note:

(A) *Characters.* List every character who appeared in your dream, including yourself. Some will be individuals whom you know personally—your friends, your co-workers, members of your family. Others may be persons you know only by sight or by name—perhaps a famous movie star, or a leading politician, or a man you saw on a bus. Still others will be persons you do not know but who appear in certain familiar roles—for example, as a physician, or a fireman, or an airplane pilot.

Record the name of every person you know and also the role in which he appears. For instance, if your best friend appears in the dream as a barber or as a bus driver, make a note of this fact. Or if a famous politician appears as your dentist or as a traffic policeman, note this also. Then record the role of every dream character whom you do not know by sight or by name—for example, note that the people in your dream included an anonymous bartender, an anonymous television announcer or an anonymous baseball player. Finally, record also the appearance in the dream of any nonhuman animals—dogs, cats, fish, birds, etc. Distinguish between animals you know individually, such as your own household pets, and animals who do not have any specific identity to you.

(B) *Objects*. List every inanimate object which appears in your dream. For example, you may dream that you are playing cards. The cards themselves will be one object which you will list. Another will be the table on which you are playing—perhaps it's your kitchen table, or a card table at a friend's house, or a picnic bench at an amusement park. Other objects may include money, if the game is being played for stakes; poker chips, if they are being used; a pencil and paper, if you happen to be keeping score (and be sure to note whether you or another dream character is the scorekeeper); food and drinks, if they are being served, and any other object which may appear in the dream. It is absolutely essential that you record every object you can remember.

(C) *Setting*. Describe the locale where the dream takes place. Are you on an airplane? In a bus? At home? Note this—and, of course, if your dream contains more than one such setting, note each setting.

(D) *Action*. Describe exactly what takes place in the dream, with special emphasis on who does what and to whom. For example, you may dream that you're riding in a car which stops at a fishing pier, after which you get out. Some of the actions which you should note are: Who is the driver of the car—you or another person? Why are you going to the fishing pier—is it your idea or someone else's? Why did you get out when the car stopped—were you asked to leave or did you do so of your own accord? Was a radio playing while you were riding? Did you see anything along the road? Who else was in the car with you? Where were these other people sitting? Did any of them do or say anything to you? Did any conversation take place which didn't involve you? What were your feelings toward the other people in the car—did you like or dislike them, were you comfortable with them, were you afraid of any of them? Was any aspect of the ride particularly pleasing or displeasing to you? All these factors are important.

We repeat, write down all these details as soon as you awake—even if it is in the middle of the night, and even if you awake several times during the same night. The importance of recording a dream immediately cannot be overstressed, for the memory of a dream tends to fade very quickly and if you wait until you get up in the morning, you may forget many important details. Also, be sure to write down *every* detail you can remember, no matter how minor or unimportant it may seem to you. A detail which may seem insignificant at first may become very significant days or weeks later when viewed in relation to other dreams.

Next, when you finally do get up in the morning, review everything you have written in your log. Perhaps you will now remember some details of your dreams which you failed to record initially. Record these new details at this time. Then put the log away until evening, by which time the emotional impact of your dreams will have worn off and you will be able to analyze the dreams objectively and in an unbiased frame of mind.

After dinner, when the cares and chores of the day are behind you, take out your dream log again and reread it. Underline every person, object, setting and action in each dream you recorded. Then look up each underlined word in the *What Your Dreams Mean*. When you have defined every underlined word on your list, you will have the raw material from which your dream analysis can be built. Most definitions in *What Your Dreams Mean* offer a variety of possible interpretations—some of which may even seem contradictory. What you must now do is decide, based on your own knowledge of yourself, which of these interpretations apply to your dream. At first this will be difficult, because the whole process of dream analysis will be new to you—and because you will not have a great many dreams in your log from which to draw conclusions. But, as days pass and as new dreams are added, you will find that certain underlined words appear in your log regularly. These recurrent words will be the key to understanding your dreams. Note the words—and the definitions—which appear most often. Soon you will see a pattern take form, and this pattern will tell you what you want to know about yourself.

A final and most important point: when interpreting your dreams, you must be completely honest with yourself. Rejection of an interpretation because it displeases you or because it doesn't conform with your image of yourself will defeat the whole purpose of your analysis. You are analyzing your dreams because you want to discover the *real you*—the you which is not apparent in your waking life, which only appears under the protective cover of dreaming. If you are willing to face the whole truth about yourself, dream analysis can help you discover that real you and, by self-discovery, you can free yourself from the inner fears and anxieties which haunt your dreams and your unconscious mind.

3 / What to Look for When Interpreting a Dream

As has been noted in the previous subsection, you should record every character, object, setting and action which appears in your dream; then you should look up each entry from your dream log in *What Your Dreams Mean*. However, not all these entries will be of equal importance when you begin interpreting your dreams. Here are some of the things to look for when trying to decide which of your entries are important and which are not:

(A) Recurrent characters and/or themes. The surest indication of a dream symbol's importance is the fact that it appears again and again in your dreams. This applies especially to characters and themes. If a certain person —say your best friend, or your employer, or even a national personality whom you do not know personally— appears regularly in your dreams, you can be sure that this person is significant in your life. The same is true on a symbolic level with character-types which do not have a specific identity to you—for example, a physician, or a cook, or a clergyman. When such characters appear with regularity in your dreams, examine the symbolism attached to them in *What Your Dreams Mean* and attempt to apply this symbolism to problems in your everyday life. Also, if themes recur in your dreams—for instance, the theme that you are being chased by someone, or that you are boarding an airplane or ship or other such conveyance—attempt to discover parallels in your life to which the symbolism of these themes will be relevant.

(B) Recurrent patterns of symbolism. Some objects and actions which appear in dreams have a great deal in common symbolically, even though they have nothing in common on a non-symbolic level. For example, a pencil, a candle, a bull and a bottle are all symbols of masculine virility, even though they are not in any way similar on a non-symbolic level. If such symbols appear regularly in

17

your dreams, explore your real life for situations, thoughts, fears or desires to which they may pertain.

(C) Familiar persons in unusual roles. If someone you know appears in your dreams, chances are that the appearance is without significance—for we often dream of people and things which are on our minds. However, if a familiar person appears in your dream in an unusual role —if, for example, your wife appears as a physician or as a bus driver, or if your best friend appears as an actor or as the President of the United States—the appearance of this person in such a decidedly unfamiliar role may be very significant. Examine the symbolism of the role in question as set forth in the *What Your Dreams Mean* and attempt to apply the dictionary's interpretation to your own life.

(D) Appearance of persons whom you ordinarily wouldn't think of in your waking life. If you dream of someone whom you normally wouldn't think of while awake—for example, a relative or friend whom you have not seen for many years—chances are that the person may represent something very significant to you.

(E) Your own appearance in an unusual role. If you appear in your own dream in an unusual role—say, as a bartender, or a dentist, or an airplane pilot—the symbolism of this role may be quite significant.

(F) Your own appearance or the appearance of another person in a different age-category or life-situation. If you are, say, forty years old, and if in your dream you appear as a teen-ager or as a child, this can be extremely significant. The same applies if another person you know appears in your dream in a different age-category or life-situation.

(G) Events which seem to have no relevance to your present life. A very common type of dream is what psychologists and psychiatrists call a "current events" dream. This is the re-creation in dreams of a situation in which you recently found yourself. Such dreams obviously are relevant to your present life and, as such, generally are not very significant—for we often dream of things which are on our minds. However, if you dream of an event which does not fit this category, an event which seems to have no relevance whatsoever to your present life, chances are very good that the dream will be significant.

(H) Dreams which provoke violent fear-reactions. Such dreams are generally described as "nightmares." The dreamer wakes in an extremely frightened state and may be unable to go back to sleep for hours. Sometimes he is so frightened that he cries out during his dream, or falls out of bed, or begins weeping profusely. Dreams which provoke such violent reactions usually are very significant.

Some other things to keep in mind when interpreting dreams:

(A) We often dream in fragments. In other words, a person will be having a certain dream, then the setting and characters will abruptly change and he will be having a different dream. When you dream in fragments of this sort, record each fragment as a separate dream and attempt to interpret it accordingly. Do not make any attempt to link together the different fragments unless there is an obvious connection.

(B) We often dream in "pictorial shorthand." In other words, events in a dream shift rapidly and often without any apparent reason. Do not be concerned with the transitions of action which you feel should be present but which are not. Record the dream as you dreamed it, and interpret it accordingly.

(C) A person may pass many nights without remembering a dream. Scientists have demonstrated that everyone dreams several times each night. However, few if any of us will remember all his dreams. You may pass several nights, or even several weeks, without remembering a dream. If this is the case, do not be concerned. Simply record all the details of each dream that you can remember. Generally you will find that the longer you work at dream analysis the more dreams you will remember and the more details you will remember of each dream.

4 / Sample Dreams and Their Interpretations

Now that you know how to keep a dream log and what to look for in a dream, let us examine a sample dream log and the interpretations which might be applied to the entries which it contains. The dreams which follow were taken from an actual dream log, kept by a twenty-two-year-old secretary, a divorcee with a four-year-old son. First we will consider the dreams just as she recorded them. Then we will interpret them in the light of what the dreamer knew about herself.

Monday night: I am on a pier with a lot of people, getting ready to board a ship. Somehow I begin to wander off by myself, and I find myself in a maze of dark buildings. I can't get out of the maze; the more I wander around, the more entangled I seem to get. Then, suddenly, I am back on the pier. But the ship has left. I can see all the others on the deck, laughing and dancing, but I can't get on board. It is too late.

Tuesday night: No dreams.

Wednesday night: I am walking down the road with my son. I am carrying an old man on my back. The man is one of the executives at the office where I work. I like him very much, and I don't mind carrying him although he is very heavy. We have a dog with us and someone else is there too; I think it is my sister. Suddenly the dog runs out into the middle of the road and I have to rescue him from an oncoming car. I still have the old man on my back and I have to keep an eye on my little boy. Even though my sister is there, I feel that I just can't cope with everything. I'm overburdened.

Thursday night: I'm in somebody's apartment with a lot of girls I know from high school. One of them is still a close friend of mine; the others I am acquainted with only vaguely—I haven't seen or thought about them in years. All the girls are dressed in rather garish negligees and are wearing a lot of make-up. They're acting out a play in which they are prostitutes. They invite me to be in the play. I am also dressed in a sexy black negligee and black stockings. I decline their invitation to take part in the play, but I really am rather flattered that they've asked me. They insist that I join them, and finally I consent. I say something to them—I don't remember what—and the others read their lines. Then, suddenly, Joey, an ex-boy friend of mine, is in the room. I go over and sit on his lap. I can't remember anything after that.

Friday night: No dreams.

Saturday night:

Dream Number One: I have somehow fallen into a black pit. I am buried beneath hundreds of bodies. It is horrible. I try to get out, but I can't because there are too many bodies on top of me. I can hardly move. Then I wake up.

Dream Number Two: I'm imprisoned inside a typewriter. I don't know whether the typewriter has been magnified to an inordinate size or whether I've been shrunk so that I can fit inside it. Whatever the case, I'm there and I can't get out. I look out through the keys and I see my son. I call to him but he doesn't hear me. Then a lot of executives from my firm come into the room. I beg to be let out of the typewriter. One of them opens the machine and lifts me out. I tell him to put me down, but he just laughs and tosses me to one of the other men. Soon they all begin to play a kind of toss-ball, with me as the ball. I plead with my son to help me, but he also laughs and joins in the game. When he catches me he carries me to a car and puts me in the back seat. Then he gets in the front and begins to drive. I'm terrified, but he won't stop. "It's all right, mommy," he says, "we aren't going anywhere."

Sunday night: I'm on a bus with a lot of other people. The driver looks familiar to me. I think he's a physician whom I went to recently. The bus is standing still, but no one can get off. It is like being in school and waiting for the teacher to tell you when you can go home. Finally I get up and tell the driver that I'm leaving. He doesn't say anything, so I go to the door, open it and get off the bus.

As we review these dreams and consult *What Your Dreams Mean* for interpretations of the symbols which they contain, a very clear picture takes form. Knowing what we know about the secretary's personal life, we are able to analyze the dreams quite meaningfully.

In the first dream, she is on a pier with a lot of people, getting ready to board a ship. By consulting *What Your Dreams Mean* we learn that the log-entry, "ship," has a number of possible interpretations. Among these are the dreamer's desire to go somewhere new, to change his present life-situation, to better himself, to "move up in the world." In the secretary's case, the last three interpretations seem most applicable. She does not necessarily want to go someplace new, at least not in the geographic sense. But she is uncomfortable in her present life-situation: she is divorced, she has to work to support herself and her four-year-old son, she thinks of herself as missing out on the many desirable things—like love and security —which she believes that most girls of her age enjoy.

A maze, we learn from *What Your Dreams Mean,* symbolizes an impossible situation—an unresolvable riddle from which the individual cannot escape. The secretary, in her dream, wanders into the maze and cannot seem to extricate herself. Then, suddenly, she is extricated and finds herself back on the pier—but now the ship has left. The maze, it seems, represents the secretary's marriage. She was very young when she married, and she now feels that she didn't know what she was getting into. Then, when the marriage ended in divorce, she found that her "ship" had already left—in other words, that she had denied herself the happiness which she originally sought to attain. The people on board the deck are laughing and dancing; they are happy. But she can't join them, because it is too late.

Wednesday night's dream seems to symbolize the secretary's present situation. She is required to care for her son, with whom she is walking down the road. But she also is burdened with her job—symbolized by the old man whom she is carrying on her back. Although the burden is heavy, she does not mind, because she likes the old man—that is, she likes her job. But she feels that the entire situation is a bit more than she can handle.

Later in the dream, a dog that is traveling with the group runs out into the road and the secretary must rescue him from an oncoming car. Consulting *What Your Dreams Mean* we learn that dogs generally indicate the dreamer's desire for companionship and affection. Applying this interpretation to the dream at hand, we may conclude that the secretary feels that she can never have companionship or affection from other people so long as she is burdened by her job and her son.

The secretary's sister also appears in the dream, and, consulting *What Your Dreams Mean,* we learn that a sister—or any one family member—may symbolize a person's entire family. Thus, viewed as a whole, the dream suggests that the secretary fears that she can never enjoy companionship or affection because she is overburdened by her present obligations and there is no one, not even her family, to whom she can turn for help.

Thursday night's dream seems to be the restatement, in a somewhat different context, of Monday night's dream. The secretary is in an apartment with some girls with whom she had been very friendly before her marriage. The girls are acting out a play in which they are prostitutes. Consulting *What Your Dreams Mean* we learn that prostitutes in a dream generally symbolize sexual promiscuity or the surrender of sexual services for a specific reward. In the secretary's dream, this latter symbol may apply; probably the secretary feels that her girl friends have kept their marriages intact for the sake of the security which marriage provides, rather than because they love their husbands. In any case, the secretary seems to feel that her girl friends are enjoying advantages which she herself does not enjoy. The girls invite her to take up the kind of life which they are leading. She declines, then acquiesces and makes an attempt to join them. But the attempt is short-lived. She is taken from the situation by her ex-boy friend. The fact that she goes to the boy friend voluntarily suggests that she was not really serious in her attempt to join the girl friends in their prostitution-play.

The interpretation of this dream can only be tentative. The symbolism of participating in a play as prostitutes rather than actually being prostitutes is confusing. There is nothing in the dream which sheds any light on this matter, and there does not seem to be anything in the girl's waking life which can clarify the situation. However, some future dream may make things easier to understand. The prostitution dream, therefore, should be filed away for future study.

The first dream on Saturday night seems to be a restatement of all the dreams which have gone before. The secretary again finds herself in a situation from which she cannot extricate herself. When the dream ends, she is no closer to a solution of her problems than she had been at its beginning.

The presence of "bodies" in this dream is interesting. Live bodies, *What Your Dreams Mean* tells us, symbolize sexual desire. Dead bodies symbolize death fears or wishes. The secretary does not remember whether the bodies in her dream are alive or dead. However, knowing what we know about her personal life, we may guess that the bodies are alive. If such is the case, it might be theorized that the secretary's sexual desires—which originally drew her into her youthful marriage—now have led to her being imprisoned in the "pit" of her present situation.

In the second dream on Saturday night, the imprisonment theme is repeated. This time the symbolism is blatantly obvious. The girl's typewriter almost certainly represents her job, which restricts her from seeking the happiness she believes she would find were she free to explore the normal avenues for establishing new social contacts.

It is significant that the executives in the dream are tossing the girl from one to another. This is an example of circular movement, and, consulting *What Your Dreams Mean*, we learn that circular movement symbolizes being restricted by the confines of a particular situation. The fact that the executives in the dream are responsible for the secretary's circular movement reveals that she unconsciously—in real life—believes them to be responsible for her situation. This impression is, of course, erroneous; actually the executives are merely employing her under an arrangement which both she and they agreed to. Thus the dream points up the irrationality of any feelings of resentment which she may presently entertain toward her employers

It is equally significant that the secretary's son joins in on the executives' game of toss-ball. By the action of the dream, the secretary reveals that she unconsciously resents the fact that her son is responsible for her being inextricably immersed in her present situation. These feelings of resentment may manifest themselves in cruelty to the boy, or perhaps in indifference to his needs and desires. By becoming aware, through dream interpretation, of the irrationality of this resentment, the secretary can check these feelings before the boy is made to suffer because of them.

Finally, the boy in the dream puts the secretary into the back seat of a car and begins to drive. Consulting the *What Your Dreams Mean* we find that a car may symbolize a dreamer's desire to get out of an awkward or unpleasant situation. We also find that the driver of a car symbolizes a person who controls the destiny of his passengers. Thus, when the secretary dreams that her son is driving the car in which she is riding, she indicates that she regards her son as the person who could get her out of her present unpleasant situation. Then, when the boy in the dream says, "We aren't going anywhere," he is telling the secretary, in effect, that he will not get her out of the situation.

Lastly, we come to Sunday night's dream, where the secretary finds herself on a bus with a lot of other people. Via *What Your Dreams Mean* we learn that a bus, like a car, a ship or any other passenger-carrying vehicle, symbolizes the desire to escape an awkward or unpleasant situation. The fact that the bus in the secretary's dream is standing still suggests that she believes that she cannot presently escape her situation. This interpretation is substantiated by the fact that, in the secretary's dream, no one can get off the motionless bus.

The driver of the bus appears to be a physician whom the secretary recently consulted. Both roles—driver and physician—symbolize authority figures, which testify to the dreamer's desire for leadership and guidance. The secretary obviously is longing for someone to extricate her from her situation. But, as the dream reveals, no one seems willing or able to do so.

Finally, however, the secretary gets up and tells the driver that she is leaving the bus—in other words, she announces to the people in authority that she is going to extricate herself from the situation. No attempt is made to stop her, so she gets off the bus. In other words, she takes the problem in her own hands and solves it. We have no indication of precisely how she solves it. But the action of the dream testifies to a very important point: the secretary evidently has come to the realization that she can turn to no one but herself to solve her problems, that she must take things into her own hands.

Now, having interpreted the individual dreams, let us note briefly some of the procedures we followed along the way:

First, we looked up each log entry in *What Your Dreams Mean* and examined each dictionary definition for the specific interpretation or interpretations which appeared best to fit the circumstances of our particular case —*knowing what we already knew about the secretary's personal life-situation.*

Then we related the interpretations to each other, in the context of the whole dream and in the context of what we knew about the secretary's personal life-situation, to construct a meaningful total-dream interpretation.

In some cases the dream symbols were bewildering— for example, the fact that in Thursday night's dream the secretary's girl friends were playing the roles of prostitutes in a play rather than simply being prostitutes. Since we were unable to relate this curious circumstance to other factors in the secretary's dreams or in her personal life, we filed away the dream for further reference. On the other hand, when dream symbols were clear, we quickly related them to the secretary's life as we knew it—and we completed our total-dream interpretation accordingly.

Whenever we encountered a character, we inquired very carefully into the role he played both in the dream and in the secretary's personal life. Thus we took note of the fact that the bus driver in Sunday night's dream was not just an anonymous bus driver but actually a physician whom the secretary had consulted in real life, now playing the role of a bus driver in the dream. The information proved valuable to us.

Also, we were careful to note the reactions of characters in the dream. Thus, we learned that the girl friends in Thursday night's dream *wanted* the secretary to participate in their play about prostitutes—they did not merely stage the play and *permit* her to participate in it. Likewise, we noted that her son in the second dream on Saturday night was indifferent to her cries for help from inside the typewriter and that later he joined in the game of toss-ball with the executives. Both of these reactions were important in our interpretation.

Of course, the interpretation which finally resulted from our analysis of all these dreams did not point the way to any solution of the secretary's problem. However, it did identify the problem—which may not have been quite so apparent to the secretary had the dreams not been analyzed. Also—and considerably more important —it revealed to the secretary her unconscious feelings of resentment toward her employers and her son. These feelings, having been recognized, could now be dealt with rationally. Had they gone unrecognized, they might have prompted the secretary to acts of indifference or cruelty which could have hurt her son and/or which could have further complicated her present problem.

The fact that dream analysis cannot—and will not— solve your problems cannot be overstressed. The problems will remain, no matter how accurately and expertly you may analyze your dreams. However, dream analysis can—and should—help you better to understand your problems, your hidden fears, your secret hopes, your anxieties and your apprehensions. This understanding can then point the way toward coping rationally with the situations you meet in everyday life.

Finally, let us point out that few dream logs will be as consistent and concise as the sample presented here. Most persons will have to record their dreams for weeks or even months before they acquire enough material to pinpoint their problems as precisely as we have pinpointed the problems of the secretary. And, more often than not, the less acute the person's problems, the longer it will take for these problems to emerge through dream symbols. Therefore, when you begin your dream analysis, be patient. If your dreams do not lend themselves facilely to interpretation, do not abandon your dream log. Continue to record your dreams and to interpret them with *What Your Dreams Mean* until such a time as a clear picture emerges—no matter how long it takes.

And continue even beyond that, for, as your personal life-situation changes, so too will your problems. Dream analysis can help illuminate these new problems as they arise. Indeed, many people discover dream analysis early in life and continue to practice it for as long as they live.

Their self-understanding increases with each year—and with the increase in self-understanding comes the ability to cope more effectively with every problematic situation one ever encounters.

5 / Lucky Dream Numbers

The psychologists and psychiatrists who developed the science of dream interpretation have not explored the question of "lucky" dreams—that is, of dreams which give the dreamer a hint about how he can better his fortunes in waking life. Nonetheless, a great many people have found that certain omens and numbers which appear in dreams can indeed be very lucky.

The most common method of using dreams to better one's fortunes involves a numerical system which will be described in the following paragraphs. There is no scientific evidence that this system can actually help you find a lucky number. However, the system is sufficiently popular for no book about dreams to be complete without mention of it.

The system is built around an alphabetical-numerical table. In the table, each letter of the alphabet is assigned a number between one and nine. To determine your lucky dream number for any given day, spell out each object which appears in your previous night's dreams, then reduce the letters involved to numbers by means of the alphabetical-numerical table.

The table is as follows:

A	B	C	D	E	F	G	H	I
J	K	L	M	N	O	P	Q	R
S	T	U	V	W	X	Y	Z	
1	2	3	4	5	6	7	8	9

To understand how this table works, let us assume that the objects in your dreams for a given night were bathtub, a pair of scissors and a car. You first obtain the numerical equivalents for all the letters in each word. In bath-tub, "b" equals two, "a" equals one, "t" equals two, "h" equals eight, "t" equals two, "u" equals three and "b" equals two. Two plus one plus two plus eight plus two plus three plus two equals twenty.

In scissors, "s" equals one, "c" equals three, "i" equals nine, "s" equals one, "s" equals one, "o" equals six, "r" equals nine and "s" equals one. One plus three plus nine plus one plus one plus six plus nine plus one equals thirty-one.

In car, "c" equals three, "a" equals one and "r" equals nine. Three plus one plus nine equals thirteen.

Here in diagram form are how these words translate into numbers:

BATHTUB

Ⓐ Ⓑ C D E F G Ⓗ I

J Ⓚ L M N O P Q R

S Ⓣ Ⓤ V W X Y Z

1 2 3 4 5 6 7 8 9

```
2—B
1—A
2—T
8—H
2—T
3—U
2—B
──
20
```

SCISSORS

A B Ⓒ D E F G H Ⓘ

J K L M N Ⓞ P Q Ⓡ

Ⓢ T U V W X Y Z

1 2 3 4 5 6 7 8 9

1—S
3—C
9—I
1—S
1—S
6—O
9—R
1—S
———
31

CAR

Ⓐ B Ⓒ D E F G H I

J K L M N O P Q Ⓡ

S T U V W X Y Z

1 2 3 4 5 6 7 8 9

3—C
1—A
9—R
———
13

Next, add *all* the numbers for all the words involved: BATHTUB, SCISSORS, and CAR. Twenty, thirty-one and thirteen:

```
                    20——BATHTUB
                    31——SCISSORS
                    13——CAR
                    ——
                    64
```

Write this figure numerically, as 64, and add both digits.

```
                         6
                         4
                        ——
                        10
```

Since we are looking for an integer as a lucky number, we must again add the digits in the figure, 10.

```
                         1
                         0
                        ——
                         1
```

Therefore, the lucky number for the day is *one*.

Generally, of course, you will have far more than three dream objects. However, no matter how many objects you have, you can always come up with a single-figure lucky number by adding the digits until they are reduced to one digit. For example, if the total of your dream numbers is two thousand nine hundred and eighty-seven, add the digits 2, 9, 8 and 7 for a total of twenty-six, then add the 2 and the 6 for a total of eight, your lucky number. No matter how big the number, it always can be reduced to a single digit if you keep on adding.

For your convenience, *What Your Dreams Mean* includes the numerical equivalent of each object defined therein. This will save you the trouble of computing the numbers yourself. Thus, if your dream includes four objects—a barber, a bartender, a bed and a boat—you can learn from *What Your Dreams Mean* that the numerical equivalents of these objects are, respectively, one, six, two and two. Adding these numbers, you get a total of eleven. Then, adding the digits, one and one, you get a total of two, your lucky number.

6 / Interpreting Your Own Dreams

And now, if you have read everything in this section and understand it completely, you are ready to begin interpreting your own dreams. Some readers will not want to attempt dream analysis until they have first read every entry in *What Your Dreams Mean*. This is a good idea because, by reading all the entries, you will get something of a "feel" for dream interpretation; you will see the wide variety of interpretations which can be attached to various dream characters, objects, settings and actions, and you will see ways in which individual interpretations can be applied to your own situation.

Occasionally your dream log may contain an entry which cannot be located in *What Your Dreams Mean*. This will often be the case if you have entered in your log a dream character, object, setting or action which is one of a large class of similar characters, objects, settings or actions. For example, you may dream of a subway conductor or of a flight engineer on an airplane. You may dream of a cocker spaniel or of the novel, *Gone With The Wind*. Your dream may be set in a bungalow or on a raft. You may dream that you are rushing somewhere or that you are toppling off a perch. The words for these characters, objects, settings and actions do not appear in *What Your Dreams Mean*. However, if you think for a moment about these words, you will realize that they have synonyms which do appear in the dictionary or are related to other words which appear in the dictionary.

When your dream log contains a word which you cannot find in the dictionary, try to determine if the word in question belongs to a large class of similar words. Then try to think of a word which describes this entire class. A cocker spaniel, for example, is a dog. A novel is a book. Both words, "book" and "dog," appear in the dictionary.

Sometimes you will find that you cannot think of a

word which describes the entire class of words similar to your log entry. Or you may find that the class-word itself does not appear. For example, a raft is both a vessel and a conveyance. A subway conductor is a trainman and a transit worker. None of these words—vessel, conveyance, trainman and transit worker—appears in the dictionary.

In a case like this, try to think of other words which describe characters, objects, settings and actions which are somewhat similar to the characters, objects, settings and actions described by the words in your log. For example, a raft is somewhat similar to a boat and to a ship. A subway conductor is in some ways similar to a bus driver. A flight engineer has many things in common with a pilot. And rushing is somewhat similar to running. The words, "boat," "ship," "driver," "pilot" and "running" all appear in *What Your Dreams Mean*. Naturally these words do not mean precisely the same thing as the words to which they are similar. But, if you keep in mind the difference between the words, you will find that you often will be able to apply some of the dictionary's interpretations for the listed words to the words in your own dream.

If even this process does not help you find an interpretation for an entry in your log, try relating the entry to other words which the log contains for the same dream. For example, let us suppose that you dreamed that you were eating a steak. The word, "steak," does not appear in *What Your Dreams Mean*, nor does the class-word, "meat," nor does the even-more-inclusive class-word, "food." You can think of dozens of words which describe foods that are in some way similar to steak—for instance, the words "chop," "roast," "sirloin," "beef," "venison," "pork," and "ham." None of these words appears in the dictionary either. However, if you relate your log entry, "steak," to the action which was performed on the steak —namely, that you were *eating* it—you will be able to interpret the dream. The word, "eating," does appear in the dictionary.

If at this point you still cannot find a dictionary listing which will shed some light on your dream, you might try interpreting the dream on your own—by applying the principles which have been applied in the writing of the dictionary. These principles will be familiar to you once you have read all the dictionary's entries. For example, let us say that you dreamed that you summoned a man to your home to exterminate some bugs and other household pests. There is no dictionary listing for "exterminator," no dictionary listing for "bugs" or "pests." You can think of no dictionary-listed class-words which pertain to any of these log entries, you can think of no synonyms or similar words which can be found in the dictionary, and you cannot relate the entries to other words for the same dream because there are no other words in the dream. However, having read the dictionary carefully from first word to last, you probably will realize instantly that the function of an exterminator is to kill things. Consulting the dictionary listing for "killings," you can come up with a valid interpretation of your own—perhaps that you want someone to help you "kill" your appetite for certain things which you feel you should not have, or that you feel that your problems are too big for you to solve without some outside assistance.

A careful reading of the dictionary from first word to last also will reveal to you that there are certain types of objects which, because of their shape, are phallic symbols, vaginal symbols or breast symbols. If you dream of a similarly-shaped object which is not listed in the dictionary—for example, a spear, a bowl or a grapefruit (none of which is listed)—you will recognize instantly that these objects also are phallic symbols, vaginal symbols and breast symbols, and you will be able to apply the dictionary interpretations for other phallic symbols, vaginal symbols and breast symbols to the symbols in your own dream.

Generally, of course, such extrapolation will be unnecessary—for *What Your Dreams Mean* contains hundreds of words which represent the most common characters, objects, settings and actions that appear in dreams. With it as your guide, you should have virtually no trouble in analyzing your dreams.

Here are several reminders to guide you in that analysis:

(A) List in your dream log *every* detail that you can remember about *every* dream you have. No detail is unimportant.

(B) Inquire diligently into the circumstances of every

dream. If someone whom you know personally appears as a dream character, be sure to make a note of the *role* in which he appears. Note also his *actions,* both with respect to you and with respect to other characters in the dream.

(C) Be alert for the appearance of *familiar* persons in *unusual* roles and for the appearance of persons whom you ordinarily wouldn't think of in waking life. Be alert also for your own appearance in an unusual role or in a different age-category or life-situation.

(D) Watch for events which seem to have *no relevance* to your present life. They generally will have symbolic significance.

(E) Be especially thorough when you are analyzing dreams which provoked *violent fear-reactions.* Their strong emotional impact on you suggests that they are very significant to your waking life.

(G) Remember that no single dream will tell you very much about yourself but that all your dreams, taken as a whole, can tell you a great deal. Relate the interpretation of each dream to the interpretation of all your other dreams, and in this manner you will be able to form a very clear picture of the hidden fears and desires, the hidden anxieties and wishes, the hidden hopes and aspirations which reveal themselves only through your unconscious mind—and only while you're dreaming.

Now begin using *What Your Dreams Mean.*

PART II

WHAT YOUR DREAMS MEAN

Common Dream Symbols from A to Z

A

ACROPOLIS (9)*—The acropolis was the center of spiritual life in ancient Greek cities, a citadel built high above the rest of the city to serve as a fortress against possible invasion. Today, the acropolis is symbolic of the glory that once was Greece. If you dream of the acropolis, chances are that you're indicating a desire to (a) visit foreign places; (b) escape to another world—and, by so doing, to rid yourself of the problems and annoyances of your present life-situation; (c) surpass your colleagues—i.e., to rise high above the crowd, as the acropolis towered above ancient Greek cities. Dreaming of the acropolis may also indicate your fear that your best days are behind you, just as the glory that once was Greece has passed although the acropolis still stands. If, of course, you happen to be a former resident of Greece or the descendent of Greek parents, dreaming of the acropolis may merely mean that you desire to return to your former home or the home of your parents—thus, to return to an earlier mode of life which was more comfortable and/or more secure than your present life-situation.

ACTOR (3) or ACTRESS (4)—If you yourself appear in one of your dreams as an actor, you probably are testifying to unconscious wishes to (a) change your own personality, as actors change their personalities when they assume different roles; (b) be someone that other people talk about and admire, as they talk about and admire popular movie stars; (c) express—i.e., "act out"—certain feelings or emotions which you have been suppressing; (d) lead a more glamorous life, a life of the sort which actors and actresses seem to lead. If someone you know appears in one of your dreams as an actor, you probably are indicating that (a) you think he is a phony; (b) you envy the glamorous life which he seems to lead; (c) you think he is more popular and worthy of emula-

---

* The figure, 9, is the numerical equivalent of the dream object, acropolis (see subsection, *Lucky Dream Numbers,* in "How to Use Your Dream Dictionary"). A numerical equivalent will appear in parentheses following each object, character or setting which is defined in this dictionary. No numerical equivalent will appear for dream actions, which do not qualify as dream symbols and which therefore do not figure into the computation of a lucky dream number.

tion than you ordinarily would admit in waking life; (*d*) you would like him to enjoy all the good things in life which actors seem to enjoy. If a popular movie star or other actor (whom you do not know personally) appears in one of your dreams, you most likely are revealing your desire to associate with a more glamorous circle of people than your present acquaintances. If such an actor is friendly to you in the dream, chances are that you feel that you are capable of being accepted socially by famous people if only you are given the opportunity to do so; if such an actor is unfriendly to you in the dream, chances are that you feel incapable of such social acceptance. Finally, a dream involving actors—no matter what their relationship to the dreamer—may indicate that the dreamer is afraid of facing reality; hence, that he is more comfortable in the world of make-believe than in the real world.

ADULTERY—Most commonly, dreams of adultery fall into the category of "current event" dreams. In other words, the person who dreams that he is committing adultery is indicating either a desire to do so or a fear that he might do so despite his intentions to the contrary; likewise, the person who dreams that his spouse is committing adultery is indicating a fear that the spouse will do so or an unconscious desire that the spouse do so—perhaps to pay him back for an adulterous act which he has committed. However, dreams of adultery may also be significant on a metaphoric level. Adultery symbolizes betrayal—not necessarily sexual—and the person who dreams that he or his spouse is committing adultery may very well be expressing desires or fears of betraying his spouse or having his spouse betray him.

AIRPLANE (4)—When a person dreams of taking a trip in an airplane, he generally is expressing a desire to go somewhere new or to change his present life-situation in a hurry. On a more metaphoric level, he may also be expressing a wish to raise his station in life, to move up in the world. However, far more significant than the mere appearance of an airplane in a dream is the status of the plane and the status of the dreamer in the plane. Thus, if a person dreams of being in an airplane which is grounded, he may feel that he is not succeeding in his career, that he just can't get "off the ground." If he dreams of being in an airplane which crashes, he may be expressing his fears of imminent disaster. If he dreams of missing a flight, he may be voicing the fear that he has failed to get "on board" with respect to his career or some other aspect of his life. If he dreams of being in an airplane which has trouble landing, he may be testifying to fears that he will be unable to complete an important project. If he dreams that he is looking down on the world through an airplane window, he may be indicating a desire to be "above" other people, to enjoy a higher station in life. If he dreams that he is the pilot of the plane, he may be indicating a desire to hold a position of great responsibility or a fear of holding such a position. If none of the above interpretations seem to apply to your airplane dream, you might also interpret the dream in the light of the fact that an airplane is, because of its cylindrical fuselage and enormous power, symbolic of virility.

ALE (9)—Ale, like all other alcoholic beverages, most commonly symbolizes good fellowship, convivial company and general merriment. However, with many individuals, alcoholic beverages have a decidedly negative connotation. This is especially the case among people who personally have a drinking problem or who are involved with other persons who have a drinking problem. Alcoholic beverages also might have a decidedly negative connotation for people who have at one time or another suffered abuse at the hands of a habitual drinker. Thus, the appearance of any alcoholic beverage in a dream can be interpreted only in the light of the dreamer's own experiences with drinking or with drinkers—and, in any case, the presence of an alcoholic beverage in a dream will be less significant than the actions of the person or persons who are drinking it, serving it, etc.

ALLEY (1)—An alley usually is a dark and secluded place. Thus, dream-events which take place in an alley generally are events which the dreamer considers shameful or frightening. Since alleys often terminate in a dead end, the dreamer who envisions himself in an alley may also be voicing unconscious fears that he has placed himself in a situation from which there is no way out.

AMBULANCE (9)—Ambulances, of course, are vehicles used for the emergency transportation of people who are critically ill or injured. Thus, if you dream of yourself or of another person being taken somewhere in an ambulance, you generally are expressing a fear or a desire that you or the other person will soon be in an emergency situation, one which could have disastrous consequences.

AMPUTATION—Amputation is the severance of a limb or other bodily part. Dreams of amputation generally testify to (a) an unconscious fear that a person's life is not complete, that "something is missing"; (b) a feeling that one is different from other people; (c) a fear of being punished for some real or imagined misdeed, or a desire to be punished for such a misdeed.

ANGEL (3)—Angels symbolize a wide variety of persons and circumstances. Probably the most common symbolism is that of one's mother. Hence, the person who dreams of an angel may actually be using the dream-figure of the angel to replace his own mother. In such a case, whatever action the angel performs can be ascribed to the dreamer's mother. Angels also symbolize purity—especially sexual purity—and death. Finally, when a person dreams of an angel he may be giving voice to unconscious feelings of inadequacy—feelings as a result of which he desires some sort of superhuman figure to provide reassurance and guidance.

APPLE (5)—Ever since the snake lured Eve away from the path of righteousness with an apple from the Tree of Knowledge, the apple has been considered symbolic of temptation. Thus, the person who dreams of giving someone an apple may be expressing a desire to tempt that person; likewise, the person who dreams of being given an apple by someone else may be expressing his fear that the other person is tempting him—possibly beyond the limits of his own endurance. Also, because of their shape, apples symbolize the female breasts. Hence a girl who dreams of giving an apple to someone or of having someone take an apple from her may be indicating a desire to share or a fear of sharing her breasts—or, on a more deeply symbolic level, her sexual participation—with that person.

APPOINTMENT (8)—An appointment is an arrangement for a meeting, and the consequences of missing one may be severe. Hence, the person who dreams of having missed an appointment may be voicing a fear of being punished for some real or imagined misdeed. Likewise, since many apointments lead to important opportunities, the individual who dreams of missing an appointment may be expressing a fear that he is missing out on an opportunity. Finally, since there is something of an obligation on the part of all parties to keep an appointment once it has been made, the person who dreams of missing one may be testifying to a fear that he is derelict in his responsibilities, or to a desire to avoid these responsibilities; similarly, the person who dreams that he is continually rushing from appointment to appointment may be revealing his feeling that he is overburdened with obligations and responsibilities.

ARROW (4)—Arrows symbolize a great many things, including truth, speed, death and the male penis. Hence, the person who dreams of shooting someone with an arrow may be expressing (a) the desire to enjoy a perfectly candid relationship with that person; (b) the desire to kill the person, or a fear that he may inadvertently kill the person; (c) the desire to do or the fear of inadvertently doing injury to the person; (d) the desire to have sexual intercourse with the person. Similarly, the person who dreams of being shot by someone else's arrow may be voicing (a) the desire to have that person tell him the truth about a particular matter; (b) the fear of being killed by the person or of being injured by him; (c) the desire to have sexual intercourse with the person. On a more metaphoric level, the dreamer who is shooting an arrow at another person may be revealing a fear that his relationship to the person is being blocked by the latter's stubbornness, indifference, dislike, etc.; in this case, the arrow represents the dreamer's attempt to "get through" to the other person by piercing the armor of his stubbornness, indifference, dislike, etc.

ASPARAGUS (4)—Asparagus, because of its shape, symbolizes a phallus.

AUTHORITY FIGURE—An authority figure is, as the name implies, a person in command of a given situation. Authority figures which commonly appear in dreams include policemen, military officers, judges, schoolteachers, clergymen, monarchs and elected heads of state. When an authority figure appears in a person's dream, the action of the figure—and his identity—almost invariably are more significant than the mere fact that he has appeared. If, for example, the dreamer pictures himself as an authority figure, he generally is expressing (a) the desire to enjoy a position of authority and responsibility; (b) the fear of assuming a position of authority and responsibility. If someone the dreamer knows appears in an authority-figure role which does not match his status in real life, the dreamer may be (a) voicing his belief that the person in question deserves to occupy a position of such authority; (b) expressing admiration for the person; (c) expressing a desire to be guided or controlled by the person; (d) expressing resentment at the belief that the person is trying to guide or control him—or the belief that the person actually is guiding or controlling him. The presence of an anonymous authority figure in a dream generally means that the dreamer either desires to submit or resents being forced to submit to someone else's authority. (For numerical equivalents of various authority figures, consult the alphabetical listings for these figures—e.g., judge, policeman, etc.)

AUTOMOBILE (5)—Automobiles, like all other passenger-carrying vehicles, signify movement—either toward a specific goal or away from an undesired situation. Generally the role of the dreamer with respect to the automobile in his dream will be more significant than the mere appearance of the automobile in the dream. Hence, a person who dreams that he is driving the automobile may be expressing the feeling that he is or should be moving toward a certain goal or away from a certain situation, while the person who dreams that he is a passenger in the automobile may be testifying to the belief that someone else is controlling his movement toward the goal or away from the situation. Similarly, a person who dreams that an automobile has pulled away before he was able to get in it may be indicating that he believes he has lost out on an important opportunity.

B

BABY (3)—The appearance of a baby in a dream lends itself to a wide variety of interpretations. In many cases, the baby represents the dreamer himself. When this is true, the dreamer may be revealing (a) that he feels helpless in a given situation; (b) feelings of inferiority with respect to his peers, next to whom he is figuratively a "babe in the woods;" (c) the desire to be pampered, as he had been when he actually was a baby; (d) craving for attention and love without reciprocal obligations—a situation which he enjoyed when he was a baby; (e) the desire to avoid or shirk responsibility. In other cases, the baby in a dream may represent an indefinite object of the dreamer's own attentions; in other words, by dreaming of a baby the dreamer may be indicating that he wants someone upon whom to lavish love and attention— someone who will not question or reject this love and attention. If the dreamer is a childless husband or wife, the dream probably is nothing more than an expression of his desire to become a parent—or, in rare cases, of his fear of becoming a parent. If the dreamer is a small child with a younger sibling, the dream may be an expression of his fear that the new arrival has supplanted him in the affection of his parents. If the dreamer is an only child, the dream may mean that he would like a younger brother or sister. If the dreamer is getting on in years, the dream may be indicative of his desire to turn life's clock back, to be once again young enough to bring up his children, who now have babies of their own. If the dreamer is a parent who has suffered the loss of a child, the dream may represent a longing for the return of that child or for the birth of another child. If the dreamer is a woman who has undergone an abortion, the dream may be an indication that she still suffers guilt stemming from that episode. If the dreamer is a man or woman who is sterile, the dream may represent a wish to be fertile. Still other interpretations are possible, depending upon the life-situation of the dreamer. Indeed, interpretations of baby-dreams are virtually limitless. The main questions to ask yourself if you have such a dream are: What is my relationship in the dream to the baby? What is my life-situation with respect to babies?

BALLOON (8)—Balloons, because of their shape, symbolize the female breast. Hence, a man who dreams of holding balloons may be expressing a desire to caress a woman's breasts —or, by extension, to have sexual intercourse with her. A man who dreams of taking balloons from a girl forcibly may be indicating a desire to rape her. A girl who dreams of giving a balloon to a man or of having him take a balloon from her may be indicating a desire to share or a fear of sharing her breasts—or, by extension, her sexual participation—with that man. Balloons also are symbolic of childhood and gaiety; thus, persons who dream of balloons may also be expressing a desire to return to the lighthearted days of their youth.

BANANA (6)—The banana is a phallic symbol. Thus, a

man who dreams of giving a banana to someone may be expressing a desire to have sexual relations with that person. A man who dreams of possessing a large stalk of bananas may be voicing unconscious fears of sexual inadequacy. A girl who deams of receiving a banana from a man may be expressing a desire to have sexual relations with him. A girl who dreams of possessing bananas may be revealing unconscious homosexual tendencies, or a desire to enjoy the power and strength which men generally enjoy in society, or a desire to overpower the men in her life (by taking possession of their virility).

BANK (1)—A bank is a symbol of security, solidity, power and strength. When a dream is set in a bank, the dreamer may be expressing a desire to lead a more stable life or a fear that his present life is lacking in excitement and adventure. The same dream may also symbolize confidence in one's own power and strength or the fear that one is not sufficiently strong and powerful to cope with one's present life-situation. Naturally, dreams which are set in a bank can be interpreted only in the light of the actions which take place in the bank.

BAR, IRON (3)—An iron bar is a barrier. Thus, when a person dreams of an iron bar he may be indicating the desire to put up a barrier—perhaps against certain problems which now beset him, or against certain persons who are important in his life—or the fear that someone else has put up a barrier which prevents him from realizing his desires. Because of its shape, an iron bar may also be a phallic symbol.

BAR [SALOON] (3)—A bar is thought of by most people as a place of good fellowship, convivial company and general merriment. However, with many individuals, bars have a decidedly negative connotation. This is especially the case among persons who have a drinking problem, who are involved with other persons who have a drinking problem, or who have at one time or another suffered abuse at the hands of an habitual drinker. Thus, the dreamer's own feelings toward drinking—and the actions which take place in the bar of his dreams—generally will be far more significant than the mere fact that the dream is set in a bar. One common interpretation of bar-dreams: since a bar is to some people a place where they can go to drown their sorrows, a dream which is set in a bar may signify the dreamer's desire to escape from the world and from its sadness and heartbreak.

BARBER (1)—Gone forever are the days in which the barber, like the one of Sevillian fame, not only cut his master's hair and shaved his beard but also ran his errands, shined his shoes, acted as his valet and confidant, and wrote his love notes. Yet, although the modern barber is strictly a shave-and-a-haircut man (and, more often than not, a haircut man only), he still serves as a confidant to many men—a willing ear into which one's troubles can be poured, a source of advice and of kind words of sympathy. Thus, the appearance of a barber in a dream often will signify the dreamer's desire for someone whom he can trust and confide in. However, a barber may also represent a Delilah-figure—i.e., a person who saps a man's strength by cutting off his hair. Therefore, the presence of a barber in a dream may also indicate the dreamer's unconscious fear of losing his strength and virility, or his desire to shirk the responsibilities which possessing that strength and virility entails.

BARTENDER (6)—The bartender not only serves up alcoholic beverages but also is a friend and confidant to many people. Thus, the appearance of a bartender in a dream may signify the dreamer's wish that there were someone in whom he could trust and confide, someone who could take care of him as the bartender ministers to the needs of his customers. On a more metaphoric level, a bartender may also symbolize the dreamer's mother—who was the first person to minister to his needs.

BASEBALL (9)—A baseball, because of its shape, is a breast symbol. Also, because of the fact that the pitcher hurls it into the catcher's vagina-like mitt, it symbolizes the male's semen—hence, virility and fertility.

BATH (4)—A bath is an operation whereby one is physically cleansed. The person who dreams of taking a bath generally is expressing unconscious feelings of guilt, as a result of which he feels he must be spiritually cleansed. The person who dreams that someone else is taking a bath probably is voicing a belief that this person has done something for which he should feel guilty.

BATHTUB (2)—A bathtub, as the receptacle in which a bath is taken, is a place where a person is physically cleansed. Its appearance in a dream generally testifies to the dreamer's belief that the individual who is bathing in it suffers guilt for which he should be spiritually cleansed. Also, because of its shape and because of the fact that it is filled with water, the bathtub symbolizes the female genitalia.

BATTLE (6)—A battle is the physical manifestation of a bitter conflict. Thus, the dreamer who envisions himself as a participant in or an observer of a battle generally is revealing that (a) he is plagued with inner conflict, (b) he possesses a secret which, if revealed, would lead to conflict. Important questions to ask yourself if you dream of a battle are: What is your role in the battle? Why is the battle being fought? If you are a participant, did you acquit yourself bravely or cowardly? If you are an observer, why aren't you a participant? Did you make any attempt to stop the battle from taking place?

BEACH (1)—To most people, the beach is a place where one can relax and enjoy oneself. Thus, dreams which are set on beaches usually are indicative of the dreamer's desire to bring more relaxation and enjoyment to his life. However, far more significant than the appearance of a beach in a dream is the action which transpires on the beach.

BED (2)—Since beds may mean so many different things to so many different people, it would be next to impossible to attempt here to provide individual interpretations of dreams in which beds appear. Suffice it to say that among the things which beds signify in dreams are rest, infancy (especially if the bed is a crib), sickness, death and sexual intercourse. The main questions to ask yourself if a bed appears in your dreams are: Who is in it? Who's in it with him? What are they doing there?

BEER (3)—Beer, like all other alcoholic beverages, generally symbolizes good fellowship, convivial company and general merriment. However, with many individuals, alcoholic beverages have a decidedly negative connotation. This is especially the case among people who personally have a drinking problem or who are involved with other persons who have a drinking problem. Alcoholic beverages also might have a decidedly negative connotation for people who have at one time or another suffered abuse at the hands of an habitual drinker. Thus, the appearance of any alcoholic beverage in a dream can be interpreted only in the light of the dreamer's own experience with drinking or drinkers—and, in any case, the presence of an alcoholic beverage in a dream will be less significant than the actions of the persons who are drinking it, serving it, etc.

BLOOD (3)—Blood is one of the most difficult dream symbols to interpret. It symbolizes life, but it also symbolizes injury and death. It rarely appears in a dream except in connection with an action as a result of which it is made to flow, and the interpreter of dreams would be wise to concentrate on the symbolism of that action rather than upon the symbolism of blood itself.

BOAT (2)—Boats, like most other vehicles, are symbolic of movement—either toward a specific goal or away from an undesired situation. The person who dreams of taking a sea voyage may be indicating that he wishes to change his life-situation, or that he believes he is on his way to attaining a certain goal, or that he feels he should be on his way toward attaining a certain goal. If you dream that you yourself are piloting a boat, you may be revealing your desire to control your own life-situation more than you presently control it—thus, to chart your own course. If you dream that you are on a boat which is adrift, you may be indicating that you fear you have no goals, that you are merely drifting through life. And if you dream that you have arrived too late to board a boat, you may be revealing your fear that you have lost out on an opportunity, that you have "missed the boat."

BODY, DEAD (1)—A dead body generally symbolizes death fears or wishes. These fears or wishes may pertain to the dreamer's own death or to the death of someone else. In some cases, however, the death in question may be metaphoric—as in the death of a love affair or of an era in the dreamer's life.

BODY, LIVE (1)—Live bodies generally symbolize sexual desire.

BOMB (5)—A bomb is an instrument of destruction. Hence,

the person who dreams of building and/or setting off a bomb generally is revealing feelings of hostility and desires to wreak destruction. Meanwhile, the person who dreams of a bomb blast which he himself did not trigger may be expressing (*a*) fear of death; (*b*) fears of helplessness; (*c*) fear of a very tense—i.e., explosive—situation.

BOOK (7)—Books are symbolic of knowledge, wisdom and understanding. The person who dreams of reading a book generally is testifying to his desires for (*a*) more knowledge, wisdom and understanding; (*b*) the solution to a perplexing problem; (*c*) the power and prestige which come from being knowledgeable, wise and understanding. However, books also provide the reader with a means of escaping the difficulties of his everyday existence; hence, the person who dreams of reading a book may also be revealing dissatisfaction with his present life-situation and a desire to escape it.

BOTTLE (2)—When bottles appear in dreams, they often represent the dreamer's first bottle—the bottle from which he was nursed. When this is the case, the dreamer generally is revealing (*a*) a desire to return to infancy, when his every need was satisfied and his every whim catered to by those around him; (*b*) the desire to be as important to other persons as the person who nursed him was important to him; (*c*) his craving for spiritual "nourishment" comparable to the physical nourishment which he received from his milk bottle as an infant. Cylindrical bottles with narrow necks are, because of their shape, phallic symbols.

BOY (6)—The appearance of a boy in a dream is of itself far less significant than the identity of the boy and the life-situation of the dreamer. In some cases, the boy will represent the dreamer himself. When this is true, the dreamer may be revealing his (*a*) desire to return to boyhood, when life was far less complex for him than it is today (*b*) feelings of inferiority with respect to his peers, next to whom he is figuratively still just a boy; (*c*) desire to be pampered and cared for, as he was when he was a boy; (*d*) craving for attention and love without reciprocal obligations—a situation which he enjoyed when he was a boy; (*e*) desire to avoid responsibilities. In other cases, the boy in a dream may represent an indefinite object of the dreamer's own attentions; in other words, by dreaming of a boy the dreamer may be indicating that he wants someone upon whom to lavish love and attention—someone who will not reject this love and attention. Small boys, when they appear in the dreams of grown men, often are symbolic of the dreamers' lost youth. Women who dream of boys usually are expressing their desire to become mothers or to return to the days when their now-grown sons were small boys.

BRIDE (2)—The appearance of a bride in a dream is far less significant than the identity of the bride, her relationship to the dreamer, and the dreamer's present life-situation. When an unmarried woman dreams of a bride she may be voicing her desire to become one—or, in rare cases, her fear of becoming one against her wishes. When a middle-aged or elderly woman dreams of a bride, she generally is expressing her desire to return to the early days of her marriage—or, if she has an unmarried daughter, she may be expressing a desire that the daughter get married. Brides also can serve as symbols of sexual innocence; hence, the woman who dreams of herself as a bride may be expressing a wish to regain her sexual innocence.

BRIDEGROOM (6)—The appearance of a bridegroom in a dream is far less significant than the identity of the bridegroom, his relationship to the dreamer, and the dreamer's present life-situation. When an unmarried woman dreams of a bridegroom, she generally is voicing her desire to get married—or, perhaps, her fear that the man she loves will marry someone else. When an unmarried man dreams of a bridegroom, he probably is expressing the wish to get married—or, in not-so-rare cases, the desire to avoid marriage or the fear of being forced into a marriage against his will. A mature married woman who dreams of a bridegroom may be revealing her inner desire to have her husband lavish on her as much affection and attention as he did when they first were married. Middle-aged or elderly persons who dream of a bridegroom may be voicing an unconscious desire to return to the days of their youth, when they were newlyweds, or to marry off a bachelor son.

BRIDESMAID (3)—The appearance of a bridesmaid in a dream is far less significant than the identity of the bridesmaid, her relationship to the dreamer, and the dreamer's present life-situation. Bridesmaid dreams per se generally are without significance unless the dreamer is an unmarried woman who pictures herself as a bridesmaid, in which case she may be expressing distress over her unmarried state and a fear that she will always stand on the sidelines watching her friends get married and have children while she herself remains husbandless and childless.

BRIDGE (9)—A bridge symbolizes (*a*) understanding, (*b*) friendship, (*c*) progress, (*d*) the desire to change one's life-situation. If you dream of crossing a bridge to meet another person, you probably are expressing a desire to form a friendship with that person. If you dream that you are unable to cross a bridge which separates you from another person, you probably are expressing the feeling that, try though you might, you cannot get through to him, you cannot understand him, you cannot persuade him to take you into his confidence. If you dream of crossing a bridge with no intention of meeting another person, you probably are revealing a desire to change your life-situation. The same dream may also mean that you believe you must surmount a certain obstacle before you can attain a desired goal. If you dream of yourself as being unable to cross a bridge, you may unconsciously feel that there is an insurmountable barrier to your attainment of success in a specific endeavor or in life generally.

BROTHER (5)—The appearance of a dreamer's brother in a dream is far less significant than the actions of the brother toward the dreamer. In some dreams, a brother may serve to represent the dreamer's entire family. Thus, if you dream that your brother has saved you from an impending catastrophe, you may be expressing the belief that your family will not let you down, no matter how serious your troubles.

BUCKET (8)—Buckets, like all containers, are vaginal symbols. If a girl dreams that she possesses a bucket which a man fills with something, she may be expressing a desire to have sexual intercourse with that man—or, conversely, a fear that she will be unable to resist the man's sexual advances.

BULL (2)—The bull is symbolic of masculine virility and strength. A man who dreams of a bull may be expressing a desire to be more virile and/or more attractive to women. A woman who dreams of a bull may be voicing the wish that she were spiritually stronger and thus more capable of handling her own affairs, or the desire for sexual intercourse, or the fear of sexual intercourse.

BUM(9)—A dreamer who pictures himself as a bum usually is voicing feelings of failure and inferiority. A dreamer who envisions a friend or acquaintance as a bum probably is revealing that he is disappointed at the failure of that person to live up to the dreamer's expectations. A dreamer who pictures his enemies or competitors as bums generally is voicing the belief that he can overcome them easily or the wish that he could overcome them more easily than he now seems able to.

BURIAL—The act of burial, naturally, signifies death. Thus, the dreamer who pictures himself being buried usually is expressing deep-seated death fears or wishes, and the dreamer who pictures another person being buried generally is voicing the wish or the fear that this other person will die. Burial may also have metaphoric significance in dreams, however. Thus, a person who dreams of being buried may also be voicing the belief that his problems are overwhelming (hence, he is being "buried" by them).

BURNING—The act of burning symbolizes both death and sexual intercourse. Thus, the person who dreams that he or that someone else is burning may be revealing death wishes or fears with respect to himself or to the other party, or he may be revealing sexual desire. To dream that an inanimate object is burning generally is to testify to a desire or a fear that the object will be destroyed.

BUS (6)—Buses, like all other passenger-carrying vehicles, signify movement—either toward a specific goal or away from an undesired situation. Generally the role of the dreamer with respect to the bus in his dream will be more significant than the mere appearance of the bus in the dream. Hence, a person who dreams that he is driving a bus may be expressing the feeling that he is or should be moving toward a certain goal or away from a certain situation, while the person who dreams that he is a passenger on a bus may be testifying to the belief that someone else is controlling his movement toward the goal or away from the situation. Similarly, a person who dreams that a bus had pulled away before he was able to board it may be indicating that he believes he has lost out or is losing out on an opportunity. A person who dreams that he is on a bus which is not moving may be expressing unconscious fears that he cannot escape his present life-situation. If he dreams of being on a bus which is involved in a bad traffic accident, he may be voicing fears that disaster is imminent in his life.

BUTCHER (5)—Butchers symbolize bloodshed and death. To dream of oneself in the role of a butcher generally is to reveal extreme feelings of aggression and hostility. To dream of another person as a butcher generally is to ascribe these aggressive and hostile tendencies to him, or to express a fear of him.

C

CAGE (7)—A cage is symbolic of restriction and confinement. Thus, a person who dreams that he is locked in a cage generally is testifying to (a) feelings of restriction or confinement in his career or personal life; (b) the desire to suppress (i.e., to lock up, as in a cage) certain of his feelings or impulses—for example, a tendency toward aggressive behavior; (c) the belief that he should be punished for a real or imagined misdeed; (d) the fear that he will be punished for a real or imagined misdeed. Cages in dreams may also have sexual significance. Superstition has it that the virgin who dreams of freeing a bird from a cage will soon lose her virginity. Whether or not this is so, most dream interpreters believe that the dream of freeing a bird from a cage is symbolic of sexual intercourse. One interpretation of the dream is that the person who frees the bird desires sexual congress—i.e., he wants to free himself of sexual inhibitions. Another interpretation is that the person who frees the bird desires to rid himself of guilt feelings stemming from a previous sexual experience; in this interpretation, the bird symbolizes the male's penis and the cage symbolizes the female's vagina: hence, the freeing of the bird from the cage represents the removal of the penis from the vagina, and, by extension, the elimination of guilt feelings which the act of sexual intercourse has inspired.

CANDLE (3)—A wide variety of interpretations can be attached to candles as dream symbols. Among the most common things which candles symbolize are (a) the male penis, (*b*) the act of growing old, (*c*) death. As is the case with all dream symbols which lend themselves to numerous interpretations, the mere presence of a candle in a dream will be far less significant than the actions of dream characters toward the candle. A common candle dream involves the burning to nothingness of a candle. This dream may signify that the dreamer fears or desires death, that he fears aging or that he desires to be more mature than he is. Among males, the same dream may also indicate a fear of losing sexual prowess.

CAR (4)—Cars, like all other passenger-carrying vehicles, signify movement—either toward a specific goal or away from an undesired situation. Generally the role of the dreamer with respect to the car in his dream will be more significant than the mere appearance of the car in the dream. Hence, a person who dreams that he is driving a car may be expressing the feeling that he is or should be moving toward a certain goal or away from a certain situation, while the person who believes that he is a passenger in the car may be testifying to the belief that someone else is controlling his movement toward the goal or away from the situation. Similarly, a person who dreams that a car has pulled away before he was able to get in it may be indicating that he believes he has lost out on an important opportunity.

CAROUSEL (4)—A carousel, of course, is an amusement-park ride which goes around in circles. The person who dreams of riding on a carousel usually is revealing the unconscious belief that his own life is directionless and without progress, that he is stuck in a rut, that *he* is going around in circles. To dream of other people riding on a carousel is to attribute these same characteristics to them, or to wish that these characteristics could be attributed to them.

CARTON (8)—Cartons, like all containers, are vaginal symbols. A common carton-dream is one in which a girl holds a carton which a man fills with various objects. This dream generally signifies the dreamer's desire for sexual intercourse or his fear that he will not be able to resist the temptation to engage in sexual intercourse.

CARVING—There are several types of carving: the carving of meat and poultry; the carving of one's initials on a piece of wood or on some other surface, and the carving of a statue or some other object. To dream of carving meat or poultry generally is to express feelings of hostility and aggression—perhaps the desire to cut up one's enemies just as one is cutting up the roast in one's dreams. The same dream may also testify to the dreamer's fear that he possesses these feelings of hostility or aggression, or that someone else possesses them and may use them against the dreamer. To dream of carving one's initials (or of carving any design) into wood or some other surface generally is to indicate the dreamer's desire to leave his imprint on something—in other words, to "make his mark" on the world. Finally, to dream of carving a statue or some other object is to express confidence in one's artistic abilities, or to express the desire that one might be more artistic than he actually is.

CASTLE (6)—Castles symbolize (*a*) strength and power, (*b*) luxury and elegant living, (*c*) a world of fantasy. Thus, the person who dreams of castles may be expressing (*a*) the belief that he is securely beyond the reach of his enemies, as a king is secure in a castle; (*b*) the desire for such security; (*c*) the desire to improve his status in life—hence, to live like a king; (*d*) his desire to escape from his present life-situation— thus, to build a "castle in the sky."

CAVE (4)—Caves symbolize both the female's vagina and the womb. Hence, to dream of being in a cave is to indicate (*a*) a desire for sexual intercourse, (*b*) a desire for security —security of the sort which one enjoyed when he was in his mother's womb, (*c*) a desire to turn back the clock to the moment of his birth—thus, a desire to relive his life.

CELL, JAIL (5)—A jail cell is symbolic of restriction and confinement. Thus, a person who dreams that he is locked in a jail cell generally is testifying to (*a*) feelings of restriction or confinement in his career or personal life; (*b*) the desire to suppress (i.e., to lock up, as in a jail cell) certain of his feelings or impulses—for example, a tendency toward aggressive behavior; (*c*) the belief that he should be punished for a real or imagined misdeed; (*d*) the fear that he will be punished for a real or imagined misdeed. Children who dream of being in jail generally are expressing the unconscious desire for more parental authority.

CEMETERY (4)—Cemeteries are symbolic of death fears or wishes.

CHERRY (5)—In everyday language as well as in dream interpretations, cherries are symbolic of virginity. Thus, the virgin who dreams of presenting a young man with a bunch of cherries generally is revealing her desire to lose her virginity to him. The non-virgin who dreams of presenting a man with a bunch of cherries probably is revealing the wish that she still had her virginity to offer him. A virgin who dreams of having cherries stolen from her probably is expressing (a) fear of losing her virginity; (b) the desire to have her virginity taken from her by force. A non-virgin who dreams of having cherries stolen from her probably is expressing (a) regret over the loss of her virginity, (b) the belief that her virginity was taken from her by force (either physical or moral) or guile. A man who dreams of taking cherries from a girl probably is indicating (a) a desire to relieve her of her virginity, (b) regret that he cannot relieve her of her virginity. A person who dreams of taking cherries from or giving cherries to a person of the same sex may be revealing (a) homosexual tendencies, (b) fear that he has homosexual tendencies, (c) the desire to lose his naivete (not necessarily sexual naivete), (d) the fear of losing his naivete (again, not necessarily sexual naivete), (e) the desire to rob someone else of his naivete (again, not necessarily sexual naivete), (f) the fear that he might inadvertently rob someone else of his naivete (again, not necessarily sexual naivete).

CHILD (9)—The appearance of a child or of children in a dream lends itself to a wide variety of interpretations. In many cases, the child represents the dreamer himself. When this is true, the dreamer may be revealing (a) that he feels helpless in a given situation; (b) feelings of inferiority with respect to his peers, next to whom he is figuratively a child; (c) the desire to be pampered, as he had been when he actually was a child; (d) a craving for attention and love without reciprocal obligations—a situation which he enjoyed when he was a child; (e) the desire to shirk responsibility. In other cases, the child in a dream may represent an indefinite object of the dreamer's own attentions; in other words, by dreaming of a child the dreamer may be indicating that he wants someone upon whom to lavish love and attention—someone who will not question or reject this love and attention. If the dreamer is a childless husband or wife, the dream probably is nothing more than an expression of his desire to become a parent. If the dreamer is getting on in years, the dream may be indicative of his desire to turn life's clock back, to be once again young enough to bring up his children, who now have children of their own. If the dreamer is a parent who has suffered the loss of a child, the dream may represent a longing for the return of that child or for the birth of another child. If the dreamer is a man or woman who is sterile, the dream may represent a wish to be fertile. Still other interpretations are possible, depending upon the life-situation of the dreamer. Indeed, interpretations to child-dreams are virtually limitless. The main questions to ask yourself if you have such a dream are: What is my relationship in the dream to the child? What is my life-situation with respect to children?

CHOKING—The act of choking may symbolize a great many things. There is choking in the literal sense, meaning strangulation; in this case, the act of choking in a dream may signify death fears or wishes, or the desire to inflict bodily harm upon someone, or the fear of having bodily harm inflicted upon oneself. There also is choking in the metaphoric sense, meaning termination, as of an unpleasant business relationship or of a phase of one's life. The main questions to ask yourself if an act of choking appears in your dreams are: Who is choking whom? What is the relationship of the assailant and the victim to each other? Why is the act of choking taking place?

CHURCH (1)—Churches, to most people, symbolize peace and tranquility. Thus, dreams which are set in churches may be interpreted to mean that the dreamer feels himself to be beset by emotional conflicts and longs to resolve them— hence, to be "at peace" with himself. Another possible interpretation is that the dreamer feels he is being persecuted and longs for a place where he will be safe—i.e., a sanctuary. Finally, dreams which are set in a church may testify to the dreamer's belief that he has not been as religious as he should be, that he has not obeyed the moral precepts to which he subscribes.

CHURN (1)—The churn, because it is a type of container, is a vaginal symbol. If the dreamer envisions the churning stick inside the churn, the dream may be symbolic of the act of coitus, since the stick, because of its shape, is a phallic symbol. However, the appearance of a churn in a dream need not be significant on a sexual level. A churn is indigenous to a dairy farm; hence, a city dweller who dreams of a churn may merely be expressing the desire to abandon the tensions of city life for the more tranquil existence of life in the country; likewise, a person who grew up on a dairy farm may merely be voicing the wish to return to the days of his youth.

CIRCLE (5)—The circle, because of its shape, is a vaginal symbol.

CIRCULAR MOVEMENT—Circular movement suggests restriction to the status quo, activity which is directionless and nonprogressive—hence, the metaphor, "going around in circles."

CLERGYMAN—The clergyman is generally thought of as a benign person who seeks to help people for purely altruistic motives. Thus, to most dreamers, the appearance of a clergyman in a dream generally indicates a desire to be helped in some way or in some way to help another person. Of course, the identity of the clergyman in a dream and the actions which he performs almost invariably will be more significant than the mere fact of his appearance. Thus, if the dreamer pictures himself as a clergyman, he may be indicating (*a*) the wish that he were a better person than he is; (*b*) the desire to have other people come to him for help; (*c*) the desire to have other people respect and admire him; (*d*) the desire to have other people think of him as good and noble. If he pictures an acquaintance as a clergyman, he generally will be (*a*) ascribing the qualities of goodness, nobility, etc., to that other person; (*b*) voicing the desire to turn to that other person for help and assistance; (*c*) indicating that the believes the other person wrongly thinks of himself as possessing clergyman-like qualities. If the clergyman in his dream is a real clergyman whom he knows personally or by name, or if the clergyman in his dream is anonymous, the dreamer generally will be testifying to a desire for help, comfort, consolation, etc. In some religions, clergymen also are authority figures. Thus, to dreamers who regard them as such, clergymen in dreams also may signify (*a*) the desire to submit to authority; (*b*) the desire to be forgiven for real or imagined misdeeds; (*c*) the desire to be punished for real or imagined misdeeds. (For numerical equivalents of various clergymen, consult the alphabetical listings for different types of clergymen—e.g., MINISTER, PRIEST, RABBI.)

CLIMBING—The act of climbing signifies upward movement. Thus to dream of climbing is to dream of (a) moving toward a specific goal, (b) escaping from one's present life-situation or from a specific problem in one's life, (c) generally bettering oneself—i.e., raising one's station in life, moving up in the world.

CLOCK (8)—The clock is an instrument for measuring time. Its appearance in a dream may mean that the dreamer (a) is afraid of death—i.e., time is running out on him; (b) feels confined by his present circumstances—i.e., time and the world are passing him by; (c) feels overburdened—i.e., he wishes there were more hours in the day so that he could discharge all his obligations; (d) inwardly resents the rigid schedule to which his present circumstances force him to adhere—i.e., he objects to "living by the clock."

CLOSET (2)—Closets generally are thought of as places where objects can be hidden from sight. Thus, dreams in which closets appear usually signify the dreamer's desire to hide something, or his fear that someone else is hiding something from him.

COCONUT (1)—Coconuts, because of their shape, symbolize the female breasts. Hence, a man who dreams of holding coconuts may be expressing a desire to caress a woman's breasts—or, by extension, to have sexual intercourse with her. A man who dreams of taking coconuts from a woman by force may be indicating a desire to rape her. A woman who dreams of giving a coconut to a man or of having him take a coconut from her may be indicating a desire to share or a fear of sharing her breasts—or, by extension, her sexual participation—with him. If a man dreams of breaking coconuts, he may be testifying to unconscious desires to destroy a woman's sexual attractiveness. Likewise, a woman who dreams of possessing cracked coconuts may be indicating an unconscious fear that she is sexually unattractive.

COMMANDER (5)—The commander of a military unit is

an authority figure. When an authority figure appears in a person's dream, the action of the figure—and his identity—almost invariably are more significant than the mere fact that he has appeared. If, for example, the dreamer pictures himself as an authority figure, he generally is expressing (a) the desire to enjoy a position of authority and responsibility; (b) the fear of assuming a position of authority and responsibility. If someone the dreamer knows appears in an authority-figure role which does not match his status in real life, the dreamer may be (a) voicing his belief that the person in question deserves to occupy a position of such authority; (b) expressing admiration for the person; (c) expressing a desire to be guided or controlled by the person; (d) expressing resentment at the belief that the person is trying to guide or control him—or the belief that the person actually is guiding or controlling him. The presence of an anonymous authority figure in a dream generally means that the dreamer either desires to submit or resents being forced to submit to someone else's authority.

CONTAINER (9)—Containers, especially those which are round in shape, are vaginal symbols. Their appearance in a dream almost invariably is far less significant than the actions of dream characters toward them.

COOK (8)—Cooks, of course, prepare and serve food, and thereby provide a person with strength and nourishment. In dream interpretation, this strength and nourishment may be of a metaphoric as well as of a literal sort. Thus, when a cook appears in a dream, his functions are (a) to make a person healthy and strong, (b) to help the person develop desired qualities of character and personality, (c) to solve whatever problems beset the person. Naturally, the significance of a cook in any given dream will depend on his identity and his actions rather than upon his mere appearance in the dream. Hence, if a person dreams of himself as a cook, he may be expressing (a) a desire to serve other people in the manner described above, (b) his resentment that other people look to him to serve them in this manner. If he dreams of a friend or acquaintance in the role of a cook, he may be voicing (a) the belief that the person is capable of serving others in this manner; (b) the desire that the person serve him in this manner; (c) the belief that the person falsely believes himself capable of serving others in this manner. If he dreams of an anonymous cook, he generally will be expressing a desire for someone—anyone—to serve him in this manner. On a more deeply symbolic level, the cook who appears in a dream may also represent the dreamer's mother, who was the first person to serve him in this manner. Thus, cook-dreams may also testify to the dreamer's desire for (a) love and affection, (b) a return to the days of childhood, when he was secure and free from cares; (c) a return to life of his deceased mother or a return to health of his ailing mother. If the dreamer feels in some way responsible for the unhappiness of his mother, the presence of a cook in his dream may also testify to guilt feelings.

CORD (3)—When a piece of cord appears in a dream, it usually symbolizes the umbilical cord, which binds a foetus to its mother. Thus, a dreamer who envisions himself tied to another person by a piece of cord may be expressing (a) the desire to be dependent upon that person, as he was dependent upon his mother before the umbilical cord was severed; (b) resentment at what he perceives to be a dependence upon that person. Meanwhile, the dreamer who pictures a broken strand of cord may be expressing (a) a desire to break free from authority or domination—i.e., to sever the cord of dependence; (b) a desire to terminate an unpleasant relationship—thus, to break the ties that bind; (c) regret that there is no one upon whom he can now depend; (d) regret at the loss of his mother.

CORPSE (4)—A corpse generally symbolizes death fears or wishes. These fears or wishes may pertain to the dreamer's own death or to the death of someone else. In some cases, however, the death may be metaphoric—as in the death of a love affair or of an era in the dreamer's life.

COTTAGE (8)—Cottages have the connotation of being cozy and homelike. Thus, dreams set in a cottage may indicate the dreamer's desire to (a) bring or restore tranquility to his life, (b) escape a problem or unpleasant situation which presently troubles him, (c) return to a period in his life when things were less hectic than they are now. Naturally, however, what transpires in the cottage which a person is dreaming about will almost invariably be more significant than the mere fact that a cottage appears in the dream.

COUNTING—The act of counting may symbolize several things. Since one of the items which we most frequently count is money, the person who dreams of counting—no matter what it is that he is counting in his dream—may be expressing a concern over financial affairs. However, the same dream may indicate the dreamer's belief that he is a failure—i.e., that he has counted up his accomplishments in life and has found that they fail to meet his expectations of himself. Also, the person who dreams of counting may be expressing self-satisfaction; in other words, he is counting his "blessings," accomplishments, good works and deeds, etc.

COURT (1)—Since a court is a place where a person is put on trial, dreams which are set in a courtroom may be indicative of the dreamer's feeling that he is being judged—either with respect to culpability for a real or imagined misdeed, or with respect to his success or failure in discharging certain obligations. However, the fact that a dream is set in a courtroom is far less significant than the role of the dreamer in the dream and the action which transpires in the courtroom.

CRAB (6)—In the vernacular, a person with an unpleasant disposition is described as a "crab." Thus, when a crab appears in a dream, it may mean (a) that the dreamer feels antagonism and/or hostility toward other characters in the dream, (b) that the dreamer fears that people think of him as "an old crab."

CRADLE (7)—A cradle connotes childbirth and infancy. Thus, a person who dreams of a cradle generally is expressing (a) a desire to enjoy the security and protection which he enjoyed as an infant, when he was "in the cradle;" (b) feelings of inadequacy and helplessness—in other words, the feeling that he is like a baby in its cradle; (c) the desire to be pampered, as he had been when he was a baby; (d) a craving for attention and love without reciprocal obligations—a situation which he enjoyed in the cradle; (e) the desire to avoid or shirk responsibility; (f) the wish to become a parent; (g) the fear that he may become a parent against his wishes. Naturally, however, the dreamer's role with respect to the cradle will be far more significant than the mere appearance of a cradle in a dream. (For further interpretations of CRADLE, see BABY.)

CREAM (4)—Cream is symbolic of luxury, affluence, the "good things" in life. Thus, the person who dreams of cream generally is expressing (*a*) the desire to lead a more affluent life; (*b*) the fear that his fortunes will take a turn for the worse; (*c*) the expectation that his fortunes will take a turn for the better; (*d*) guilt stemming from the belief that he enjoys more affluence than he feels he is rightfully entitled to; (*e*) resentment and envy stemming from the belief that he does not enjoy as much affluence as he feels he is rightfully entitled to.

CRIB (5)—A crib connotes childbirth and infancy. Thus, a person who dreams of a crib generally is expressing (*a*) a desire to enjoy the security and protection which he enjoyed as a baby, when he was confined to a crib; (*b*) feelings of inadequacy and helplessness—in other words, the feeling that he is like a baby in its crib; (*c*) the desire to be pampered, as he had been when he was a baby; (*d*) a craving for attention and love without reciprocal obligations—a situation which he enjoyed in the cradle; (*e*) the desire to avoid or shirk responsibility; (*f*) the wish to become a parent; (*g*) the fear that he may become a parent against his wishes. Naturally, however, the dreamer's role with respect to the crib will be far more significant than the mere appearance of a crib in a dream. (For further interpretations of CRIB, see BABY.)

CRIME (3)—The person who dreams that he himself is committing or has committed a crime generally is voicing (*a*) feelings of guilt about a real or imagined misdeed; (*b*) fears of being discovered as the perpetrator of some real or imagined misdeed; (*c*) fears of having hurt someone whom he holds dear. The person who dreams that someone else is committing or has committed a crime generally is expressing (*a*) distrust for that person; (*b*) fears that he himself will soon be wronged, either by the person he is dreaming about or by someone else; (*c*) the belief that he has been wronged, either by the person he is dreaming about or by someone else.

CROWN (1)—A crown symbolizes wealth, power and authority. Thus, the person who dreams of a crown usually is expressing (*a*) the desire to become rich, powerful and authoritative; (*b*) the fear that he is not as rich, powerful and authoritative as he should be. Naturally, the mere appearance of a crown in a dream will be far less significant than the function of the crown. Thus, a father who dreams that he is a king whose crown has been stolen may be testifying to the belief that his family does not pay sufficient attention to his opinions, while an unmarried girl who dreams that her boy friend is wearing a crown may be expressing a desire that the boy friend be more rich, powerful and/or authoritative than he is.

CRYING—The act of crying signifies pain or sorrow. Thus, the person who dreams that he is crying generally will be expressing sorrow over the event which takes place in the dream. However, crying may also have a reverse significance —in other words, it may be evidence of a dreamer's unconscious pleasure over an event which he consciously knows to be unpleasant or even tragic. Thus, the man who pictures himself crying at his wife's deathbed may actually desire her death; because he is ashamed of this desire, he disguises his true feelings by assuming a posture of grief. The question to ask yourself if you envision yourself crying in a dream is: Do I have good reason to believe that the event I am crying about actually will come about in the very near future? If the answer is no, chances are that you actually want the event to come about, your posture of grief notwithstanding.

CUCKOLD (6)—A cuckold is a man whose wife has been unfaithful to him. The man who dreams that he has been cuckolded generally is expressing (a) a fear that his wife will betray him; (b) his belief that his wife already has betrayed him; (c) guilt over having betrayed her (as a result of which betrayal he feels that he deserves to be betrayed in turn). The woman who dreams of cuckolding her husband generally is voicing (a) feelings of guilt for having done so; (b) fears that she will do so in the near future; (c) the belief that he has betrayed her (as a result of which betrayal he deserves to be betrayed in turn). However, dreams of cuckolding and/or being cuckolded may also be significant on a metaphoric level. Hence, the same fears, guilt feelings, beliefs and desires listed above may pertain to nonsexual betrayal—for example, a husband's lying to a wife or vice-versa while competing for the affections of their children.

CUCUMBER (4)—Cucumbers, because of their shape, are phallic symbols. Thus, a man who dreams of giving a cucumber to someone may be expressing a desire to have sexual relations with that person. A man who dreams of possessing a large cucumber—or a bountiful supply of cucumbers—may be voicing unconscious feelings of sexual inadequacy. A girl who dreams of receiving a cucumber from a man may be expressing a desire to have sexual relations with him. A girl who dreams of possessing a supply of cucumbers of her own may be revealing unconscious homosexual tendencies, or a desire to enjoy the power and strength which men generally enjoy in society, or a desire to overpower the men in her life (by taking possession of their virility).

CUP (4)—Cups, because they are containers, are vaginal symbols. A common cup-dream is one in which a girl holds a cup which a man fills with a liquid. This dream generally signifies the dreamer's desire for sexual intercourse or his fear that he will not be able to resist the temptation to engage in sexual intercourse.

CUTTING—Dreams in which the act of cutting takes place may be interpreted in several ways. One interpretation is that the dreamer wishes to inflict injury upon himself or upon someone else. Another is that the dreamer desires to sever a personal or business relationship. If the dreamer envisions himself cutting or attempting to cut the body of another person, he may be exhibiting hostility toward that person; also, he may be expressing an unconscious desire to lessen the other person's power or authority over him. Likewise, if the dreamer is the person being cut, he generally is testifying to the fear that other persons feel hostility toward him or that others are trying to diminish his power or authority over them. As is the case with most actions, the action of cutting itself is generally of far less significance than the identity of the person who is performing it, the identity of the person (or the nature of the object) upon whom (or which) it is being performed, and the circumstances under which the performance takes place.

D

DAM (9)—A dam is a barrier against the forces of nature, a man-made instrument by means of which the otherwise uncontrollable is brought under control. Thus, when a person dreams of a dam, he usually is expressing unconscious feelings about a situation or a relationship which he believes requires very rigid control. If the dreamer dreams that he is constructing a dam, he probably is expressing the belief that he should exercise greater control in an area in which he previously has exercised insufficient control. If he dreams that a dam is breaking, he generally is expressing his fear that he is losing control.

DANCING—Dancing is symbolic of youth, joy and victory. Thus, when a person dreams that he is dancing, he generally is voicing (a) feelings of happiness with respect to some specific achievement or victory; (b) feelings of contentment with life in general; (c) the desire for happiness and contentment. However, dancing also has sexual connotations. Thus, if you dream of dancing with someone, you may also be indicating your desire for sexual intercourse with that person.

DENTIST (1)—The removal of a tooth symbolizes death, for an extracted tooth leaves a gap in the midst of other teeth in precisely the same way that a person who dies leaves a gap in his family. Thus, when a person dreams of going to a dentist to have a tooth extracted, he may be expressing his unconscious desire for or fear of death. Similarly, the person who dreams that a friend or acquaintance is having a tooth extracted may be revealing an unconscious death wish or death fear with respect to that person. However, dreams involving dentists may also be "current event" dreams; thus, if you presently are having trouble with your teeth, you may merely be reaffirming in your dreams a concern which you already are aware of in waking life. Finally, since most people regard all dental work as a necessary evil, a dream of going to a dentist for purposes other than tooth extraction may be symbolic of the dreamer's feelings that he must face up to an unpleasant responsibility. In such a dream, the dentist may represent a person whom or a situation which the dreamer fears, dislikes and/or resents.

DEPUTY (8)—A deputy is an assistant, a helpmate, a subordinate. Thus, the person who casts himself in the role of a deputy generally is indicating his desire to be of assistance in a specific situation or to pursue a career in which he will be of assistance to others. Similarly, the dreamer who casts another person in the role of a deputy may be indicating a desire to receive aid or assistance from that person. On the other hand, the person who dreams of himself as a deputy may also be revealing an inner resentment at being forced to play "second fiddle" in a business or romantic relationship. Likewise, the person who casts someone else in the role of a deputy may be revealing a desire to have power and/or authority over that person. Finally, the dreamer who casts someone else in the role of a deputy may be expressing his belief that the other person is in some way inferior to himself.

DESERT (8)—The desert, arid and devoid of life, is symbolic of death on both the literal and metaphoric levels. Thus, a person who dreams of a desert may be expressing death fears or wishes, or the fear that his own creativity, talent and/or emotions have "gone dry." Also, the barrenness of a desert may have sexual significance. Hence, the woman who dreams of a desert may be expressing a fear of being barren or a wish that she were in fact barren, and a man who dreams of a desert may be expressing similar fears of or desires for sterility.

DIAMOND (6)—Diamonds, like all other gems, symbolize both love and money. The love symbolism is more common among men. However, the mere appearance of diamonds in a dream is generally far less significant than the actions of the dream characters with respect to the diamonds. Thus, if a woman dreams that a man or another woman is wearing a diamond, she may be expressing her desire for the man's love or her belief that the man or woman wearing the diamond is affluent. If a woman dreams that she has been given a gift of diamonds, she probably is expressing her desire for the love of the person who gave her the gift or her belief that the person does in fact love her. If she dreams that another woman has stolen her diamond, she most likely is revealing a fear that the other woman has stolen the love of the man whom she—the dreamer—loves. Likewise, if a man dreams that another man or a woman is wearing a diamond, he probably is expressing his belief that the person in question is affluent. If he dreams of giving a diamond to a woman, he probably is expressing his love for that woman.

DICE (3)—Dice are instruments used in games of chance. Thus, dreams involving dice may indicate the dreamer's (a) desire to take a chance on a certain business venture or romantic involvement; (b) fear of taking a chance on a certain business venture or romantic involvement; (c) belief that he should take greater risks than he thus far has been taking; (d) fear that he recently has been pushing his luck too far. Naturally, the appearance of dice in a dream will generally be far less significant than the identities of the persons using the dice and the actions of these persons with respect to the dice.

DIGGING—The act of digging lends itself to a wide variety of interpretations. A person who dreams of digging may be expressing his desire to uncover the true facts about a certain situation or to reveal someone else's true feelings toward himself. The same dream may be indicative of the dreamer's desire to hide the facts about a certain situation or to hide his feelings toward a certain person. Also, dreams of digging may mean that the dreamer is afraid that someone will "dig up" certain facts which he wants to conceal. Finally, dreams of digging may be indicative of the dreamer's fear that someone else will uncover the dreamer's feelings toward that person.

DINING—Food symbolizes love, strength, power and virility. Thus, dreams of dining are generally related to desires for love, strength, power and/or virility. If a person dreams of eating an extremely satisfying meal, he probably is expressing his satisfaction with the status quo. If he dreams of eating endlessly, he may be testifying to the fact that his hunger for love, strength, power and/or virility remains unsatisfied. If he dreams of serving food to another person, he most likely is revealing his love for that person or his desire to help the person become stronger or more powerful. This latter dream, however, may also mean that the dreamer resents his relationship with another person—that is, he resents the fact that he must contribute to that person's strength and power, or he resents the fact that he is giving love to the person without receiving love in return.

DIRT (6)—Dirt symbolizes both guilt—especially sexual guilt—and death. The person who dreams that he is being covered with dirt or has been covered with dirt probably is revealing deep-seated death wishes or fears (related to the fact that a dead person's coffin is covered with dirt) or feelings of guilt with respect to a specific act (especially a sexual act, since sexual intercourse is regarded by many people as "dirty"). The person who dreams that he is covering some-one else with dirt may (*a*) wish the other person's death, (*b*) fear that he is in some way responsible for the other person's death or ill fortune, (*c*) feel that he has "dirtied" the other person sexually.

DIVORCE—The act of divorce serves to terminate a marital relationship. In dreams, divorce may pertain to other relationships as well. Dreams of divorce thus may be indicative of the dreamer's desire to terminate a business or romantic relationship, or of his fear that a business or romantic relationship will be terminated by his associate or partner in that relationship.

DOCTOR (3)—The doctor—be he physician, educator, psychologist, philosopher or what-have-you—is an authority figure, a person to whom one can turn for guidance, leadership and wisdom, a person in whom one can confide and trust. When a person envisions himself as a doctor, he generally is expressing his desire to possess these qualities. When he envisions another person as a doctor, he may be (*a*) voicing his belief that the person in question possesses these qualities; (*b*) expressing general admiration for the person; (*c*) expressing a desire to be guided, led, counseled, etc., by that person; (*d*) expressing resentment at the belief that the person is trying to guide, lead and/or control him against his wishes—or the belief that the person actually is guiding, leading and/or controlling him. The presence of an anonymous doctor in a dream may mean that the dreamer either desires to submit or resents being forced to submit to someone else's authority, guidance, leadership, control, etc.

DOG (8)—To dream of a dog is generally to express unconscious desires for companionship and affection. In some cases, the same dream may mean that the dreamer desires companionship and affection without the responsibilities which these things ordinarily entail—for a dog usually is loyal to his master, even if the master is not loyal to the dog.

DOLL (7)—Dolls often appear in dreams as replacement figures for children. When such is the case, the dream may have the same significance as a dream in which children actually do appear. (For interpretation of such dreams, consult

BABY.) However, to dream of a doll may also be to reveal a desire to return to the carefree days of childhood—when one played with dolls.

DOOR (7)—Doors are extremely common dream symbols which lend themselves to a wide variety of different interpretations. If a person dreams of opening a door, he generally is expressing a desire to enter into a business or romantic relationship or to escape from an unpleasant situation. Similarly, the person who dreams of closing a door is probably revealing a desire to terminate a certain relationship—i.e., to "close the door" on a certain portion of his life. Doors also symbolize barriers. Thus, the person who dreams of trying to unlock a door may be expressing his desire to (a) break down a barrier between himself and another person; (b) overcome the obstacles which separate him from the attainment of a specific goal; (c) discover the true facts about a certain situation—i.e., to unlock the door to truth. If in this dream the person finds himself unable to unlock the door, he probably is indicating his fear that he will not be able to surmount the barrier in question; if he dreams that someone helps him unlock the door, he probably is revealing his dependence upon that person for assistance in attaining his goal. As is so often the case with dream objects, the actions of characters in the dream usually are far more important than the mere appearance of the object in the dream.

DOUGHNUT (7)—Doughnuts, because of their shape, are vaginal symbols. If a woman dreams of giving a doughnut to a man, she generally is testifying to a desire to have sexual intercourse with him. If she dreams that a man has taken a doughnut from her by force, she probably is revealing the fear or the desire that he will rape her. Likewise, a man who dreams that a woman has given him a doughnut probably is revealing that he hopes she will welcome him sexually or that he is aware of her sexual attraction toward him. The man who dreams that a woman has refused to give him a doughnut probably is voicing the belief that she will not welcome him sexually. The man who dreams of taking a doughnut from a woman by force probably is revealing his desire to overcome the woman sexually by force or his belief that the only way he can enjoy her sexually is to overcome her by force.

DRIFTING—The act of drifting suggests a number of things. The person who dreams of drifting through space—or of being in a boat which is adrift—generally is expressing the belief that he is "drifting" through life, that he never will be successful at anything. Another interpretation of such a dream is that the dreamer longs to stop drifting—that is, to settle down to a particular career or way of life, to "establish roots" somewhere. Finally, dreams of drifting may signify the desire to drift—i.e., the desire to rebel against the rigid routine of daily life.

DRINKING—The act of drinking may be significant on several levels. Since the drinking of alcoholic beverages generally brings to mind good fellowship, convivial company and general merriment, the person who dreams of drinking may merely be expressing a desire to live a happier, more cheerful life. However, with many individuals, alcoholic beverages have a decidedly negative connotation. This is especially the case among people who have a personal drinking problem or who are involved with other persons who have a drinking problem. Alcoholic beverages also might have a decidedly negative connotation for people who have at one time or another suffered abuse at the hands of an habitual drinker. Thus, to dream of drinking might also be to voice feelings of dissatisfaction about the dreamer's perceived lack of will power, self-control, etc. Of course, alcoholic beverages are not the only beverages which one may drink. Thus, dreams of drinking may also pertain to such drinking as is necessary for the body's sustenance and growth—the drinking, for example, of water, milk and other liquids. Dreams of this sort, like dreams of dining, generally are related to desires for love, strength, power and/or virility. (See DINING for detailed interpretations.) Finally, drinking may be symbolic of infancy, at which time the individual's sole nutritional intake was of a liquid nature. Thus, the person who dreams of drinking—especially straight-from-the-bottle—may be expressing an unconscious desire to return to the days of his childhood, when he was loved and protected by those around him, when all his needs and desires were satisfied by others, and when he did not have to cope with the harsh realities of everyday existence. In this context, a person who dreams of drinking may also be disclosing unconscious feelings of resentment toward a parent, friend or spouse for treating him like a baby. Similarly, the dreamer who envisions another person in the act of drinking may be testifying to his belief that the other person is immature, or may be expressing his unconscious desire to pamper or "baby" the other person. Because of the inordinately wide variety of interpretations which can be attached to dreams of drinking, it is essential in interpreting these dreams to relate the act of drinking to the identities of the persons involved in the dream and to the dreamer's feelings toward these persons.

DRIVER (4)—The driver of a vehicle is the person who controls the destiny of his passengers. Thus, the dreamer who pictures himself as the driver of a vehicle may be expressing (a) the belief that he is in fact the controller of his own destiny; (b) the fear that he is not the controller of his own destiny but should be; (c) the desire for responsibility over other people (his passengers). Similarly, the dreamer who envisions another person as the driver of a vehicle may be expressing (a) his desire that this person guide or control his life; (b) his resentment at the belief that the person does in fact guide or control his life, or is trying to.

DROWNING—A variety of interpretations may be attached to dreams of drowning. One interpretation is that the dreamer feels that life is overwhelming him—i.e., that he is "drowning" in an ocean of personal problems. Another interpretation is that the dreamer unconsciously desires or fears death. A third interpretation is sexual: since bodies of water symbolize the female genitalia, the male who dreams that he is drowning may be expressing a desire for sexual intercourse. If it is another person rather than the dreamer who is drowning, the dreamer may be expressing a death wish with respect to that person or a fear that the person will die.

E

EARTHQUAKE (8)—Earthquakes symbolize both destruction and coital orgasm. Thus, to dream of an earthquake may be to express (a) feelings of hostility and aggression; (b) feelings of guilt (as a result of which the dreamer wants to be punished by being destroyed in an earthquake); (c) feelings of general hatred toward mankind (hence, the desire for mankind's destruction in an earthquake); (d) the desire for sexual satisfaction; (e) fears of being unable to achieve sexual satisfaction. Naturally, the circumstances under which an earthquake takes place in a dream and the actions of characters in the dream will be of more significance than the mere fact that an earthquake takes place in a dream.

EATING—Food symbolizes love, strength, power and virility. Thus, dreams of eating are generally related to desires for love, strength, power and/or virility. If a person dreams of eating an extremely satisfying meal, he probably is expressing his satisfaction with the status quo. If he dreams of eating endlessly, he may be testifying to the fact that his hunger for love, strength, power and/or virility remains unsatisfied. If he dreams of serving food to another person, he most likely is revealing his love for that person or his desire to help the person become stronger or more powerful. This latter dream, however, may also mean that the dreamer resents his relationship with another person—that is, he resents the fact that he must contribute to that person's strength and power, or he resents the fact that he is giving love to the person without receiving love in return.

EEL (4)—Eels, because of their shape, are phallic symbols.

EGG (1)—Eggs, because of their shape, symbolize the male's testicles. Since the testicles are the storehouse of the male's virility, dreams involving eggs lend themselves to a wide variety of interpretations. If a man dreams of giving eggs to a woman, he may be expressing (a) a desire to have sexual intercourse with her; (b) the feeling that he has surrendered his power to her. If a woman dreams of giving eggs to a man, she may be expressing (a) a belief that it is she who is responsible for his virility—and, by extension, for his success in life; (b) resentment over the fact that he enjoys certain prerogatives which she does not; (c) a desire to help him, to contribute to his strength and power. If a man dreams of taking eggs from a woman, he may be voicing (a) the belief that he is dependent upon her; (b) the desire to render her weak and powerless. If a woman dreams of taking eggs from a man, she may be voicing (a) the desire to have sexual intercourse with him; (b) the desire to strip him of his power. If a man dreams of breaking eggs, he may be revealing (a) a lack of confidence in his strength, power and virility; (b) sexual guilt—evidenced by the fact that he wants to destroy the source of his sexual energy; (c) a fear that he will lose his sexual potency or his physical strength. If a woman dreams of breaking eggs, she may be revealing (a) a desire to overpower men (by depriving them of their strength and virility), (b) an abhorrence of sexual intercourse (as evidenced by the fact that she is destroying the source of man's sexual energy).

ELEVATOR (8)—Elevators symbolize upward movement. Thus, if you dream that you are in an ascending elevator, you may be expressing your belief or hope that your fortunes are rising, or you may be giving testimony to your desire to go up in the world. However, elevators—like everything else which rises—must also come down. Hence, if you picture yourself riding in a descending elevator, you may be expressing the fear that your career is going downhill, that your fortunes are falling, or that you will not be successful in a specific venture or in life generally. A dreamer who envisions himself in an elevator which is stuck may be expressing the feeling that his life has come to a standstill, that a particular business or romantic relationship is stuck in a rut. Finally, when a child dreams of riding in an elevator, he is probably expressing a desire to grow up.

EMBER (7)—An ember is a glowing fragment of coal or some other flammable material—especially such a fragment smoldering in ashes. As such, it signifies death, both literal and metaphoric. Thus, to have a dream in which embers appear is generally to reveal (a) fears or wishes with respect to one's own death or to the death of another party; (b) the desire to terminate (i.e., to "burn out," or to put to death figuratively) a business or social relationship; (c) the belief that a certain business or social relationship is about to be terminated; (d) the fear that a certain business or social relationship will be terminated against one's wishes; (e) the fear that one's health is failing (i.e., that one's life is "burning out"); (f) the fear that someone else's health is failing, or the desire that it fail; (g) the fear or the belief that one's fortunes are declining, or are about to decline; (h) the fear, belief or wish that someone else's fortunes are declining or are about to decline. However, as is generally the case with dream objects of this sort, the mere appearance of an ember or of embers in a dream usually is far less significant than the circumstances under which the object appears, the actions and identities of the characters who populate the dream, and the presence of other dream objects. For example, if you dream that your best friend has dropped something into a fire's embers and that you have retrieved it, you may be voicing the desire to have that person turn to you in times of trouble, or the resentment that the person is in fact dependent upon you. Likewise, if you dream that you have extinguished a smoldering fire by pouring water on its embers, you may be expressing the belief that you must take a more active role in bringing about the termination of some business or social relationship which you presently find undesirable. On the other hand, if you dream of sitting around the embers of a fire with a compatible group of friends, you may merely be indicating a desire to enjoy the company of these friends, or contentment at the fact that they are your friends.

EMBRACING—The action of embracing, in real life as well as in dreams, signifies love and affection. Thus, to dream of embracing someone is generally to express love and affection for that person, or the desire to have a loving and affectionate relationship with that person. Naturally, the questions to ask yourself if embracing takes place in one of your dreams are: Who is embracing whom? Under what circumstances? What are the reactions of the persons embracing to each other? What are the reactions of other characters who may populate the dream.

EMERALD (4)—Emeralds, like all other gems, symbolize both love and money. The love symbolism is more common among women, the money symbolism more common among men. However, the mere appearance of emeralds in a dream is generally far less significant than the actions of the dream characters with respect to the emeralds. Thus, if a woman dreams that a man or another woman is wearing an emerald, she may be expressing her desire for the man's love or her belief that the man or woman wearing the emerald is affluent. If a woman dreams that she has been given a gift of emeralds, she probably is expressing her desire for the love of the person who gave her the gift or her belief that the person does in fact love her. If she dreams that another woman has stolen her emerald, she most likely is revealing a fear that the other woman has stolen the love of the man whom she—the dreamer—loves. Likewise, if a man dreams that another man or a woman is wearing an emerald, he probably is expressing his belief that the person in question is affluent. If he dreams of giving an emerald to a woman, he probably is expressing his love for that woman.

EMPTINESS—The quality of emptiness frequently is related to objects which appear in a dream. For example, a person may dream of holding an empty glass, or of being in an empty room, or of riding in a bus or other conveyance which is (except for his presence) empty of people. When the dream object which is empty is essentially a container—e.g., a glass, a box, a dish, an oven—the dreamer generally is testifying to fears or desires regarding the usual contents of the container. These fears and desires may also be significant on a metaphoric level; hence, the person who dreams of an empty glass may be expressing the belief that his life is without meaning (i.e., empty) or that his talents have been dissipated. When the dream object which is empty is essentially a setting rather than a container—e.g., a room, a bus, etc.—he generally is testifying to fears of loneliness or to the desire to be alone. Because of the wide variety of interpretations which can be attached to the quality of emptiness in dreams, such dreams should be analyzed very carefully and with keen attention toward such details as the identities and actions of dream characters, the symbolism of the dream object itself which is empty, and the symbolism of other objects which appear in the dream.

ENGINE (9)—An engine is, of course, an apparatus which makes a machine work. The mere appearance of one in a dream generally is without significance except insofar as it relates to actions which transpire in the dream. Thus, to dream of being on a bus, plane or other conveyance which is having engine trouble may be to express the fear that one's plans, desires, etc., cannot be fulfilled without difficulty. To dream that someone else is repairing an engine for the dreamer is generally to voice the desire that that person (or that any person) assist the dreamer in an enterprise; the same dream, by extension, may signify the dreamer's feelings of inferiority or inadequacy—i.e., he cannot manage his own affairs, and therefore requires outside help. (To some people, the term, "engine," connotes the vehicle which pulls a train. For interpretations in this context, see LOCOMOTIVE.)

ENGINEER (5)—An engineer is a scientist who designs and/or constructs mechanical apparatus. The phrase, "engineer," also is employed to describe the person who operates a locomotive. When the engineer who appears in a person's dream is of the scientist variety, his appearance in the dream generally is without significance except insofar as his actions affect dream objects or dream characters. However, if one's dream-engineer is a person who operates a locomotive, the dream may be symbolic with respect to the engineer's function as a person who controls the destiny of his passengers. Thus, the dreamer who pictures himself as a locomotive engineer may be expressing (a) the belief that he is in fact the controller of his own destiny; (b) the fear that he is not the controller of his own destiny but should be; (c) the desire for responsibility over other people (his passengers). Similarly, the dreamer who envisions another person as a locomotive engineer may be expressing (a) his desire that this person guide or control his life; (b) his resentment at the belief that this person does in fact guide or control his life, or is trying to.

ESCAPING—The action of escaping, in real life as well as in dreams, accomplishes the extrication of a person from an undesired situation. When escaping takes place in one of your dreams, ask yourself: Who is escaping? From what? Under what circumstances? Is anyone helping him? Is anyone trying to hinder him? Is his attempt to escape successful?

EXPLOSION (3)—An explosion symbolizes destruction. Thus, to dream of an explosion may be to express (a) feelings of hostility and aggression; (b) feelings of guilt (as a result of which the dreamer wants to be punished, as by an explosion in which he and/or his property are destroyed); (c) feelings of general hatred toward mankind (ergo, the desire to see the human race go up in an explosion); (d) fears that his desires will be thwarted (i.e., that his wishes will be "exploded"). Naturally, the circumstances under which an explosion takes place in a dream, and the actions of characters in the dream, will be of more significance than the mere fact that an explosion takes place in a dream.

F

FACTORY—Since a factory is a place where things are manufactured, dreams set in factories may be indicative of the dreamer's desire to manufacture a new life for himself, or to be creative, or to enjoy general success in life. However, as is the case with all dream settings, the fact that a factory appears in a dream is far less significant than the characters who populate the factory and the activities which transpire therein.

FALLING—Falling is one of the most common of all dream actions, and lends itself to a variety of interpretations. More often than not, it signifies downward movement. Thus, the person who dreams that he is falling may be expressing (a) the belief or fear that his career is rapidly declining; (b) the belief or fear that a relationship in which he is involved is coming to an end; (c) death fears or wishes. However, falling may also have metaphoric significance. Thus, the person who dreams that he is falling may be voicing (a) the fear that he is succumbing to a romantic or erotic temptation; (b) the hope that another person will succumb romantically or erotically to him. Falling in a dream may also signify that the dreamer fears that he is unable to cope with his present problems—in other words, that he is unable to stand on his own two feet.

FATHER (4)—The father is an authority figure. In dreams he represents a person to whom the dreamer can turn for leadership or guidance, or a person in whom the dreamer wishes to trust and confide. He may also represent a person or persons whom the dreamer resents or fears. When the dreamer envisions himself as a father, he may be expressing his desire to be someone whom other people can turn to for leadership and guidance, or someone in whom other people can trust and confide; or he may be revealing a desire for a position of power and authority. In other cases, to dream of oneself as a father is to give voice to the desire to have children or the fear that one might become a father against one's wishes. When the dreamer's own father appears in a dream, there generally is no symbolic significance. However, if the dreamer casts another person in the role of his father, he may be expressing feelings of hostility toward his real father.

FENCE (6)—Fences symbolize both confinement and privacy. Thus, dreams in which fences appear may signify both the dreamer's feelings of restriction and confinement in his business and/or personal life or the dreamer's desire to keep other people from intruding upon his personal affairs. Also,

dreams of fences may have metaphoric significance in that
the dreamer may be voicing the desire to contain inner feelings and desires of which he is ashamed.

FINGER (5)—Fingers are, because of their shape, phallic
symbols. Thus, if a man dreams of stroking a woman with
his fingers, he probably is expressing a desire to have sexual
intercourse with her. Likewise, if a woman dreams of fon-
dling a man's fingers, she probably is expressing a desire to
fondle his penis—or, by extension, to have sexual intercourse
with him.

FIRE (2)—Fire symbolizes both death and sexual intercourse. Thus, the person who dreams that he or someone else
is on fire may be revealing death wishes or fears with respect
to himself or to the other party, or he may be revealing sexual desire. To dream that an inanimate object is on fire is
generally to testify to a desire or fear that the object will be
destroyed.

FIREMAN (3)—The fireman, as a person who extinguishes
fires, signifies a great many things in dreams. He is, first of
all, a person to whom one can turn for help. He is, second of
all, a guardian of property. And he is, third of all, a symbol
of masculine strength and virility. Naturally, the mere appearance of a fireman in a dream will be far less significant
than the identity of the fireman and the role which he plays
with respect to other dream characters. If a dreamer envisions himself as a fireman, he may be expressing (a) his desire to be the type of person who inspires confidence and
trust in others; (b) his desire to be generally helpful to people; (c) his desire to be competent and efficient, or his belief
that he is competent and efficient; (d) his desire for sexual
intercourse. If a dreamer envisions another person as a fireman he may be expressing (a) his admiration for the person;
(b) his belief that he can trust and confide in the person; (c)
his desire to be helped by the person; (d) his belief that the
person is competent and efficient; (e) his belief that the person wrongfully thinks himself to be the possessor of the qualities just described. If the dreamer is a woman, she may also
be expressing a desire to have sexual intercourse with the fireman in question—i.e., her desire to have him "douse the
fires" of her passion.

FISH (6)—Fish, because of their shape, are phallic symbols. Hence, if a man dreams of bringing fish to a woman, he may be expressing his desire to have intercourse with her. Likewise, if a woman dreams of receiving fish from a man, she may be expressing her desire to have sexual intercourse with him—or her desire to rob him of his virility by taking away his penis. To dream of eating fish generally is to dream of increasing one's strength and power. To dream of fish which are foul-smelling is to voice unconscious feelings of disgust with sex. And, if a woman dreams of scaling fish, she may be testifying to a desire to strip men of their masculinity. However, the presence of fish in dreams need not have sexual significance. If, for example, a man dreams of going fishing, he may merely be expressing his desire to relax a little, to get away from the troubles of his present life-situation.

FISHING ROD (1)—Fishing rods are, because of their shape, phallic symbols. Their appearance in a dream generally will be far less significant than the actions which are performed with them. If, for example, a man dreams that he had just acquired a new fishing rod, he may be expressing (a) fears of sexual inadequacy—as evidenced by the fact that his old fishing rod was no longer satisfactory and had to be replaced; (b) the feeling that he has gained a new lease on life—witness the fact that the rod which he now has is brand new; (c) the desire to enjoy the sexual favors of a new woman. Likewise, if a woman dreams that a man has hit her with a fishing rod, she may be testifying to (a) her belief that men in general are sadistic; (b) her fear of sex; (c) her desire to be treated roughly in the sexual situation.

FLAGPOLE (2)—Flagpoles are, because of their shape, phallic symbols. As is the case with most phallic symbols, their appearance in a dream generally will be far less significant than their relationship to characters in the dream and the actions which are performed with and around them.

FLYING—The act of flying symbolizes both movement and freedom. The person who dreams that he is flying through the air probably is indicating (a) a desire to escape the multitude of problems which beset him daily; (b) a desire to attain a specific goal; (c) the wish to be stronger and more powerful than he actually is—in other words, to have power over even the immutable physical laws, like the law of gravity. Naturally, in dreams of this sort, the circumstances under which one is flying will be far more significant than the mere fact that one is flying. (For interpretations of dreams about flying in an airplane see AIRPLANE.)

FOUNTAIN (1)—The most common symbolism for fountains is longevity—as in the famed Fountain of Youth for which Ponce de Leon unsuccessfully searched. Thus, if a fountain appears in your dream, chances are that you (a) fear that you are growing too old too quickly; (b) would like to return to the days of your youth. However, fountains also may symbolize sexual power. Thus, the man who dreams of a fountain may be giving voice to the unconscious desire to be more virile.

G

GAMBLER (4)—Gamblers are people who take chances. Thus, when a dreamer pictures himself as a gambler, he may be expressing his desire to take a risk on a certain business venture or romantic involvement, or to be bolder and more daring in all his business and/or personal relationships. Likewise, if he envisions a friend or acquaintance as a gambler he may be expressing (a) admiration of the person's daring and venturesomeness; (b) envy of these qualities in the person; (c) the belief that the person should be more daring and venturesome than he actually is; (d) the belief that the person should be less daring and venturesome than he actually is. Meanwhile, if a dreamer envisions himself as an onlooker, or "kibitzer," in a gambling establishment, he may be indicating his desire to "play it safe" in life or his fear of taking more chances than he actually does take. By the same token, if he envisions another person in the kibitzer's role, he may be expressing (a) the belief that the other person is afraid to take chances; (b) resentment at the other person's unwillingness to take chances; (c) envy or admiration of the other person's ability to refrain from taking chances.

GARDEN (4)—A garden, as the setting for a dream, lends itself to a variety of interpretations. Since gardens generally are thought of as places of beauty wherein one may relax and enjoy himself, a person whose dream is set in a garden may be expressing (a) his desire to bring more beauty and enjoyment to his life; (b) his desire to escape from the hustle and bustle of everyday existence; (c) his feelings of contentment with the status quo of his life-situation. Gardens also remind many people of their youth—especially when the people in question are city dwellers who grew up in a rustic setting. To such individuals, dreams set in gardens may signify a desire to turn back the clock to the days when they were carefree and unburdened with responsibilities. Finally, gardens may have metaphoric significance: since a garden is a place where plants and flowers grow, dreams set in gardens may testify to the dreamer's desire to "cultivate" something—a new talent, an interest in some previously unexplored subject, a family, etc.

GIRL (1)—The appearance of a girl in a dream is of itself far less significant than the identity of the girl and the life-situation of the dreamer. In some cases, the girl will represent the dreamer herself. When this is true, the dreamer may be revealing her (a) desire to return to girlhood, when life was far less complex for her than it is today; (b) feelings of inferiority with respect to her peers, next to whom she is figuratively still just a girl; (c) desire to be pampered and cared for, as she was when she was a little girl; (d) craving for attention and love without reciprocal obligations—a situation which she enjoyed when she was a girl; (e) desire to avoid responsibilities. In other cases, the girl in a dream may represent an indefinite object of the dreamer's own attentions; in other words, by dreaming of a girl the dreamer may be indicating that she (or he) wants someone upon whom to lavish love and attention—someone who will not reject that love and attention. Small girls, when they appear in dreams of grown women, often are symbolic of the dreamers' lost youth. Older men who dream of young girls usually are expressing their desire to become fathers or to return to the days when their now-grown daughters were young girls.

GUN (6)—Guns are symbolic of death, violence and the male's penis. In those dreams in which a gun is phallically symbolic, it is usually associated in some fashion with violent or brutal sexuality.

H

HAND (9)—Dreams of hands are extremely common and lend themselves to a wide variety of meanings. Generally the appearance of hands in a dream is far less significant than the identity of the person to whom they belong, the manipulations which they perform and the circumstances under which they appear. A common hand-dream involves two people shaking hands. As in waking life, this gesture is symbolic of friendship. Another common hand-dream involves a pair of hands folded in prayer. The dreamer who envisions hands in this position generally is revealing (*a*) a desire for a solution to a current problem or an emotional conflict; (*b*) a deep-seated faith in a supreme being; (*c*) a desire for supernatural assistance in one's everyday troubles; (*d*) gratitude for the benefits which one presently enjoys. Still another hand-dream involves hands which are grasping or clutching at something. This dream may reveal the dreamer's fear of death (the hands are clutching at life) or his fear that something which he desires intensely may slip out of his grasp. Because dreams of hands can have so many different meanings, they must be analyzed very carefully with special emphasis on any other dream objects which may be present, the setting of the dream, and the personalities and actions of the dream characters. (See also, FINGER.)

HARVEST (4)—A harvest is the gathering of a crop. If the dreamer was raised on a farm, his dream of a harvest may represent a desire to return to the days of his youth, when his cares were fewer and his problems more easily solved. If the dreamer is presently engaged in farming, his dream of a harvest probably will be a "current event" dream—that is, a dream which reflects problems and aspirations which presently confront him. For non-farmers, dreams of a harvest most likely will have metaphoric significance: the dreamer may be expressing a desire to bring to fruition a particular plan or project, or to "harvest" a crop of his own—i.e., to raise a family.

HEARTH (3)—The hearth symbolizes warmth and comfort. The person who dreams of a hearth may be expressing either satisfaction with his present domestic existence or a desire for a happier home life.

HILL (5)—Hills are common dream settings. They are usually without symbolic significance. However, the action which takes place on a hill may be very meaningful in terms of dream interpretation. To dream that an object or person is at the top of the hill is to express one's belief that the object or person is beyond the dreamer's reach, or unattainable. To dream of an object falling or rolling down a hill is to hope that the object will become available to the dreamer. Finally, to dream of falling down a hill is to reveal a fear that one's fortunes are in jeopardy or that one's health is failing.

HITTING—Dreams which involve hitting usually indicate feelings of aggression and hostility or fear of violence. The dreamer who envisions himself hitting another person is revealing his own feelings of hostility and aggression. The dreamer who envisions being hit by another person probably is expressing a fear of that person—or, in some cases, a desire to be punished for a real or imagined misdeed. The dreamer who appears in the role of a witness to a fight between two or more persons may be expressing (a) a dislike of the participants in the fight (as evidenced by his desire to see them inflict injury upon each other); (b) feelings of aggression and hostility which he himself lacks the courage to act upon; (c) an abhorrence of violence. As is generally the case with all actions in dreams, the action of hitting is in itself less significant than the identities of the people involved and the circumstances under which their fight takes place. If you have a dream involving the act of hitting, ask yourself these questions: Who is hitting whom? Why? If you are an observer to the fight, what are your feelings toward the fighters?

HOLE (5)—Holes are vaginal symbols.

HORSE (2)—The horse is symbolic of masculinity and male sexual prowess. If a man dreams of horses, he probably is giving voice to an unconscious desire to be more virile and attractive to women or to an unconscious fear that he is losing his virility and his ability to attract women. If a woman dreams of horses, she is probably expressing her desire for sexual intercourse, or her desire to be accepted by men as an equal. The woman who dreams of being chased by a horse may be revealing a fear of sexual intercourse. The man who dreams of being chased by a horse may be giving voice to fears that he has homosexual tendencies.

HOSE (2)—Hoses are, because of their shape, phallic symbols.

HOSPITAL (1)—A hospital, of course, is a place where one goes when one is seriously ill. When a person dreams of being hospitalized he may be expressing his fear of ill health or of death. Similarly, when the dreamer envisions someone else being hospitalized he generally is displaying his concern over that person's health. However, in this latter case, the dreamer may also be revealing a desire that the persons whom he envisions in a hospital suffer ill health or die. On a more deeply symbolic level, the person who dreams of himself as a patient in a hospital may be revealing a desire to be pampered and taken care of. Likewise, the person who dreams of someone else as a hospital patient may be evidencing a desire to have that person in such a position that the person will be dependent on the dreamer for help.

HOUSE (5)—Since houses provide the setting for a majority of dreams, their appearance in most dreams is without significance. However, when a specific type of house appears in a dream, such as a castle (see CASTLE) or a cottage (see COTTAGE), then it may be of symbolic value.

HUNTING—Hunting is an activity in which a person, either for purposes of obtaining food or, more commonly, for sport, kills game. The same term, applied metaphorically, signifies searching—as in "hunting" for a lost object. With respect to hunting as an activity in which a person kills game, to dream of hunting generally is to express (a) feelings of hostility and aggression (the game being killed symbolize people, whom the dreamer would like to kill, maim or otherwise hurt); (b) the desire to be thought of as ruggedly masculine (the hunter, in killing game, ostensibly subjects himself to certain perils which less masculine persons avoid; (c) the desire to enjoy the comraderie of ruggedly masculine men (the hunter, presumably, is accepted as an equal by other hunters). With respect to hunting as a metaphor for searching, to dream of hunting generally is to indicate the desire to discover something. In dreams of this sort, the questions to ask yourself are: What are you hunting for? If it is an object rather than a person, does the object in question have symbolic significance (e.g., a key)? Are you being helped in your search? Is anyone impeding or trying to impede your search? What are the identities and actions of other dream characters who may be present? What is the setting of the dream?

I

ICE (8)—Ice is symbolic of death and of sexual frigidity. As is usually the case with dream objects of this sort, the role of the object in the dream is far more significant than the object's mere appearance in the dream.

ILLNESS—When a person dreams that he himself is ill, he generally is revealing (a) the fear that he soon will be ill or will die; (b) the belief that he isn't taking good enough care of his health; (c) the unconscious desire to be pampered and nursed, as an ill person is pampered and nursed. When a person dreams that someone else is ill, he generally is revealing (a) the fear that the other person soon will be ill or will die; (b) the desire that the other person soon will be ill or will die; (c) the belief that the other person isn't taking good enough care of his health; (d) the desire to pamper and nurse the other person; (e) the belief that the other person desires to be pampered and nursed.

ISLAND (5)—Islands symbolize isolation and loneliness. Thus, dreams set on an island generally signify (a) the dreamer's desire to isolate himself from people who are trying to get close to him; (b) the dreamer's desire to escape from a specific situation or from his life-situation in general; (c) the dreamer's belief that he is somehow isolated or cut off from his friends and associates or from society in general; (d) the dreamer's feelings of loneliness, either for a specific person or for any person who would offer him affection and companionship.

J

JAIL (5)—Jails symbolize restriction and confinement. Thus, the person who dreams that he is incarcerated in a jail generally is testifying to (a) feelings of restriction or confinement in his career or personal life; (b) the desire to suppress (i.e., to lock up, as in a jail cell) certain of his feelings or impulses —for example, a tendency toward aggressive behavior; (c) the belief that he should be punished for a real or imagined misdeed; (d) the fear that he will be punished for a real or imagined misdeed. If the dreamer envisions someone else in jail, he probably is revealing sentiments like those above with respect to the other person. If he dreams of himself as the warden of a jail, as a jail guard or as some other sort of prison official, he generally is expressing the desire to (a) enjoy authority over others; (b) punish his enemies; (c) escape punishment for real or imagined misdeeds of his own. Children who dream of being in jail generally are expressing the unconscious desire for more parental authority.

JEWELRY (8)—Jewelry symbolizes both love and money. The love symbolism is more common among women, the money symbolism more common among men. However, the mere appearance of jewelry in a dream is generally far less significant than the actions of the dream characters with respect to the jewelry. Thus, if a woman dreams that a man or another woman is wearing jewelry, she may be expressing the desire for the man's love or her belief that the man or woman wearing the jewelry is affluent. If a woman dreams that she has been given a gift of jewelry, she probably is expressing her desire for the love of the person who gave her the gift, or her belief that the person does in fact love her. If she dreams that another woman has stolen her jewelry, she most likely is revealing a fear that the other woman has stolen the love of the man whom she—the dreamer—loves. Likewise, if a man dreams that another man or a woman is wearing jewelry, he probably is expressing his belief that the person in question is affluent. If he dreams of giving jewelry to a woman, he probably is expressing his love for that woman.

JUDGE (2)—A judge is a person who decides the fate of others. When such a figure appears in a person's dream, the action of the figure—and his identity—almost invariably are more significant than the mere fact of his appearance. If, for example, the dreamer pictures himself as a judge, he may be expressing (a) the desire to stand in judgment of another person or persons; (b) fear of standing in judgment over another person or persons; (c) anxiety over a decision which he is about to make; (d) the desire to have power and authority over others. If someone the dreamer knows appears as a judge, the dreamer may be (a) voicing his belief that this person holds the dreamer's fate in his hands; (b) expressing his desire for this person's approval; (c) expressing his fear that the person will disapprove of something which the dreamer has said or done; (d) voicing his admiration for the person (by believing that the person is in fact qualified to stand in judgment over others); (e) expressing his resentment over the fact that the person wants to stand in judgment over the dreamer or over others; (*f*) expressing his resentment over the fact that the person does in fact stand in judgment over the dreamer or over others; (*g*) expressing his anxiety over the decision which the person is about to make; (*h*) expressing the belief that the person believes himself wrongly to be qualified to stand in judgment over others. If an anonymous judge appears in a dream, the dreamer generally is testifying to his own (*a*) fear that he himself is about to be judged for something he has said or done; (*b*) fear of being punished for a real or imagined misdeed; (*c*) desire to be punished for a real or imagined misdeed.

K

KEY (5)—Keys have a wide variety of meanings when they appear in dreams. One of the most common interpretations of a key dream is that the dreamer is seeking a solution to a specific problem or to the problems of life in general—in other words, he wants to find the "key" to the problem or problems. Another interpretation is that the dreamer desires to overcome some sort of barrier—just as the person with the proper key can overcome the barrier of a locked door. A third interpretation is that the dreamer suffers feelings of inferiority or inadequacy; thus, he cannot cope with his problems unless he has some special help—the key to the problems. Dreams of keys may also have sexual significance. A key is a phallic symbol and a keyhole is a vaginal symbol. Thus, the appearance of a key in a dream may indicate the dreamer's desire to have sexual intercourse with a specific person—i.e., he wishes to "unlock" the person's passions—or his desire for sexual satisfaction in general. Understandably, however, the mere appearance of keys in a dream generally will be far less meaningful than the actions which take place involving the keys and the identities of the characters performing the actions. Thus, if a man dreams that a woman is unlocking the door, he may be revealing (*a*) his belief that the woman desires him sexually (i.e., that she is attempting to open the door of his emotions); (*b*) his resentment over what he perceives to be her attempts to intrude upon his personal life; (*c*) his desire to have her pay attention to him. Conversely, if he dreams of a woman locking a door, he may be revealing (*a*) his fear that she does not desire him sexually (she is locking the door of her emotions to him); (*b*) his belief that she is trying to hide something from him; (c) his resentment over the secretiveness which she displays toward him in waking life. (For further interpretations, see DOOR.)

KILLING—The act of killing, when it takes place in dreams, generally symbolizes death fears and/or wishes or feelings of aggression and hostility. The main questions to ask yourself if killing takes place in one of your dreams: Who is killing whom? Why? What is the relationship of the killer and his victim? What is your reaction to the event?

KING (5)—The king is both an authority figure and a father figure. Thus, the appearance of a king in dreams may be symbolic on several levels. When the dreamer envisions himself as a king, he may be expressing (a) his desire for power; (b) his desire to be someone whom other people can turn to for leadership and guidance; (c) his belief that he is far more capable than people generally give him credit for being; (d) his fear that he is not as capable as he should-be; (e) his desire to become a father. If he envisions someone else in the role of a king, he may be voicing (a) his belief that this other person desires power; (b) his desire to turn to the other person for leadership and guidance; (c) his admiration for the person; (d) his resentment at what he perceives to be the other person's erroneously high opinion of himself. If the king in one's dreams is a real king and if the dreamer pictures himself as one of the king's associates, the dreamer probably is testifying to (a) a desire to associate with important and powerful individuals; (b) the fear that he is incapable of associating with important and powerful individuals. Finally, in many cases, the king who appears in a dream may actually represent the dreamer's own father. In these cases, all the actions and emotions which the king displays are actions and emotions which the dreamer attributes to his own father.

KNIFE (9)—Knives are symbolic of violence, death, sexual aggression and the male's penis. As is usually the case in dreams involving objects of this sort, the use to which the object is put in the dream generally is far more significant than the fact that the object appears in the dream.

L

LABORATORY (1)—A laboratory is a place where experiments are conducted. Thus, dreams which are set in laboratories generally indicate (*a*) the dreamer's dissatisfaction with his present life-situation (hence, his desire to experiment with new things); (*b*) the dreamer's desire to test his relationship with someone; (*c*) the dreamer's belief that another person is trying to put him to a test. However, dreams which are set in laboratories may also signify merely that the dreamer desires to become involved in scientific pursuits, or that he would like to bring more order to his life (order of the sort which generally is found in a laboratory).

LADDER (8)—Ladders are instruments by means of which a person gains access to higher places. Thus, the presence of a ladder in a dream may signify the dreamer's (*a*) desire to improve his lot in life (i.e., to "rise up" in the world); (*b*) wish to escape from his present life-situation or from a specific problem in his life; (*c*) desire to attain a certain goal. However, as is the case with all dream symbols of this sort, the mere appearance of a ladder in a dream generally is far less significant than the actions of dream characters with respect to the ladder. Questions to ask yourself if a ladder appears in your dreams: Is someone using the ladder? If so, is he climbing or descending? Is anyone interfering with his progress? Who is the person who is using the ladder? What is at the top of the ladder? What is at the bottom?

LAKE (2)—Lakes, like all bodies of water, are vaginal symbols.

LAMP (6)—Since lamps are sources of light, their appearance in dreams usually is indicative of the dreamer's desire to discover the truth about a particular situation—i.e., to shed light on the subject.

LANTERN (3)—Since lanterns are sources of light, their appearance in dreams usually is indicative of the dreamer's desire to discover the truth about a particular situation—i.e., to shed light on the subject.

LAUREL (6)—Laurels are symbolic of victory. Thus, the

person who dreams of wearing a laurel generally is expressing his desire to succeed in life or to be victorious in a specific situation. Likewise, the person who dreams that someone else is wearing a laurel generally is expressing (a) the belief that this other person is a success; (b) his admiration for the person; (c) his belief that the other person has been or will soon be victorious in a specific situation; (d) his resentment over the other person's knack for coming out on top in a situation.

LETTUCE (5)—Heads of lettuce are, because of their roundness, symbolic of the female breasts. Hence, a man who dreams of holding a head of lettuce or of eating lettuce may be expressing a desire to caress a woman's breasts—or, by extension, to have sexual intercourse with her. A man who dreams of taking lettuce from a woman by force may be indicating a desire to enjoy her sexually by force. A woman who dreams of serving lettuce to a man may be indicating a desire to share or a fear of sharing her breasts—or, by extension, to have sexual intercourse—with him.

LIGHTNING (1)—The appearance of lightning in a dream may be an indication of the dreamer's desire to discover the truth about a particular situation—i.e., to shed light on the subject. However, lightning also symbolizes death and destruction. Thus, the person who dreams of lightning may be expressing feelings of aggression and hostility toward the persons who are present when the lightning flashes, or feelings of antipathy toward the place where the lightning flashes. Among persons who in waking life have a fear of lightning, the appearance of lightning in a dream may also testify to deep-seated fears of death.

LIQUOR (2)—Liquor, like all other alcoholic beverages, most commonly symbolizes good fellowship, convivial company and general merriment. However, with many individuals, alcoholic beverages have a decidedly negative connotation. This is especially the case among people who have a personal drinking problem or who are involved with other persons who have a drinking problem. Alcoholic beverages also might have a decidedly negative connotation for people who have at one time or another suffered abuse at the hands of an habitual drinker. Thus, the appearance of any alcoholic beverage in a dream can be interpreted only in the light of

the dreamer's own experiences with drinking or with drinkers
—and, in any case, the presence of an alcoholic beverage in a
dream will be less significant than the actions of the person
or persons who are drinking it, serving it, etc.

LOCK (5)—Locks have a wide variety of meanings when
they appear in dreams. One of the most common interpretations of a lock-dream is that the dreamer has something to
hide—in other words, that he wants to lock his secret away
from the rest of the world. Another interpretation is that the
dreamer wants to erect some sort of barrier against other
people—perhaps to keep other people from getting close to
him emotionally or sexually. A third interpretation is that the
dreamer suffers feelings of persecution; thus, he must lock
the doors of his life, lest his enemies find him vulnerable.
Dreams of locks may also have sexual significance. The key-
hole-type lock is a vaginal symbol, and the key is a phallic
symbol. Thus, the appearance of a lock in a dream may indicate the dreamer's fear of sexual intercourse. Finally, in contemporary society with its soaring crime rate, the appearance
of a lock in a dream may testify to the dreamer's concern
over the safety of his home, his person and the lives of those
he holds dear.

LOCKING—The action of locking may symbolize a great
many feelings and emotions. The questions to ask yourself if
the action takes place in one of your dreams are: What is
being locked up? Who is doing the locking? What are the actions of dream characters with respect to the locking? If you
dream of locking someone else in a room, you may be expressing (a) unconscious feelings of jealousy (i.e., you desire
to keep that person away from the rest of the world so that
you can have him all to yourself); (b) your desire to chastise
or take vengeance upon the person; (c) your desire to limit
or curtail the person's activities; (d) your fear of the person
(you are locking him up so that he can no longer be a threat
to you). If you dream of locking yourself in a room, you
may be voicing (a) the desire for privacy; (b) the desire to
erect a barrier against other people—perhaps to keep other
people from getting close to you emotionally or sexually; (c)
your fear that other people are trying to harm you; (d) your
fear that you soon will be punished for some real or imagined misdeed; (e) your belief that you should be punished
for some real or imagined misdeed; (f) your belief that you

are too open with other people (hence, your desire to "lock up" your emotions). If you dream that someone else has locked you in a room, you may be disclosing (a) your feeling that your current way of life is too confining; (b) your belief that the person who locked you in the room dislikes you (hence, wants to punish you); (c) your belief that the person who locked you in the room wants to curtail or limit your activities; (d) your desire to be punished for some real or imagined misdeed; (e) your fear that you soon will be punished for some real or imagined misdeed; (f) your belief that the person who locked you in the room fears you (he is locking you up so that you can no longer be a threat to him); (g) your belief that the person who locked you in the room is jealous of others who may love you (he desires to keep you away from the rest of the world so that he can have you all to himself). Finally, if you dream that you have been locked out of a room, you probably are expressing the feeling that (a) you are being discriminated against; either by a certain group of people or by society in general; (b) the person who locked you out of the room desires to erect a barrier between you and him—perhaps to keep you from getting close to him emotionally or sexually; (c) your sexual desires for the person will not be answered by his sexual desires for you.

LOCOMOTIVE (3)—A locomotive is a vehicle which pulls a train. As such, it symbolizes strength and power. Thus, the appearance of a locomotive in your dream may signify that (a) you desire to be stronger and more powerful than you are; (b) you fear that you are not strong and powerful enough to fulfill demands being made upon you; (c) you feel the need for help (as the other cars in a train require the help of the locomotive if they are to move). However, the mere appearance of a locomotive in a dream almost invariably will be less significant than the circumstances surrounding its appearance. Thus, if you dream of a locomotive which is having trouble pulling cars up a steep slope, you may be testifying to your feelings of inadequacy and/or inferiority (i.e., your own powers of locomotion are insufficient to the tasks before you). If you dream of a locomotive which has broken loose from the cars it is supposed to be pulling, you may be testifying to (a) a desire to escape the burdens of your present life-situation; (b) a desire to avoid coping with a specific problem; (c) the fear that you lack the fortitude to fulfill your obligations. If you dream of a locomotive which has crashed, you may be indicating the belief that (a) you have let someone down who was counting on you; (b) you will soon suffer some sort of disaster. (For dreams involving a locomotive engineer, see ENGINEER.)

LOLLIPOP (8)—Lollipops may be significant in dreams either as symbols of childhood or as objects upon which one sucks. For interpretations involving the former, see CHILD; for interpretations involving the latter, see SUCKING.

LUGGAGE (6)—The term, "'luggage," is used to describe the containers in which one carries his personal effects when he is traveling. Dreams involving luggage, therefore, may be significant with respect to the luggage's container-function (all containers are vaginal symbols) or with respect to the luggage's role as an accouterment for travel. The questions to ask yourself if luggage appears in your dream: Whose luggage is it? What actions take place with respect to it? Is it packed or unpacked? Is it a hindrance to the traveler who carries it? Does it get lost? What other dream objects appear? What is the setting of the dream? What dream characters are present? If you dream of packing someone else's luggage, you may be revealing a desire to have sexual relations with that person. Likewise, if you dream of someone packing your luggage, you may be revealing the belief that that person desires to have sexual relations with you. If you dream that someone steals your luggage, you may be revealing (a) the fear that others are trying to prevent you from achieving a romantic and/or sexual relationship with a person; (b) the belief that others are trying to interfere with your life; (c) the belief that others are trying to prevent you from achieving a specific goal (they are stealing your luggage to prevent you from traveling according to your original plans). Obviously, because such a wide variety of interpretations can be attached to the appearance of luggage in dreams, such dreams should be analyzed very carefully and only in the light of the circumstances under which luggage appears in a dream.

M

MAID (9)—A maid is a person who cleans houses and puts things in order. Thus, the presence of a maid in a dream may indicate the dreamer's (a) desire to cleanse himself of guilt; (b) belief that his life is disorganized and confused, and that he needs someone to help him set his house in order. However, as is the case with most dream characters of this sort, the fact that a maid appears in a dream is far less significant than the actions of the maid with respect to other dream characters and the identity of the maid. If you cast yourself in the role of the maid, you may be testifying to (a) the desire to be helpful to other people; (b) the desire to help other people organize their lives; (c) the belief that you are inferior to other people (i.e., that you must function as their servant). If you cast a friend or acquaintance in the role of a maid, you may be expressing (a) your belief that the person is a generally helpful sort; (b) your desire to have the person help you, either with respect to a particular problem or with respect to life's problems in general; (c) your belief that the person is a busybody—one who seeks to influence people's lives against their will; (d) the belief that the person is inferior to you; (e) your wish that the person actually were inferior to you. If you cast your mother in the role of the maid, you may be testifying to feelings of guilt toward her—feelings, in other words, that you treated her as a maid, and not with the respect which she deserved.

MAZE (9)—A maze is a confusing and baffling network of paths and avenues. When a maze appears in dreams, it symbolizes an impossible situation—an unresolvable riddle from which the dreamer cannot escape. Questions to ask yourself if a maze appears in your dreams: Who is trapped in the maze? How did he get there? What are his feelings about being there? If and when he finally gets out, how did he accomplish his escape? What did he escape to?

MELTING—Melting is the process whereby a solid is changed into a liquid; in other words, the process whereunder matter dissolves. Dreams, therefore, in which melting takes place generally signify the dreamer's desire to destroy the solidity of something or his fear that the solidity of something he cherishes may be destroyed. For example, a melting-dream may indicate that the dreamer wants to wear down a person's resistance to an idea or plan, or it may reveal the dreamer's fear that another person will wear down the dreamer's own resistance to temptation. Such dreams will be particularly significant if the dream-object which melts is a phallic symbol, a breast symbol or a vaginal symbol. In any case, if you dream a melting-dream, ask yourself: What is your relationship to the object which is melting? Who are the other characters in the dream and what is their relationship to the object? What is causing the object to melt? What is your reaction to the fact that the object is melting? What are the reactions of other characters to the fact that the object is melting?

MERRY-GO-ROUND (2)—A merry-go-round, of course, is an amusement-park ride which goes around in circles. The person who dreams of riding on a merry-go-round generally is revealing the unconscious belief that his own life is directionless and without progress, that he is stuck in a rut, that *he* is going around in circles. To dream of other people riding on a merry-go-round is to attribute these same characteristics to them, or to wish that these characteristics could be attributed to them.

MICROPHONE (3)—A microphone is an instrument for amplifying sound. Thus, if you dream of a microphone, you may be expressing (*a*) the desire to draw attention to yourself and/or some cause which you espouse (as the man with a microphone draws attention); (*b*) the fear that you are not forceful enough (hence, you need a microphone to make yourself heard); (*c*) the desire to acquire power over others (as the man with a microphone enjoys power over his listeners). However, the mere appearance of a microphone in a dream generally is of far less significance than the circumstances surrounding its appearance. Thus, if a microphone appears in your dream, ask yourself: Who is using it? Why is he using it? What are the reactions of other dream characters to him? What is the setting of the dream?

MICROSCOPE (8)—A microscope is an instrument for examining objects which cannot be seen by the naked eye. Thus, if you dream of a microscope, you may be expressing (*a*) the desire to penetrate certain barriers which presently stand in the way of your achieving a certain goal (as the man with a microscope penetrates the barrier of smallness when he examines the objects he is viewing); (*b*) the desire to be generally more perceptive, knowing, etc. (*c*) the belief that certain persons are hiding something from you (hence, you need a microscope to find what it is that they are hiding); (*d*) the fear that you are incapable of keeping up with your associates (hence, you need a microscope to see things which they can see without a microscope). However, the mere appearance of a microscope in a dream generally is of far less significance than the circumstances under which it appears. Thus, if a microscope appears in your dream, ask yourself: Who is using it? Why is he using it? What is he examining with it? What are the reactions of other dream characters to him? What is the setting of the dream?

MILK (9)—Milk is a food—indeed, if we believe the claims of the dairy industry, it is the world's most perfect food. Also, it is the only food which we consume during the largest portion of our infancy. Thus, as a dream symbol, milk may represent (a) strength, virility and power—qualities associated with all foods when they appear in dreams; (b) the dreamer's infant state. (For more detailed interpretation, see BABY, EATING and DRINKING.)

MINISTER (8)—The word minister may suggest a clergyman or a high governmental official. The clergyman is generally thought of as a benign person who seeks to help people for purely altruistic motives. Thus, to most dreamers, the appearance of a clergyman in a dream generally indicates a desire to be helped in some way or in some way to help another person. Of course, the identity of the clergyman in a dream and the actions which he performs almost invariably will be more significant than the mere fact of his appearance. Thus, if the dreamer pictures himself as a clergyman, he may be indicating (a) the wish that he were a better person than he is; (b) the desire to have other people come to him for help; (c) the desire to have other people respect and admire him; (d) the desire to have other people think of him as good and noble. If he pictures an acquaintance as a clergyman, he generally will be (a) voicing the desire to turn to that person for help and assistance; (b) ascribing the qualities of goodness, nobility, etc., to that other person; (c) indicating that he believes the other person wrongly thinks of himself as possessing clergyman-like qualities. If the clergyman in his dream is a real clergyman whom he knows personally or by name, or if the clergyman in his dream is anonymous, the dreamer generally will be testifying to a desire for help, comfort, consolation, etc. When the minister in question is of the high-governmental-official variety, he generally serves the dreamer as an authority figure. An authority figure is, as the name implies, a person in command of a given situation. When an authority figure appears in a person's dream, the action of the figure—and his identity—almost invariably are more significant than the mere fact that he has appeared. If, for example, the dreamer pictures himself as an authority figure, he generally is expressing (a) the desire to enjoy a position of authority and responsibility; (b) the fear of assuming a position of authority and responsibility. If someone the dreamer knows appears in an authority-figure role which does not match his status in real life, the dreamer may be (a) voicing his belief that the person in question deserves to occupy a position of such authority; (b) expressing his admiration for the person; (c) expressing a desire to be guided or controlled by the person; (d) expressing resentment at the belief that the person is trying to guide or control him—or the belief that the person actually is guiding or controlling him. The presence of an anonymous authority figure in a dream generally means that the dreamer either desires to submit or resents being forced to submit to someone else's authority.

MONEY (9)—Money is symbolic of power, strength and virility. Thus, when a person dreams of money he generally is expressing (a) the desire to be stronger, more powerful and more virile; (b) confidence in his own strength, power and virility; (c) doubt in his own strength, power and virility. However, as is the case with all dream symbols of this sort, the role which money plays in a dream generally is far more significant than the mere fact that money has appeared in a dream. For example, if a person dreams that he has suddenly acquired a great deal of money, he may be voicing (a) anxiety over a crisis which presently besets him (he needs power, strength and virility to survive the crisis); (b) satisfaction over a recent triumph (the money represents his victory). By the same token, if a person dreams that he is losing money, he may be expressing (a) the belief that he is losing his power in the business world or in his own home; (b) the belief that his abilities are waning; (c) the fear that he is losing or will soon lose his virility or his sexual attractiveness; (d) the fear that his fortunes are undergoing a general decline. If a person dreams that someone has stolen money from him, he probably believes that this other person (a) is trying to undermine his success; (b) is trying to weaken him; (c) has done him some sort of harm. If a person dreams that he has stolen money from someone else, he probably feels that he himself (*a*) is trying to undermine the other person's success; (*b*) is inferior to the other person (hence, he is trying to weaken him). If a man dreams that a woman has stolen or otherwise wrongfully taken money from him, he probably feels that she (*a*) is trying to exploit him; (*b*) is trying to sap him of his virility. If a woman dreams that she has stolen or otherwise wrongfully taken money from a man, she probably (*a*) feels that he has been trying to dominate her (by taking his money, she is weakening him and thereby rendering him incapable of dominating her in the future); (*b*) is expressing general hostility toward him, or toward men in general. Obviously, since dreams of money are open to such a wide variety of interpretations, they should be analyzed very carefully and with great attention to such factors as other symbols appearing in the same dream, the setting of the dream, and the personalities and actions of the dream characters.

MOUNTAIN (8)—Mountains are common dream settings. They are usually without symbolic significance. However, the action which takes place on a mountain may be very meaningful in terms of dream interpretation. To dream that an object or person is at the top of a mountain is to express one's belief that the object or person is beyond the dreamer's reach, or unattainable. To dream of an object falling or rolling down a mountain is to hope that the object will become available to the dreamer. Finally, to dream of falling down a mountain is to reveal a fear that one's fortunes are in jeopardy or that one's health is failing.

MULE (6)—The mule is symbolic of stubbornness. Thus, if a mule appears in your dream, you probably are expressing (*a*) the belief that you are too stubborn for your own good; (*b*) the fear that you are not stubborn enough—i.e., that you cannot stand pat against temptation.

MURDER—The act of murder, when it takes place in dreams, generally symbolizes death fears and/or wishes or feelings of aggression and hostility. The main questions to ask yourself if murder takes place in one of your dreams: Who is murdering whom? Why? What is the relationship of the murderer and his victim? What is your reaction to the event?

MUSIC (2)—Music is symbolic of joy and merriment. If

music appears in one of your dreams, you should ask yourself: Who is playing the music? For whose benefit is it being played? What are the reactions of the characters in the dream who hear it? Thus, if you dream that a girl is playing the piano for you, you probably are voicing your belief that the girl wants to make you happy. If in the same dream you envision someone else complaining about the girl's music, you may be expressing the belief that this other person wants to prevent you from being happy and/or that the other person objects to your relationship with the girl. If you further dream that you do not like the music the girl is playing, you may be testifying to the fact that you reject her affection for you.

MUSTARD (6)—Mustard, because of its color and texture, occasionally will appear in a dream as a symbol for feces. This significance generally will apply, however, only when the dream involves the smearing, dropping or other use of mustard out of context with its normal function as a seasoner of foods. When the significance does apply, the dreamer may be expressing (a) the desire to deface, damage or otherwise harm someone or something (as he would deface, damage or otherwise harm the person or object were he to cover it with feces); (b) the fear that someone else desires to damage, deface or otherwise harm something which is dear or important to the dreamer. If such a significance seems to apply in your dream, observe very carefully the identities and actions of dream characters who may be present. Also, note carefully the setting of the dream and the appearance of other dream objects. Again, the significance of mustard as a symbol for feces will apply only *occasionally* to dreams. In the vast majority of cases, the appearance of mustard in a dream will be without symbolic significance.

MUTE (5)—To be mute is to lack the power to speak and to hear. Thus, to dream of being mute may be to express (a) the belief that one's opinions are of no importance to others; (b) the desire to impress others with one's importance (which desire, in the dream, is being thwarted by one's muteness); (c) the fear that one is missing out on something which is very important to him (hence, he is like a mute, unable to hear); (d) the desire to blot out some past experi-

ence (if he were a mute, he might not have been aware of
this past experience); (e) feelings of guilt (resulting in his
desire to blot out the guilt-causing act or episode); (f) the
desire to place his destiny in someone else's hands (as a mute
must necessarily place his destiny in the hands of those who
can speak and hear); (g) the fear that others are conspiring
to render him helpless (i.e., to make him a mute); (h) the desire to conceal a secret (if he were a mute, he would not be
able to reveal the secret). To dream of someone else's being
mute is to voice similar beliefs, fears or desires with respect
to him.

N

NAIL (9)—Nails are, because of their shape, phallic symbols. The most common nail-dreams are (a) those in which a
person is hammering a nail into something; (b) those in
which a person is extracting a nail from something; (c) those
in which a person injures himself on a nail. If a man dreams
of hammering a nail into something, he probably is expressing a desire to participate in a violent act of sexual intercourse. If a woman dreams of a man hammering a nail into
something, she probably is expressing a desire to have this
man assault her sexually; if she dreams that she herself is
hammering a nail into something, she may be expressing (a)
the desire to be more masculine, forceful and aggressive; (b)
unconscious homosexual tendencies; (c) feelings of hostility
and destructiveness. If a man dreams that he is having difficulty hammering a nail into something, he probably is testifying to (a) fears of sexual impotence; (b) the belief that he
is unattractive to women; (c) the fear that he is losing his
attractiveness to women; (d) the belief that he is encounter-
ing insurmountable obstacles in some facet or another of his
everyday dealings. If a woman dreams that a man is having
difficulty hammering a nail into something, she may be expressing (a) the desire that he become sexually impotent; (b)
the wish that he were not as attractive to her as he is; (c) the
belief that she herself is sexually frigid; (d) the hope that the
man will encounter insurmountable obstacles in some facet or
another of his everyday dealings; (e) her abhorrence of having sexual intercourse with the man. If she dreams that she
herself is having difficulty hammering a nail into something,
she probably is expressing (a) the fear that, try though she

might, she cannot become as forceful and aggressive as she would like to be; (*b*) her fear that a woman upon whom she has sexual designs will repulse her advances. If either a man or a woman dreams of extracting a nail from something, he or she probably is expressing (*a*) sexual guilt; (*b*) the desire to withdraw from a sexual or emotional entanglement. If a person of either gender dreams of injuring himself or herself on a nail, he or she probably is expressing (*a*) an aversion to sexual contact; (*b*) a fear that he or she will be punished for certain sexual indulgences; (*c*) the desire to be punished for certain sexual indulgences.

NIGHT (4)—Dreams which involve nighttime as a setting may be an indication of the dreamer's wish to hide certain feelings, desires and/or deeds of which he is ashamed. However, since many events in a person's life do take place at night, the fact that a dream involves a nighttime setting need not be symbolically significant. Obviously, all such dreams should be analyzed very carefully, with special attention to the physical setting of the dream, the dream-objects which appear, and the actions and identities of the dream characters.

NUDITY (3)—Nudity symbolizes sexual desire, honesty and candor. Thus, the person who dreams of himself as being naked may be expressing (*a*) the desire to be less inhibited sexually; (*b*) the desire to tell the truth about some matter in his waking life; (*c*) the fear that he is hypocritical, or that other people think of him as hypocritical; (*d*) the fear that certain facts or emotions which he wished to keep secret have been revealed to another person or persons. If, of course, it is a person other than the dreamer himself who appears nude in a dream, the dreamer may be expressing similar sentiments about this other person. The main questions to ask yourself if nudity is involved in one of your dreams: Which characters in the dream are nude? Why are they nude? Which, if any, characters in the dream have refused to denude themselves? Why have they refused? What are the reactions of the various characters toward each other? What is your reaction toward each of the characters?

NUN (4)—A nun is a woman who takes religious vows, most commonly the vows of poverty, "chastity" (i.e., sexual abstinence) and obedience. She also is a woman who performs works without expectation or desire of a material reward. Thus, dreams involving nuns generally will reveal the dreamer's desire to be cast or fear of being cast in one or more of the roles attributed to a nun. Naturally, the identity of a nun in a particular dream and the actions which she performs in the dream almost invariably will be of more significance than her mere appearance in the dream. Thus, if a woman envisions herself as a nun, she may be expressing (a) the desire to be sexually abstinent; (b) guilt over past sexual indulgences; (c) fears of sexual inadequacy (if she were a nun, she would not be expected to seek sexual satisfaction or to bring satisfaction to others); (d) the desire to overcome her attachment to material things; (e) the desire to avoid making her own decisions (thus, of being obedient to a higher authority, who will make the decisions for her); (f) the desire to help other people; (g) the desire to have other people think of her as a person who can help them; (h) the desire to be a "better" person than she is; (i) the desire to have other people think of her as a "better" person than she is. To dream of another woman as a nun generally is to express similar desires, beliefs or fears with respect to that other person. Meanwhile, if the nun in a person's dream is a real nun whom the dreamer knows personally or by name, or if the nun in the dream is anonymous, the dreamer may be testifying to (a) a desire for help—especially in overcoming sexual temptations; (b) a desire for comfort and consolation (such as might be offered by a nun into whose care one is entrusted); (c) the desire to be dominated by someone (as a nun who teaches in a parochial school dominates her pupils).

NURSE (5)—The nurse is a person who comforts and aids the sick. To many people she also serves as an authority figure. Dreams involving nurses lend themselves to a wide variety of interpretations, depending upon the life-situation of the dreamer, the identity of the nurse who appears in the dream and the actions of the nurse in the dream. If a young girl dreams of nurses, she may merely be expressing the desire to become a nurse when she grows up. If a middle-aged or elderly woman dreams of nurses, she may be voicing (a) fears about her health (as a result of which she believes she may soon require the care of a nurse); (b) the desire to have one of her daughters become a nurse; (c) regret that she herself is not a nurse. The appearance of nurses in dreams—regardless of the age, life-situation and gender of the dreamer—may also indicate the dreamer's (*a*) unconscious desire to be pampered and nursed; (*b*) desire to pamper and nurse others; (*c*) desire to be regarded by friends and acquaintances as a source of comfort and assistance. However, as has been pointed out, the identity of the dream-nurse and the actions which she performs are of great importance in interpreting nurse-dreams. Thus, a person who dreams that he (or she) is nursing someone else may be expressing (*a*) the unconscious desire that that person will become dependent upon him (or her); (*b*) the unconscious desire that that person will fall ill or die; (*c*) the desire to be helpful to that person; (*d*) the hope that that person will think of the dreamer as a source of comfort and assistance. Likewise, a person who dreams that someone else is nursing him (or her) may be voicing (*a*) feelings of dependence toward that person; (*b*) resentment at being dependent upon the person; (*c*) the belief that the person is a source of comfort and assistance; (*d*) the belief that the person wrongfully thinks himself (or herself) to be a source of comfort and assistance; (*e*) the desire to be pampered and nursed by the person.

NUT (1)—Nuts are symbolic of the male's testicles. Since the testicles are the storehouse of the male's virility, dreams involving nuts lend themselves to a wide variety of interpretations. If a man dreams of giving nuts to a woman, he may be expressing (*a*) his desire to have sexual intercourse with her; (*b*) the feeling that he has surrendered his power to her. If a woman dreams of giving nuts to a man, she may be expressing (*a*) a belief that it is she who is responsible for his virility—and, by extension, for his success in life; (*b*) resentment over the fact that he enjoys certain prerogatives which she does not; (*c*) a desire to help him, to contribute to his strength and power. If a man dreams of taking nuts from a woman, he may be voicing (*a*) the belief that he is dependent upon her; (*b*) the desire to render her weak and powerless. If a woman dreams of taking nuts from a man, she may be voicing (*a*) the desire to have sexual intercourse with him; (*b*) the desire to strip him of his power. If a man dreams of cracking nuts, he may be revealing (*a*) a lack of confidence in his strength, power and virility; (*b*) sexual guilt—evidenced by the fact that he wants to destroy the source of his sexual energy; (c) a fear that he will lose his sexual potency or his physical strength. If a woman dreams of cracking nuts, she may be revealing (a) a desire to overpower men (by depriving them of their strength and virility); (b) an abhorrence of sexual intercourse (as evidenced by the fact that she is destroying the source of man's sexual energy).

O

OAR (7)—Oars are phallic symbols. The role which they play in a dream almost invariably will be far more significant than the mere fact that they have appeared in a dream. If, for example, a man dreams that he is using oars to row vigorously across a lake, he probably is expressing (a) confidence in his sexual ability; (b) the desire to be more capable sexually than he actually is. If, on the other hand, he dreams that he is rowing a boat with only one oar, he may be voicing (a) fears of sexual inadequacy; (b) the fear that he is sexually unattractive. If a woman dreams that she is rowing a boat across a lake, she may be revealing (a) unconscious desires to take a more aggressive role in her sexual relations; (b) unconscious homosexual tendencies. If a woman dreams that she and a man are in a rowboat and that the man drops the oars into the water, she may be revealing (a) a desire for sexual intercourse with the man (the union of oars—phallic symbols—and the water—a vaginal symbol); (b) her belief that the man is sexually incompetent; (c) her desire that the man become impotent; (d) her wish that the man were not as attractive sexually to her as he actually is.

OFFICER (8)—An officer—whether military, police, corporate or whatever—is an authority figure. When an authority figure appears in a person's dream, the action of the figure—and his identity—almost invariably are more significant than the mere fact that he has appeared. If, for example, the dreamer pictures himself as an authority figure, he generally is expressing (a) the desire to enjoy a position of authority and responsibility; (b) the fear of assuming a position of authority and responsibility. If someone the dreamer knows appears in an authority-figure role which does not match his status in real life, the dreamer may be (a) voicing his belief that the person in question deserves to occupy a position of such authority; (b) expressing admiration for the person; (c) expressing a desire to be guided or controlled by the person; (d) expressing resentment at the belief that the person is trying to guide or control him—or the belief that the person actually is guiding or controlling him. The presence of an anonymous authority figure in a dream generally means that the dreamer either desires to submit or resents being forced to submit to someone else's authority. However, dreams involving military, police, corporate and other officers may be significant on a non-symbolic level also. For example, the dreamer who has a son in the military service and who dreams of a military officer may be expressing (a) the desire that his son advance rapidly up the ranks; (b) the fear that his son has been killed or wounded in combat (news of which misfortune the officer has come to bring). Likewise, to dream of the vice president of one's bank might be to testify to fears that one's fortunes are declining or to the fear that one's less-than-ethical financial manipulations will be discovered. If you have a dream involving an officer of any sort, try to rule out all non-symbolic interpretations before accepting the authority-figure interpretation.

OGRE (9)—The presence of an ogre in a dream generally indicates that the dreamer has certain inner feelings or desires which he considers ugly and frightening. Naturally, however, the actions of the dream-ogre and the reactions of other dream characters to him will generally be far more significant than the mere fact that an ogre has appeared in the dream.

OIL (1)—Oil symbolizes slyness and cunning, and also sexual intercourse. Thus, dreams involving oil may indicate (a) the dreamer's desire to reap a profit through sly and/or unethical means; (b) the dreamer's fear that someone with whom he is involved is a "slick" character; (c) a desire for sexual intercourse. However, as is generally the case with dream symbols of this sort, the role which oil plays in a dream is far more significant than the mere fact that oil has appeared in a dream. If, for example, a person dreams of striking oil, he probably is expressing a desire to "strike it rich"—i.e., to obtain a great deal of wealth through luck rather than through hard work. On the other hand, if a person dreams that someone else has drained the oil from the dreamer's car, he may be indicating that he believes the other person is trying to drain him of his energy.

ONE (7)—The figure one is, because of its shape, a phallic symbol. To dream of the figure itself or of single quantities of a great many objects is generally to indicate a desire for sexual intercourse. Naturally, however, such dreams can be interpreted only in the light of the characters involved and their actions in the dream.

ORANGE (6)—Oranges are, because of their shape, breast symbols. Hence, a man who dreams of holding oranges may be expressing a desire to caress a woman's breasts—or, by extension, to have sexual intercourse with her. A man who dreams of taking oranges from a woman by force may be indicating a desire to rape her. A man who dreams of squeezing oranges may be expressing feelings of hostility toward a woman or toward women in general (he wants to destroy her —or their—breasts, and thus her—or their—sexual attractiveness). Likewise, a woman who dreams of giving an orange to a man may be indicating a desire to share her breasts —and, by extension, her sexual participation—with him. A woman who dreams of having a man take an orange from her by force may be expressing (a) the fear of being raped; (b) the desire to be taken sexually by force. A woman who dreams of squeezing oranges may be expressing (a) feelings of sexual guilt (she wants to destroy her breasts, which represent her sexuality); (b) the fear that dissolute living is causing her to lose her sexual attractiveness.

OVEN (1)—Ovens, because they are warm and dark, symbolize both the female's vagina and her womb. If you have a dream in which an oven appears, ask yourself: Is anything in the oven? If so, what? Who put it there? What actions are taking place which involve the oven? What are the reactions of dream characters to these actions? If an unmarried woman dreams of putting something in an oven, she may be expressing a fear that she will become or has become pregnant. If a married woman dreams of putting something in an oven, she may be expressing the desire to become pregnant or the fear that she will become or has become pregnant. If a pregnant woman dreams of taking something out of an oven, she may be revealing (a) a desire to become a mother; (b) the desire to have an abortion. If a pregnant woman dreams that something she is cooking in an oven has become burned, she may be voicing fears of having a miscarriage. Dreams involving ovens may also have nonsexual significance. For interpretations involving ovens as an apparatus for cooking, see COOK and EATING.

OWL (5)—Owls symbolize wisdom. Thus, the appearance of an owl in a dream may signify the dreamer's desire for wisdom in general or his desire to solve a specific problem.

P

PAINTING—The significance of the act of painting when it appears in a dream depends largely on whether the painting is of the house-maintenance variety or the artistic variety. The person who dreams that he is doing painting of the house-maintenance variety probably is indicating (a) the desire to conceal—i.e., to cover over—certain feelings or facts which he does not want others to know about; (b) the belief that his health is waning—hence, he requires some form of preventive maintenance. The person who dreams that someone else is doing this sort of painting probably is indicating that he believes the other person to be (a) trying to hide something from him; (b) a phony—i.e., one who presents the world with a shiny new facade which does not reflect accurately the true state of his character and personality. The dreamer who envisions himself doing painting of the artistic variety generally is voicing (a) the desire to be more creative; (b) the belief that he should beautify his surroundings. The dreamer who envisions someone else doing this sort of painting probably is expressing (a) admiration for the person's creativity; (b) the belief that the person wrongfully thinks himself to be creative.

PARK (1)—A park is a place of beauty where people may relax and enjoy themselves. Thus, dreams set in parks generally signify the dreamer's desire for a more relaxing and attractive environment at work or at home. The same dream may testify to the dreamer's desire to escape his present life-situation—i.e., to retire to a park, where things are relaxed and easygoing.

PEACH (6)—The peach is a vaginal symbol. The woman who dreams of giving a peach to a man is generally expressing a desire to have sexual intercourse with him. The woman who dreams that a man has taken a peach from her by force generally is voicing (a) the fear of being raped; (b) the desire to be taken sexually by force. The woman who dreams that a man is eating a peach which she has given him may be expressing a desire to engage in cunnilingus with him. Likewise, the man who dreams that a woman has given him a peach generally is expressing a desire that the woman offer herself sexually to him. The man who dreams of taking a peach from a woman by force generally is voicing the desire to rape her. The man who dreams that he is eating a peach which a woman has given him may be expressing a desire to engage in cunnilingus with her.

PEN (8)—Pens are, because of their shape, phallic symbols. To dream of a pen which has run out of ink is to express (a) fears of sterility; (b) fears of impotence.

PENCIL (5)—Pencils are, because of their shape, phallic symbols. A man who dreams of giving a pencil to a woman generally is voicing a desire to have sexual intercourse with her. Likewise, a woman who dreams of being given a pencil by a man generally is voicing a desire to have sexual intercourse with him. If a man dreams that he has broken the point of his pencil, he may be testifying to fears of impotence. If a man dreams that he has a pencil which won't write, he may be indicating that he doubts his sexual prowess or his sexual attractiveness.

PHYSICIAN (5)—The physician is a person who heals the sick—or at least tries to. To many people he also serves as an authority figure. Dreams involving physicians lend themselves to a wide variety of interpretations, depending upon the life-situation of the dreamer, the identity of the physician who appears in the dream and the actions of the physician in the dream. If a young man dreams of physicians, he may merely be expressing the desire to become a physician when he grows up. If a middle-aged or elderly person dreams of a physician, he may be voicing (a) fears about his health (as a result of which he believes he may soon require a physician's care); (b) the desire to have his son become a physician; (c) regret that he himself is not a physician, or, by extension, regret that his occupation is not one of prestige, power and high financial reward. The appearance of a physician in dreams—regardless of the age, life—situation and gender of the dreamer—may also indicate the dreamer's (a) unconscious desire to be fussed over and cared for; (b) desire to fuss over and care for others; (c) desire to be regarded by friends and acquaintances as a source of comfort and assistance. However, as has been pointed out, the identity of the dream-physician and the actions which he performs are of great importance in interpreting physician-dreams. Thus, a person who dreams that he (or she) is serving someone else in the capacity of a physician may be expressing (a) the unconscious desire that the person will fall ill or die; (b) the unconscious desire that the person will become dependent upon the dreamer; (c) the desire to be helpful to the person; (d) the hope that the person will think of the dreamer as a source of comfort and assistance. Likewise, a person who dreams that someone else is serving him in the capacity of a physician may be voicing (a) feelings of dependency toward that person; (b) resentment at being dependent upon the person) (c) the belief that the person wrongfully thinks himself (or herself) to be a source of comfort and assistance; (d) the desire to be cared for by the person.

PIER (3)—A pier is a structure which extends over water. Piers are used as platforms from which to board ships, from which one may fish, and, occasionally, off which to dive into water when swimming. Since each of these activities has its own set of dream interpretations, the actions which take place on the pier in a person's dream almost invariably will be far more significant than the mere fact that a dream has a pier for a setting. (See SHIP, FISH, and SWIMMING.)

PILOT (9)—A pilot is the person who controls the destiny of his passengers. Thus, the dreamer who pictures himself as a pilot may be expressing (a) the belief that he is in fact the controller of his own destiny; (b) the fear that he is not the controller of his own destiny but should be; (c) the desire for responsibility over other people. Similarly, the dreamer who envisions another person as a pilot (especially as the pilot of an airplane on which the dreamer himself is a passenger) may be expressing (a) his desire that this person guide or control his life; (b) his resentment at the belief that the person does in fact guide or control his life, or is trying to.

POLICEMAN (1)—Policemen, when they appear in dreams, serve a variety of functions. As upholders of the law, they may symbolize justice. As persons who track down wrongdoers, they may also symbolize vengeance and retribution. Because some policemen have been known to be unnecessarily rough with their captives, policemen also may symbolize cruelty, hostility and aggression. And finally, to some people, policemen are authority figures. Because of this wide variety of interpretations which may be attached to the appearance of a policeman or of policemen in a dream, the dream can be analyzed only in the context of (a) the dreamer's feelings with respect to policemen; (b) the dreamer's standing with respect to the law; (c) the action of the policeman or policemen who appear in the dream; (d) the identity of the policeman or policemen who appear in the dream. If the dreamer envisions himself as a policeman, he may be expressing (a) the desire to see justice done in a certain situation; (b) the desire to be instrumental in bringing about the downfall of someone he considers an evildoer; (c) the desire to punish his enemies; (d) the desire to be feared and/or respected; (e) the belief that he doesn't enjoy the respect he deserves, or that people are not as afraid of him as they should be; (f) feelings of aggression and hostility; (g) the desire to enjoy a position of authority and responsibility; (h) fear of assuming a position of authority and responsibility. If the dreamer envisions someone he knows in the role of a policeman, he may be expressing (a) fear of the person; (b) the belief that the person wants to be feared; (c) respect for the person; (d) the belief that the person is aggressive and hostile; (e) a desire to be protected by the person; (f) the belief that the person is someone to whom he can turn for protection. The presence of an anonymous policeman in a dream may mean that the dreamer (a) is afraid of being caught for having perpetrated some real or imagined misdeed; (b) wants to be caught for having perpetrated some real or imagined misdeed; (c) wants someone to protect him; (d) fears that there really is no one to whom he can turn for protection.

POND (1)—Ponds, because they are bodies of water, are vaginal symbols.

PRESIDENT (2)—A president, whether of a country or a corporation, is an authority figure and a symbol of success. When such a character appears in a person's dreams, the action of the character—and his real-life identity—almost invariably are more significant than the mere fact that he has appeared. If, for example, the dreamer envisions himself as a president, he generally is expressing (a) the desire to enjoy a position of authority and responsibility; (b) fear of assuming a position of authority and responsibility; (c) the desire to be generally successful in his professional, financial and personal life; (d) the desire to be thought of by others as successful. If someone the dreamer knows appears in a presidential role which does not match his status in real life, the dreamer may be (a) voicing his belief that the person in question deserves to occupy a position of such authority; (b) expressing admiration for the person; (c) expressing a desire to be guided or controlled by the person; (d) expressing resentment at the belief that the person is trying to guide or control him—or the belief that the person actually is guiding or controlling him; (e) voicing the belief that the person deserves to be successful in his professional financial and personal life; (f) voicing resentment over the person's success; (g) expressing the belief that the person wants to be thought of as successful, even though he is not. The presence of an anonymous president in a dream generally means that the dreamer (a) desires to submit to someone else's authority; (b) resents being forced to submit to someone else's authority; (c) wants desperately to become a success himself (d) resents the successes of others; (e) feels inferior with respect to the successful people who surround him.

PRIEST (6)—The priest is generally thought of as a benign person who seeks to help other people for purely altruistic motives. However, because he is authorized by his church to forgive the sins of his parishioners and to interpret the tenets of his religion, he also serves as a judge-figure and as an authority-figure. Naturally, the identity of the priest in a particular dream and the actions which he performs in the dream almost invariably will be more significant than the mere fact of his appearance. If the dreamer envisions himself as a priest, he may be indicating (*a*) the wish that he were a better person than he is; (*b*) the desire to help other people; (*c*) the desire to have other people think of him as someone who can help them; (*d*) the desire to have other people think of him as good and noble; (*e*) the desire to stand in judgment over another person or persons; (*f*) fear of standing in judgment over another person or persons; (*g*) the desire to enjoy a position of authority and responsibility; (*h*) the fear of assuming a position of authority and responsibility. If he pictures an acquaintance as a clergyman, he generally will be (*a*) ascribing qualities of goodness, nobility, etc., to that other person; (*b*) voicing the desire to turn to that other person for help and assistance; (*c*) indicating that he believes the other person wrongly thinks of himself as possessing priest-like qualities; (*d*) voicing his belief that the other person holds the dreamer's own fate in his hands; (*e*) expressing his desire for the person's approval; (*f*) expressing his fear that the person will disapprove of something which the dreamer has said or done; (*g*) voicing his admiration for the person (by believing that the person is qualified to stand in judgment over others); (*h*) expressing his resentment over the fact that the person wants to stand in judgment over the dreamer or over others; (*i*) expressing his resentment that the person does in fact stand in judgment over the dreamer or over others; (*j*) expressing his anxiety over a decision which the person is about to make; (*k*) expressing his belief that the person wrongly believes himself to be qualified to stand in judgment over others; (*l*) voicing a fear that the person wants to punish him (as a priest, by prescribing a penance, "punishes" a sinner); (*m*) accusing the person of being a hypocrite (i.e., accusing him of playing the role of a holy man when actually he is not one); (*n*) voicing his belief that the person deserves to occupy a position of authority and responsibility; (*o*) expressing admiration for the person; (*p*) expressing a desire to be guided and controlled by the person; (*q*) expressing resentment at the belief that the person is trying to guide or control him—or the belief that the person actually is guiding or controlling him. If the priest in his dream is a real priest whom he knows personally or by name, or if the priest in his dream is anonymous, the dreamer generally will be testifying to (*a*) a desire for help, comfort, consolation, etc.; (*b*) the desire to submit to authority; (*c*) the desire to be forgiven for real or imagined misdeeds; (*d*) the desire to be punished for real or imagined misdeeds.

PRISON (1)—Prisons symbolize restriction and confinement. Thus, the person who dreams that he is incarcerated in a prison generally is testifying to (*a*) feelings of restriction or confinement in his career or personal life; (*b*) the desire to suppress (i.e., to lock up, as in a prison) certain of his feelings or impulses—for example, a tendency toward aggressive behavior; (*c*) the belief that he should be punished for a real or imagined misdeed; (*d*) the fear that he will be punished for a real or imagined misdeed. If the dreamer envisions someone else in prison, he probably is revealing sentiments like the above with respect to the other person. If he dreams of himself as the warden of a prison, as a prison guard or as some other sort of prison official, he generally is expressing the desire to (*a*) enjoy authority over others; (*b*) punish his enemies; (*c*) escape punishment for real or imagined misdeeds of his own.

PROSTITUTE (1)—Prostitutes generally symbolize sexual promiscuity or the surrender of sexual services for a specific monetary reward. A woman who dreams of herself as a prostitute generally is expressing (*a*) guilt feelings about her sexual behavior; (*b*) the desire to be less inhibited sexually. A woman who dreams of another woman as a prostitute may be expressing (*a*) her belief that the woman is sexually promiscuous; (*b*) her belief that the woman places a low value on her sexual participation; (*c*) her fear that the woman may capture the affections of someone whom the dreamer herself loves; (*d*) her envy of the woman's lack of sexual inhibitions. A man who dreams of a woman as a prostitute may be expressing (*a*) a desire that her sexual favors were more easily attainable; (*b*) his belief that the woman is sexually promiscuous; (*c*) his belief that the woman places a low value on her sexual participation. A woman who dreams of an anonymous prostitute may be expressing (*a*) the desire to be less inhibited sexually; (*b*) her fear that the man she loves may be having a sexual relationship with someone else. A man who dreams of anonymous prostitutes probably is voicing (*a*) the wish that his sex life were more active; (*b*) the fear that he will succumb to sexual or other temptations. Occasionally, the appearance of a prostitute in a dream may also signify the dreamer's belief that he or someone else is "prostituting" his talents.

PUPPET (4)—The appearance of a puppet in a dream usually is indicative of the dreamer's (a) desire to manipulate or exert power over another person or persons; (b) fear that he is being manipulated by someone else.

PURSE (7)—Purses, because they are receptacles, are vaginal symbols. A man who dreams of putting something in a woman's purse is generally expressing a desire to have sexual intercourse with the woman. Likewise, a woman who dreams that a man is putting something in her purse is generally expressing a desire to have sexual intercourse with the man. If a woman dreams that her purse is full, she probably is voicing the belief that she is sexually attractive or the fear that she is pregnant. If she dreams that her purse is empty, she probably is voicing (a) fears of sterility; (b) fears of frigidity; (c) the belief that she is sexually unattractive. If a woman who is pregnant dreams that she is emptying her purse, she may be testifying to (a) a desire to give birth; (b) a desire to have an abortion.

Q

QUEEN (8)—The queen is both an authority figure and a mother figure. Thus, the appearance of a queen in dreams may be symbolic on several levels. If a woman dreams of herself as a queen, she may be expressing (a) her desire for power; (b) her desire to be someone to whom other people can turn for leadership and guidance; (c) her belief that she is far more capable than people generally give her credit for being; (d) her fear that she is not as capable as she should be; (e) her desire to become a mother. If a dreamer envisons someone else in the role of queen, he (or she) may be voicing (a) the belief that this other person desires power; (b) the desire to turn to the other person for leadership and guidance; (c) admiration for the person; (d) resentment at what is perceived to be the other person's erroneously high opinion of herself. If the queen in one's dreams is a real queen and if

the dreamer pictures himself (or herself) as one of the
queen's associates, the dreamer probably is testifying to (a) a
desire to associate with important and powerful individuals;
(b) the belief that the dreamer is incapable of associating
with important and powerful individuals. Finally, in many
cases, the queen who appears in a dream may actually represent the dreamer's own mother. In these cases, all the actions
and emotions which the queen displays are actions and emotions which the dreamer attributes to his (or her) own
mother.

QUEST—The dreamer who envisions himself on a quest for
something may be disclosing his desire to find the solution to
a specific problem. However, he may also be revealing his
wish to "find" himself—i.e., to discover the career or way of
life which will afford him the greatest happiness and contentment.

QUILT (7)—Quilts are symbolic of warmth. Thus, the person who dreams of a quilt is generally expressing an unconscious desire for affection and/or security.

QUORUM (6)—A quorum is a specified number of members of a political body or other organization whose presence
is required for the transaction of all legal business. Although
few persons other than politicians and parliamentarians have
ever heard of quorums, let alone dream of them, the presence
of a quorum in a dream might indicate the dreamer's desire
for the support of a great many people in a particular situation, or the dreamer's fear that a position or plan which he
advocates will face severe opposition.

R

RABBI (5)—The rabbi is generally thought of as a benign
person who seeks to help people for purely altruistic motives.
Thus, to most dreamers, the appearance of a rabbi in a
dream generally indicates a desire to be helped in some way
or in some way to help another person. Of course, the identity of the rabbi in a dream and the actions which he performs almost invariably will be more significant than the
mere fact of his appearance. Thus, if the dreamer pictures

himself as a rabbi, he may be indicating (*a*) the wish that he were a better person than he is; (*b*) the desire to have other people come to him for help; (*c*) the desire to have other people respect and admire him; (*d*) the desire to have other people think of him as good and noble. If he pictures an acquaintance as a rabbi, he generally will be (*a*) ascribing the qualities of goodness, nobility, etc., to that other person; (*b*) voicing the desire to turn to the other person for help and assistance; (*c*) indicating that he believes the other person wrongly thinks of himself as possessing rabbi-like qualities. If the rabbi in his dream is a real rabbi whom he knows personally or by name, or if the rabbi in the dream is anonymous, the dreamer generally will be testifying to a desire for help, comfort, consolation, etc.

RABBIT (7)—Rabbits are known to be extremely prolific sexually. Thus, the person who dreams of rabbits may be expressing (*a*) fears of sexual inadequacy (the dreamer desires to be more like a rabbit, hence more capable sexually); (*b*) the desire to become a parent; (*c*) the fear of becoming a parent; (*d*) the desire to be more prolific with respect to one's occupational output. If a man dreams of a woman petting a rabbit, he probably is revealing (*a*) his belief that she is sexy; (*b*) his desire to have sexual intercourse with her.

RAT (3)—Rats connote dirt, squalor and disease. Thus, the appearance of a rat in a dream may testify to the dreamer's (*a*) guilt feelings about some real or imagined misdeed (dirt is symbolic of guilt); (*b*) fear that his health or the health of someone he holds dear is failing; (*c*) fear that his fortunes soon will fail.

RAVEN (8)—Ravens are symbolic of death fears or wishes. If you dream of a raven rapping on your chamber door, don't bother to write a poem about it; it's already been done.

RICE (8)—Rice, of course, is a food. It is also something which wedding guests throw at the bridegroom and bride. It is also symbolic of fertility. To persons in whose diet rice plays an important part, the appearance of rice as a dream symbol may indicate (*a*) the desire to be stronger and more powerful than one is; (*b*) the fear that one is not as strong and powerful as he should be. To most other persons, the appearance of rice in a dream will relate to the marriage or fertility symbolism. If you dream that someone is throwing rice at you, you probably are revealing (a) your belief that the person wishes you happiness; (b) your belief that the person wants you to get married, or is trying actively to arrange for your marriage. If you dream of throwing rice at someone else, you probably are revealing similar sentiments toward that person. If you dream of eating rice, you probably are expressing (a) the desire to become a parent; (b) the fear that you may become a parent against your wishes; (c) the fear that you are sterile.

RIDING—The importance of the action of riding in a dream will depend, of course, on precisely what is being ridden and who is riding it. Dreams of riding on a bus, in a car, on a ship or in some other conveyance, generally indicate the desire to achieve a specific goal or to escape from an unpleasant situation. (For more detailed interpretations, see AIRPLANE, BOAT, SHIP, CAR, BUS, AUTOMOBILE.) Dreams of riding on an animal's back—especially on the back of a horse or a bull—indicate (a) the desire for sexual intercourse; (b) the fear of sexual intercourse. If a person dreams that he and another person are riding together on a horse, he almost invariably is expressing a desire for sexual intercourse with that person. (This symbolism is one of the strongest in all dream analysis.)

RIVER (9)—A river, as a body of water, symbolizes the female genitalia. Also, because of the fact that it flows, it suggests forward movement—i.e., progress. As is the case with all dream symbols of this sort, the actions of the characters in a river-dream—and the identities of the characters—generally will be far more significant than the mere fact that a river appears in a dream. If, for example, you dream that you are floating, swimming, rowing or otherwise moving downstream on a river, you may be revealing (a) the belief that your health or your fortunes are declining; (b) uneasiness over the fact that you seem to be progressing toward your goals a bit too easily; (c) the desire to take things easy, to follow the path of least resistance; (d) the belief that you are overworking yourself (hence, that you should relax and take things easier); (e) the fear that you are weak-willed (i.e., you float along with the tide). If you dream that you are swimming, rowing or otherwise moving upstream, you may be expressing (a) resentment over the fact that things come with more difficulty for you than for other persons; (b) the belief that you are stubborn (hence, you persist in bucking the tide); (c) the belief that you are overcoming all the obstacles which separate you from the achievement of a goal; (d) the belief that people are deliberately placing obstacles in your path; (e) the fear that you are naturally unlucky; (f) the belief that you are strong-willed (hence, that you go after what you want, no matter how difficult the going may be). If you dream of crossing a river, you probably are revealing (a) the desire to achieve a specific goal (you are crossing the river to get at whatever it is that is on the other side); (b) the desire to escape an unpleasant situation or the unpleasantries of your general life-situation; (c) the desire to terminate an uncomfortable business or personal relationship; (d) the desire to be more knowledgeable and wise (you are crossing the river to find out what is on the other side). If you are standing on a river bank, you may be expressing (a) feeling of inadequacy (you are afraid to cross the river); (b) satisfaction with the status quo of your present life-situation (you have no desire to cross the river). Some questions to ask yourself if you dream of a river: What is your relationship to the river—are you crossing it, swimming in it, watching it flow, etc.? Why is your relationship what it is? What are the relationships of other dream characters to the river? Why are these relationships what they are? What is your reaction to the other characters in the dream and their reaction to you? What dream objects are present?

ROPE (9)—When a piece of rope appears in a dream, it usually symbolizes the umbilical cord, which binds a foetus to its mother. Thus, a dreamer who envisions himself tied to another person by a piece of rope may be expressing (a) the desire to be dependent upon that person; (b) resentment at what he perceives to be a dependence upon that person. Meanwhile, the dreamer who pictures a broken strand of rope may be expressing (a) a desire to break free from authority or domination—i.e., to sever the cord of dependence; (b) a desire to terminate an unpleasant relationship—thus, to break the ties that bind; (c) regret that there is no one upon whom he can now depend; (*d*) regret at the loss of his mother.

ROSE (3)—A rose symbolizes the female genitalia. If a man dreams of giving a rose to a woman, he probably is expressing a desire to have sexual intercourse with her. If he dreams of taking a rose forcibly from her, he probably is expressing the desire to rape her. Likewise, if a woman dreams of giving a rose to a man, she probably is voicing a desire to have sexual intercourse with him. If she dreams that a man is taking a rose from her by force, she probably is expressing the fear that he will rape her or the desire that he will take her sexually by force. Among persons who are fluent in French, the appearance of a rose in a dream may also symbolize the desire for oral sex; the French idiom, *faire la rose,* describes the act of cunnilingus.

ROUNDNESS—The quality of roundness makes an object a breast symbol. For interpretations of breast symbols, see CO-CONUT, BALLOON, ORANGE.

RUM (7)—Rum, like all other alcoholic beverages, generally symbolizes good fellowship, convivial company and general merriment. However, with many individuals, alcoholic beverages have a decidedly negative connotation. This is especially the case among people who have a personal drinking problem or who are involved with other persons who have a drinking problem. Alcoholic beverages also might have a decidedly negative connotation for people who have at one time or another suffered abuse at the hands of an habitual drinker. Thus, the appearance of any alcoholic beverage in a dream can be interpreted only in the light of the dreamer's own experience with drinking or drinkers—and, in any case, the presence of an alcoholic beverage in a dream will be less significant than the actions of the persons who are drinking it.

RUNNING—Generally when a person is running, he either is running toward something or away from something. Dreams in which the dreamer is running toward something usually signify his (*a*) desire to attain a specific goal quickly; (*b*) fear that he will be unable to attain a specific goal as quickly as he should or as quickly as he wants to. Dreams in which the dreamer is running away from something usually signify his (a) desire to escape an unpleasant situation or the unpleasantness of his general life-situation; (b) fear that he is about to be punished for a real or imagined misdeed. If the action of running appears in your dream, ask yourself: Who is running? Why? Is anyone pursuing him? Is he pursuing someone else? Does either the person being pursued or the person who is doing the pursuing have any symbolic significance—i.e., is he an authority-figure, a judge-figure, etc.? What is the setting in which the running takes place? Are any other characters present? If so, what is their reaction to the running? What is the reaction of the runner or runners? What dream objects are present?

S

SAND (2)—Sand, when it appears in dreams, may signify a great many things. Most commonly, it is a symbol for time —as in the expression, "the sands of time." When this is the case, the person who dreams of sand probably is expressing (a) fears of death (i.e., the belief that time is "running out" on him as sand runs through an hourglass); (b) the belief that he is not progressing as quickly as he should toward a certain goal (hence, that time is passing him by); (c) the fear that his health is failing; (d) the fear that his fortunes are going to take a turn for the worse. The appearance of sand in a dream may also signify the dreamer's desire to do something important and noteworthy—i.e., to make his footprints in the "sands" of time. Because sand is found on beaches, dreams of sand may also indicate the dreamer's desire for rest and relaxation, or his desire to escape from an unpleasant life-situation—for beaches are places where one may rest and relax and avoid the cares of the everyday world. Finally, since sand is connected with a child's sandbox, dreams of sand may indicate the dreamer's (a) desire to return to the days of childhood, when he had little more on his mind than playing in his sandbox; (b) belief that he is inferior to other people—i.e., that they treat him like a child; (c) preoccupation with unimportant things (he is playing in the sand when he should be out working). Obviously, because of the wide variety of interpretations which can be applied to sand as a dream symbol, dreams involving sand should be analyzed carefully in the light of the characters which are present, the actions which they perform and the presence of dream objects.

SCALE (4)—A scale is a device for the measurement of weight. However, scales also symbolize justice—as in the Scales of Justice. If an overweight or underweight person dreams of scales, he probably is merely voicing concern over his health and/or appearance. If someone else dreams of scales, he may be expressing (a) the belief that he is being cheated in some transaction or other, or by life in general; (b) concern with financial matters; (c) the fear of being punished for a real or imagined misdeed; (d) the desire to be punished for a real or imagined misdeed.

SCHOOL (9)—Schools connote learning, childhood and examinations. Thus, if you dream of a school, you may be expressing (a) the desire to be more wise and knowledgeable; (b) the fear that you are not as wise and knowledgeable as you should be; (c) the fear that, because of your ignorance, someone will soon get the better of you in a business transaction or personal relationship; (d) the desire for the solution to a perplexing problem; (e) the desire for the power and prestige which come from being knowledgeable and wise; (f) feelings of insecurity (you want to return to your schooldays, when your problems were far less burdensome than they are now); (g) your fear that you are about to be tried and found wanting (as one is tried and found wanting in an examination at school); (h) the belief that someone is trying to test his (or her) relationship with you; (i) the desire to test your relationship with someone else. Obviously, as in all dream settings of this sort, dreams of schools can be interpreted only in the light of the dreamer's role in the dream, the roles of other characters, and the actions which take place in the dream. Questions to ask yourself if one of your dreams is set in a school: Are you a teacher or a pupil? Are any of the other dream characters symbolic—i.e., are they authority-figures, father-figures, judge-figures, etc.? What is your reaction to the other characters, and what is their reaction to you? Why are you in a school at the present time? Is your age in the dream the same as your real age?

SEARCHING—The dreamer who envisions himself in the act of searching for something may be disclosing his desire to find the solution to a specific problem. However, he may also be revealing his wish to "find" himself—i.e., to discover the career or way of life which will afford him the greatest happiness and contentment.

SCISSORS (4)—Since scissors are instruments which are used for cutting, the appearance of scissors in a dream generally indicates the dreamer's (a) wish to inflict injury upon himself or upon someone else; (b) desire to sever a personal or business relationship; (c) feelings of hostility and aggression; (d) desire to lessen another person's power over him; (e) fear that other people are trying to lessen the dreamer's power over them. As is the case with most dream symbols of this sort, the presence of a pair of scissors in a dream generally is of far less significance than the identity of the person using it, the object upon which it is being used and the circumstances under which it is being used. A very common scissors-dream is one in which a woman is cutting clothes which belong to a man; this dream generally symbolizes the woman's desire figuratively to castrate the man—i.e., to overcome his strength and virility—or her fear of sex in general (by symbolically castrating men, she is freeing herself from the responsibility of relating to them sexually).

SHIP (7)—Ships, like most other vehicles, are symbolic of movement—either toward a specific goal or away from an undesired situation. The person who dreams of taking a sea voyage may be indicating that he wishes to change his life-situation, or that he believes he is on his way to attaining a certain goal, or that he feels he should be on his way toward attaining a certain goal. If you dream that you yourself are the captain of the ship, you may be revealing your desire to control your own life-situation more than you presently control it—thus, to chart your own course. If you dream that you are on a ship which is adrift, you may be indicating that you fear you have no goals, that you are merely drifting through life. And if you dream that you have arrived too late to board a ship, you may be revealing your fear that you have lost out on an opportunity, that you have "missed the boat."

SISTER (9)—The appearance of a dreamer's sister in a dream is far less significant than the actions of the sister toward the dreamer. In some dreams, a sister may serve to represent the dreamer's entire family. Thus, if you dream that your sister has saved you from an impending catastrophe, you may be expressing your belief that your family will not let you down, no matter how serious your troubles.

SNAKE (5)—Snakes, when they appear in dreams, may symbolize a great many things. Because many snakes in real life are poisonous and/or deadly, one of the most common symbolisms attached to snake-dreams is death. Because snakes are generally thought of as slippery and slimy, another common symbolism is guile. Because it was a snake who tempted Eve to eat from the Tree of Knowledge, snakes also symbolize temptation—especially sexual temptation. And finally, because of their shape, snakes may serve as phallic symbols. Thus, if a snake appears in your dreams, you may be expressing (a) death fears or wishes; (b) concern about your health; (c) the fear that someone is about to perpetrate a misdeed against you; (d) the belief that you are shrewd and cunning; (e) the fear that someone who is shrewd and cunning will get the better of you in a business deal; (f) the fear that you are about to succumb to some sort of temptation; (g) the desire to succumb to a certain temptation; (h) the desire for sexual intercourse; (i) the fear of sexual intercourse. Naturally, as is the case with most dream symbols of this sort, the appearance of a snake in a dream generally will be far less significant than the actions of the snake, the identities and the actions of the dream characters, and the circumstances under which the snake appears in your dream.

SNOW (8)—Snow is a symbol of purity—especially sexual purity. To dream of a snowfall is generally to testify to the belief that you are honorable and good (hence, pure), or to the fear that you are not as honest and good as you should be. To dream of tracking through previously untouched snow is generally, if the dreamer is a man, to voice the desire to have sexual intercourse with a woman, and, if the dreamer is a woman, to express the desire to have sexual intercourse with a man. To dream of snow which is tracked up, dirty and/or soiled is to express (a) feelings of guilt—especially sexual guilt; (b) the belief that you—or another person—is not as good as you (he) should be (hence, that you—or he —is morally "stained;" (c) the belief that you or another person is a hypocrite; (d) the desire to be more cunning or less inhibited than you are. To dream of melting snow is generally to express (a) the desire to shed your inhibitions; (b) the belief that you are sexually despoiled; (c) fears of failing health or impending death; (d) the desire that someone else will suffer a decline of fortunes, a decline of health, or death. As is the case with most dream symbols of this sort, the appearance of snow in dreams generally will be far less significant than the identities and actions of the dream characters and their relationship to the snow.

SOAP (6)—Soap is a symbol of cleanliness. Thus, to dream of soap is generally to express (a) feelings of guilt (hence, the desire to be cleansed); (b) the desire to perform some act which violates your moral code (after the performance of which you will feel the need to be cleansed).

SUCKING—The action of sucking lends itself to a variety of interpretations when it appears in dreams. Because an individual draws all nourishment during the first months of his life by sucking on his mother's breast (or, in modern times, on a bottle), the act may symbolize (a) the desire to become stronger and more powerful than one is (as, during infancy, he became stronger and more powerful by sucking on his mother's breast or on his bottle); (b) feelings of helplessness in a given situation (he needs the help of a mother-figure, who can nourish him and make him stronger and more powerful); (c) feelings of inferiority with respect to his peers (next to whom he is figuratively still a baby—i.e., still sucking on his mother's breast); (d) the desire to be pampered, as he had been when he was a baby; (e) a craving for attention and love without reciprocal obligations—a situation which he enjoyed when he was a baby; (f) the desire to shirk or to avoid responsibility. Likewise, because the act of fellatio (penis-mouth sexual intercourse) involves sucking, dreams of sucking may reveal (a) homosexual tendencies on the part of a male dreamer (who is substituting a phallic symbol in his dream for the male penis which he really would like to suck); (b) the desire for heterosexual fellatio on the part of a female dreamer (who is substituting a phallic symbol in her dream for the male penis which she really would like to suck). Finally, the dream act of sucking may be significant on a metaphoric level—i.e., the dreamer fears being sapped of his energies (hence, "sucked" dry), or desires to sap others of their energies, or in some other way either fears or desires any of the types of loss which might be incurred by an object of sucking. Naturally, in all dreams of sucking, the most important consideration will be the nature of the object being sucked. Is it a phallic symbol? A breast symbol? Is it an actual phallus or an actual breast? Other very important considerations will include (a) the identity of the person who is doing the sucking; (b) the circumstances under which the act takes place; (c) the actions and reactions of other dream characters; (d) the setting of the dream.

SUN (9)—The sun symbolizes life. Thus, if the sun appears in your dreams, you may be expressing (a) death fears or wishes; (b) concern about your health; (c) the belief that you are about to perform some act which will jeopardize your health or your general well-being. Also, to dream of the sun may be to voice (a) contentment with your present life-situation (hence, everything is "sunny"); (b) eagerness to begin a certain project (metaphorically, to participate in a "sunrise"); (c) the desire to complete a project (metaphorically, to observe the setting sun). However, since the sun generally shines during the daytime and since many events in a person's life do take place during the daytime, the fact that the sun appears in a person's dream need not be symbolically significant. Obviously, all such dreams should be analyzed very carefully, with special attention to the physical setting of the dream, the dream objects which appear, and the actions and identities of the dream characters.

SWIMMING—Since swimming can be done only in bodies of water, and since bodies of water symbolize the female genitalia, to dream of swimming is generally to express the desire for sexual intercourse. However, as is usually the case with dream actions of this sort, the circumstances under which swimming takes place—and the identities and actions of the dream characters involved—generally will be far more significant than the mere fact that the action of swimming takes place in a dream. Thus, if a person dreams that he is an expert swimmer, he may be testifying to the belief that he is sexually attractive and/or competent. If he dreams that he is swimming toward someone or something, he may be expressing (a) the desire to achieve a specific goal; (b) sexual desire for a person toward whom he is swimming. If he dreams that he is swimming away from someone or something, he may be voicing (a) the desire to escape an uncomfortable situation or to escape his life-situation in general; (b) the desire to repulse the sexual advances of a particular person; (c) the belief that people are making demands upon him which he cannot possibly fulfill (hence, his desire for escape). If the action of swimming appears in your dream, ask yourself: Who is swimming? Why? What characters other than the dreamer appear in the dream? What is their relationship to the swimming which is being done? What are their actions? What are their reactions toward each other and toward the dreamer? What dream objects appear in the dream?

I

TAIL (6)—The tail of an animal is a phallic symbol. Tail in the metaphoric sense (as in the "tail" end of a line) symbolizes defeat and/or exclusion. Thus, dreams involving tails may indicate (a) the dreamer's desire for or fear of sexual intercourse; (b) the dreamer's fear that he is being left behind; (c) the dreamer's feelings of inadequacy (as a result of which he finds himself at the "tail end" of things). However, as is usually the case with dream symbols of this sort, the mere fact that a tail appears in a dream is generally far less significant than the dreamer's actions toward the tail, the actions and reactions of other dream characters and the setting of the dream. If a woman dreams that she is playing with an animal's tail, she may be expressing a desire to fondle a man's penis—or, by extension, to engage in sexual intercourse with the man. If she dreams of cutting off an animal's tail, she may be expressing (a) fears of sexual intercourse (hence, she wants to castrate men so that she will not be obliged to relate to them sexually); (b) the desire for strength and power (by rendering men weak through castration, she becomes comparatively stronger and more powerful). If a man dreams of an animal with a large tail, he may be voicing (a) fears of sexual inadequacy (his penis is not as large as the animal's tail); (b) confidence in his sexual attractiveness and/or ability (his penis is as large as the animal's tail).

TEACHER (6)—A teacher is someone who contributes to the education of his pupil. He is also an authority-figure and, because he administers examinations which pupils either pass or fail, a judge-figure. When a teacher appears in a person's dream, the action of the figure—and his identity—almost invariably are more significant than the mere fact that he has appeared. If, for example, the dreamer envisions himself as a teacher, he generally is expressing (a) the desire to help others by contributing to their education; (b) the belief that he is capable of helping others; (c) the desire to enjoy a position of authority and responsibility; (d) the fear of assuming a position of authority and responsibility; (e) the desire to stand in judgment over another person or persons; (f) fear of standing in judgment over another person or persons; (g) anxiety over a decision which he is about to make. If someone the dreamer knows appears as a teacher, the dreamer may be expressing (a) the belief that this person can be helpful to him by contributing to his education; (b) the desire to relate to the person as a pupil relates to a teacher; (c) the belief that the person in question deserves to occupy a position of authority and responsibility; (d) a desire to be guided or controlled by the person; (e) resentment at the belief that the person is trying to guide or control him—or the belief that the person actually is guiding or controlling him; (f) the belief that the person holds the dreamer's fate in his hands; (g) desire for the person's approval; (h) the fear that the person will disapprove of something which the dreamer has said or done; (i) the belief that the person actually is qualified to stand in judgment over others; (j) resentment over the fact that the person wants to stand in judgment over others; (k) resentment over the fact that the person does in fact stand in judgment over others; (l) anxiety over a decision which the person is about to make; (m) the belief that the person wrongly deems himself qualified to stand in judgment over others. If an anonymous teacher appears in a dream, the dreamer generally is expressing (a) feelings of inadequacy and/or inferiority (he needs a teacher to educate and guide him); (b) the desire to submit to someone else's authority; (c) resentment over the fact that he presently is compelled to submit to someone's authority; (d) the fear that he is about to be judged for something he has said or done; (e) the fear of being punished for a real or imagined misdeed; (f) the desire to be punished for a real or imagined misdeed.

TEN (3)—The figure ten comprises the digits one and zero. Since one is a phallic symbol and zero a vaginal symbol, the union of these digits in the figure ten symbolizes coitus.

TENT (5)—A tent is a covering. Hence, the person who dreams of a tent may be expressing (a) the desire to conceal a secret; (b) the belief that he is inadequate or inferior (he must conceal his faults by covering them, as with a tent). However, dreams of tents need not necessarily be symbolic. Since tents are shelters which one uses on camping trips and similar excursions, the dreamer may merely be expressing the desire to get away from the hustle and bustle of everyday life —just as the camper gets away from his problems by camping out.

THIEF (3)—A thief, of course, is a person who steals. When a thief appears in a person's dream, the actions of the thief—and his identity—almost invariably are more significant than the fact that he has appeared. Thus, if the dreamer pictures himself as a thief, he may be expressing (a) the desire to get something for nothing; (b) the belief that he is a parasite (as a thief is a parasite on law-abiding society); (c) envy for the possessions—whether spiritual or material—of those who surround him. Likewise, if a dreamer pictures an acquaintance as a thief, he generally is voicing (a) the belief that the person in question is trying to get something for nothing; (b) distrust for the person; (c) the belief that the person envies the dreamer himself; (d) the desire to be the sort of person whom other people envy. If an anonymous thief appears in his dreams, he probably is expressing (a) the fear that others are trying to take what is rightfully his; (b) concern for the welfare of his family and other persons whom he holds dear.

TOMATO (3)—Tomatoes are, because of their shape, symbolic of the female's breasts. Hence, a man who dreams of holding or eating tomatoes may be expressing a desire to caress or suck a woman's breasts—or, by extension, to have sexual intercourse with her. A man who dreams of taking tomatoes from a woman by force may be indicating a desire to rape her. A woman who dreams of giving a tomato to a man or having him take a tomato from her is generally indicating a desire to share or a fear of sharing her breasts—or, by extension, her sexual participation—with him.

TOMB (5)—A tomb is symbolic of death fears or wishes.

TOOTH (6)—Dreams involving teeth generally involve the extraction or filling of a tooth. The extraction of a tooth symbolizes death, for an extracted tooth leaves a gap in the midst of other teeth in precisely the same way that a person who dies leaves a gap in his family. Thus, when a person dreams of having a tooth extracted, he may be expressing his unconscious desire for or fear of death. Similarly, the person who dreams that a friend or acquaintance is having a tooth extracted may be revealing an unconscious death wish or death fear with respect to that person. To dream of having a tooth filled is generally to express (a) the fear that one must face up to an unpleasant situation (having a tooth filled is almost invariably unpleasant); (b) the desire to become a parent (the filling of the tooth symbolizes pregnancy, in which the womb of a woman is "filled" with the foetus). However, dreams involving teeth may also be "current event" dreams; thus, if you presently are having trouble with your teeth in real life, you may merely be reaffirming in your dreams a concern of which in waking hours you are already aware.

TUB (7)—A tub, because of its shape and because of the fact that it is filled with water or other liquids, symbolizes the female genitalia. Understandably, however, the type of tub which appears in your dream, the use to which it is put, and the actions of dream characters with respect to it will generally be of far more significance than the mere fact that a tub has appeared in the dream.

U

UNDERCLOTHING—The appearance of underclothing in a dream lends itself to a wide variety of interpretations. Because undergarments are the items in a person's wardrobe which are worn closest to his body, to dream of a person wearing underclothing generally is to express (a) the desire to get closer to the person, to know him or her better; (*b*) the desire for sexual intercourse with the person; (*c*) the belief that the person is trustworthy (hence, he exposes himself to you); (*d*) the belief that the person is trying to keep a secret from you (hence, he refuses to appear nude—i.e., to show you everything). To dream of yourself wearing underclothing generally is to voice (*a*) the desire to have other people get close to you; (*b*) the desire for sexual intercourse with somebody; (*c*) the desire to share a secret with somebody; (*d*) the desire to keep a secret from somebody. To dream that your own underclothing or someone else's underclothing is soiled is generally to express (*a*) the belief that the person in question lacks self-control (i.e., he is unable to control bodily waste elimination); (*b*) general repulsion for the person; (*c*) the belief that the person is generally unclean; (*d*) the belief that the person desires sexual intercourse with you. (For numerical equivalents of underclothing-dreams for lucky number computations, compute a single-digit number based on the individual item or items of underclothing which appear in your dream—e.g., panties, bra, shorts, slip, T-shirt, etc.)

URINATION—The act of urination, as an act whereby the body expels its liquid wastes, generally symbolizes (*a*) feelings of guilt (the dreamer wishes to purge himself of his guilt feelings by expelling the impurities which are in his body); (*b*) the desire to confide in someone (the dreamer wishes to get a matter "off his chest," just as he is getting the liquid wastes out of his body).

V

VAULT (4)—A vault is a repository for valuables. It is also a container which cannot be opened unless one knows the combination. Hence, to dream of vaults is generally to express (*a*) the belief that good fortune lies ahead, if only one can figure out a certain problem (how to open the vault); (*b*) the desire to achieve a specific goal; (*c*) the belief that one's attempts to achieve his goals are being thwarted by fate, or by other people; (*d*) the desire to get to know someone better. As is usually the case with dream symbols of this sort, the presence of a vault in a dream generally is of far less significance than the circumstances of the dream. Thus, if you dream of a vault, ask yourself: What is in the vault? Do you want to open it? Does someone else want to open it? Do you know the combination? Does someone else know the combination? What are the identities and actions of other persons who appear in your dream? What other dream symbols are present? Vaults, because they are containers, also symbolize the female genitalia and the womb. Thus, to dream of a vault may also be to express (*a*) the desire for or the fear of sexual intercourse; (*b*) the desire to become a parent; (*c*) the fear of becoming a parent.

VEIL (3)—Because a veil is used to conceal something, the appearance of a veil in your dream will generally mean (*a*) that you want to conceal something from somebody; (*b*) that you are afraid other people are concealing something from you; (*c*) that you suffer guilt feelings for some real or imagined misdeed (hence, you wish to conceal the misdeed).

VIOLIN (9)—The violin, as a musical instrument, symbolizes joy and merriment. Because violin music often is romantic, the appearance of a violin in a dream may also symbolize love. If you dream of a violin, you should ask yourself: Who is playing it? For whose benefit is it being played? What are the reactions of the dream characters who hear it being played? For example, if you dream that a girl is playing the violin for you, you probably are voicing your belief that the girl loves you and/or wants to make you happy. If in the same dream you envision someone else complaining about the girl's violin-playing, you may be expressing the belief that this other person wants to prevent you from being happy and loved, and/or that the other person objects to your relationship with this particular girl. If you further dream that you yourself do not like the girl's violin-playing, you may be testifying to the fact that you reject her affection for you.

W

WASHING—The act of washing, because it is a process whereby one is physically cleansed, generally testifies to the dreamer's unconscious feelings of guilt, as a result of which he feels a need to be spiritually cleansed. The person who dreams that someone else is washing is probably voicing a belief that this other person has done something for which he should feel guilty.

WATER (4)—Water is one of the most common—and difficult to interpret—dream symbols. Among the things which it symbolizes are birth, death and cleansing. Also, if it appears in the form of a lake, pond or other body of water, it may symbolize the female genitalia. If water appears in your dream, you should ask yourself: What form does it take? For what purpose is it being used? Who is using it? What are the identities and actions of dream characters who are present? What other dream symbols appear? With respect to water's birth-death symbolism, the person who dreams of water may be testifying to (a) death fears or wishes; (b) the fear that his health is failing; (c) the desire to change his personality (i.e., to start life anew by being metaphorically reborn); (d) the desire to achieve a specific goal (i.e., the goal of being reborn); (e) the desire to become a parent; (f) the fear that one may become a parent against his wishes. For interpretations involving other types of water-symbolism, see WASHING, DRINKING, SHIP, BOAT, PIER, RIVER, POND.

WHISKY (1)—Whisky, like all other alcoholic beverages, generally symbolizes good fellowship, convivial company and general merriment. However, with many individuals, alcoholic beverages have a decidedly negative connotation. This is especially the case among people who have a personal drinking problem or who are involved with other persons who have a drinking problem. Alcoholic beverages also might have a decidedly negative connotation for people who have at one time or another suffered abuse at the hands of an habitual drinker. Thus, the appearance of any alcoholic beverage in a dream can be interpreted only in the light of the dreamer's own experience with drinking or drinkers—and, in any case, the presence of an alcoholic beverage in a dream will be less significant than the actions of the persons who are drinking it.

WHITE (9)—The color white is symbolic of purity and innocence. Its appearance in a dream generally indicates the dreamer's belief that the character who is wearing the color or that the object which is so colored is good, desirable, pure, innocent, etc.

WINDOW (7)—Windows symbolize the female genitalia. Their appearance in dreams may also be significant on the metaphoric level—i.e., with respect to parallels to window-functions in real life. Thus, a person who dreams of a window or windows may be indicating (*a*) the desire to learn the solution to a particular problem (i.e., to shed light on the problem, by opening a window); (*b*) the desire to escape from an uncomfortable situation or from one's life-situation in general (as one escapes through a window); (*c*) feelings of guilt (which may be purged by the opening of a window, as one cleans out the stale air in a room by opening the windows); (*d*) the desire for or the fear of sexual intercourse. As is usually the case with dream objects of this sort, the mere fact that a window appears in your dreams is generally far less significant than the circumstances surrounding its appearance. Thus, if you dream of a window or windows, ask yourself: Is it open or closed? Why is it open or closed? What are your actions and the actions of other dream characters with respect to it? What other dream objects are present?

WINE (6)—Wine, like all other alcoholic beverages, generally symbolizes good fellowship, convivial company and general merriment. However, with many individuals, alcoholic beverages have a decidedly negative connotation. This is especially the case among people who have a personal drinking problem or who are involved with other persons who have a drinking problem. Alcoholic beverages also might have a decidedly negative connotation for people who have at one time or another suffered abuse at the hands of an habitual drinker. Thus, the appearance of any alcoholic beverage in a dream can be interpreted only in the light of the dreamer's own experience with drinking or drinkers—and, in any case, the presence of an alcoholic beverage in a dream will be less significant than the actions of the persons who are drinking it.

Y

YELLOW (2)—The color yellow is symbolic of cowardice. If a dream object is yellow, the fact probably will be of no significance. But if the dreamer or some other dream character is wearing the color yellow, the dreamer may be indicating his belief that the person in question (including himself) is cowardly.

YOUTH—The state of being a youth is symbolic of adventurousness, strength, good health, virility and joy. Thus, to dream of yourself as a youth or to dream of other people as youths is generally to apply one or more of these characteristics to them. Dreams involving anonymous youths probably indicate the dreamer's (a) desire to return to the days of his youth, when he was adventurous, strong, healthy, virile and joyful; (b) fear of death (as evidenced by the fact that his youth is far behind him); (c) the desire to grow intellectually, as youths grow intellectually; (d) belief that his sexual powers are waning (he no longer can hold his own with youth); (e) belief that his intellectual abilities are waning (he can no longer hold his own with youth).

Z

ZERO (1)—The figure zero is, because of its shape, a vaginal symbol. To dream of the figure is generally to indicate a desire for sexual intercourse. However, the appearance of a zero or of several zeros in a person's dream may also indicate (a) feelings of intellectual, spiritual emptiness (i.e., the dreamer is a zero, he has nothing inside him); (b) the fear that one's fortunes or one's health is failing (i.e., coming to naught); (c) destructive tendencies (the desire to reduce things to nothingness).

ZOO (2)—A zoo, of course, is a place where animals are kept, and dreams of animals generally indicate the dreamer's desire for companionship and affection. Hence, to dream of a zoo probably is to voice (a) unconscious desires for companionship and affection; (b) the fear that one is not worthy of receiving companionship and affection. However, zoo-dreams may also be symbolic of childhood—the period in one's life when one generally was taken to a zoo. Thus, dreaming of a zoo may reveal the dreamer's (a) feelings of helplessness in a given situation (i.e., he feels like a child); (b) feelings of inferiority with respect to his peers (next to whom he is figuratively a child; (c) the desire to be pampered, as he had been when he actually was a child; (d) a craving for attention and love without reciprocal obligations—a situation which he enjoyed when he was a child; (e) the desire to shirk responsibility. (Many times zoo-dreams contain cages; in this case, consult CAGE for further interpretations).

PART III

YOUR DREAM LOG

A one-week starter to record your dreams. After the first week you may wish to continue with your own dream log in a special notebook.

YOUR DREAM LOG FOR THE WEEK OF ....

MONDAY

Characters	Name	Objects	Setting	Action

DREAM

DREAM

YOUR DREAM LOG FOR THE WEEK OF ....

TUESDAY

Characters	Name	Objects	Setting	Action

DREAM

DREAM

YOUR DREAM LOG FOR THE WEEK OF..........

WEDNESDAY

Characters	Name	Objects	Setting	Action

DREAM

DREAM

YOUR DREAM LOG FOR THE WEEK OF......................

THURSDAY

Characters	Name	Objects	Setting	Action

DREAM

DREAM

YOUR DREAM LOG FOR THE WEEK OF ·················

FRIDAY

Characters	*Name*	*Objects*	*Setting*	*Action*

DREAM

DREAM

YOUR DREAM LOG FOR THE WEEK OF ....

SATURDAY

Characters	Name	Objects	Setting	Action
DREAM				
DREAM				

YOUR DREAM LOG FOR THE WEEK OF..........

SUNDAY

Characters	*Name*	*Objects*	*Setting*	*Action*

DREAM

DREAM

PSYCHIC WORLD

Here are some of the leading books that delve into the world of the occult—that shed light on the powers of prophecy, or reincarnation and of foretelling the future.

Special Offer
Buy a Bantam Book
for only 50¢.

Now you can have an up-to-date listing of Bantam's hundreds of titles plus take advantage of our unique and exciting bonus book offer. A special offer which gives you the opportunity to purchase a Bantam book for only 50¢. Here's how!

By ordering any five books at the regular price per order, you can also choose any other single book listed (up to a $4.95 value) for just 50¢. Some restrictions do apply, but for further details why not send for Bantam's listing of titles today!

Just send us your name and address and we will send you a catalog!

CATHERINE AIRD

For 15 years, Catherine Aird's mysteries have won praises for their brilliant plotting and style. Established alongside other successful English mystery ladies, she continues to thrill old and new mystery fans alike.

- ☐ 25191 HARM'S WAY $2.95
- ☐ 25414 PARTING BREATH $2.95
- ☐ 23677 LAST RESPECTS $2.50
- ☐ 25109 A SLIGHT MOURNING $2.95
- ☐ 25110 SOME DIE ELOQUENT $2.95

Prices and availability subject to change without notice.

The  **POCKET**Guide

CALIFORNIA

California: Regions and Best places to see

★ Best places to see 24–45

■ Featured sight

■ San Francisco 49–63

■ Northern California 64–81

■ Central Coast 82–89

■ Los Angeles 90–103

■ Southern California 104–129

Written and updated by Richard Minnich

© AA Media Limited 2008
First published 2008. Reprinted June 2010.

ISBN: 978-0-7495-5750-8

Published by AA Publishing, a trading name of AA Media Limited, whose registered office is Fanum House, Basing View, Basingstoke, Hampshire RG21 4EA. Registered number 06112600.

Colour separation: Keenes, Andover
Printed and bound in Italy by Printer Trento S.r.l.
Front cover images: (t) AA/K Paterson; (b) AA/C Sawyer
Back cover image: AA/P Wood

A04523
Maps in this title produced from mapping © MAIRDUMONT / Falk Verlag 2010
Transport map © Communicarta Ltd, UK

About this book

This book is divided into four sections.

Planning pages 10–23
Before you go; Getting there; Getting around; Being there

Best places to see pages 24–45
The unmissable highlights of any visit to California

Exploring pages 46–129
The best places to visit in California, organized by area

Maps pages 133–144
All map references are to the atlas section. For example, San Jose has the reference ✚ 135 C8 – indicating the page number and grid square in which it can be found

Contents

PLANNING

10 – 23

BEST PLACES TO SEE

24 – 45

EXPLORING

46 – 129

INDEX & ACKNOWLEDGEMENTS

130 – 132

MAPS

133 – 144

Planning

Before you go   12–15

Getting there   16

Getting around   17–19

Being there   20–23

Before you go

WHEN TO GO

JAN	FEB	MAR	APR	MAY	JUN	JUL	AUG	SEP	OCT	NOV	DEC
13°C	14°C	17°C	18°C	19°C	21°C	22°C	22°C	23°C	22°C	18°C	14°C
55°F	57°F	63°F	64°F	76°F	70°F	72°F	72°F	73°F	72°F	64°F	57°F

🌧️ High season   🌥️ Low season

California is known for its diversity of climates. Generally speaking, the south is warmer and the north cooler. The bay areas are renowned for their fog. The mountainous areas are known for pleasant summers and snowy winters at the higher elevations.

The San Joaquin and Sacramento valleys are extremely hot during the summer months and cool and foggy the rest of the year. The rainy season is usually from November through April. As a rule, most parts of the state are cool in the evenings.

WHAT YOU NEED

● Required
○ Suggested
▲ Not required

Some countries require a passport to remain valid for a minimum period (usually at least six months) beyond the date of entry – check before you travel.

	UK	Germany	USA	Netherlands	Spain
Passport (or National Identity Card where applicable)	●	●	▲	●	●
Visa (regulations can change – check before you travel)	▲	▲	▲	▲	▲
Onward or Return Ticket	●	●	▲	●	●
Health Inoculations (tetanus and polio)	▲	▲	▲	▲	▲
Health Documentation (► 13, Health Insurance)	●	●	●	●	●
Travel Insurance	○	○	○	○	○
Driving License (national)	●	●	●	●	●
Car Insurance Certificate (if own vehicle)	○	○	○	○	○

WEBSITES

www.gocalifornia.ca.gov
www.visitcalifornia.com
www.onlyinsanfrancisco.com
www.touringca.com
www.disneyland.com

www.lawa.org/lax
www.flysfo.com
www.nps.gov/redw/
www.nps.gov/yose/

TOURIST OFFICES AT HOME

In the UK

Visit USA Association
☎ 09069 101020
(consumer line)
www.visitusa.org.uk

In the USA

California Division of Tourism
801 K Street, Suite 1600,
Sacramento, CA 95812
☎ 916/444-4429,
call-free 800/862-2543

HEALTH INSURANCE

There is no agreement for medical treatment between the US and other
countries and all travelers MUST be covered by medical insurance (for an
unlimited amount of medical costs is advisable). Treatment will be refused
without evidence of insurance.

Medical insurance will cover you for dental treatment. In the event of
any emergency, see your hotel concierge or consult the Yellow Pages for
an emergency dentist.

TIME DIFFERENCES

| GMT | California | Germany | USA (NY) | Netherlands | Spain |
| 12 noon | 4AM | 1PM | 7AM | 1PM | 1PM |

California is on Pacific Standard Time (PST); eight hours behind Greenwich
Mean Time (GMT–8), but from early April, when clocks are put forward
one hour, to late October, Daylight Saving Time (GMT–7) operates.
California is also three hours behind the east coast of the USA (Eastern
Standard Time/EST).

NATIONAL HOLIDAYS

Jan 1 *New Year's Day*	Jul 4 *Independence Day*	Nov (4th Thu) *Thanksgiving Day*
Jan (3rd Mon) *Martin Luther King Jr's Birthday*	Sep (1st Mon) *Labor Day*	Dec 25 *Christmas Day*
Feb 12 *Lincoln's Birthday*	Oct (2nd Mon) *Columbus Day*	
Feb (3rd Mon) *President's Day*	Nov 11 *Veteran's Day*	On these days shops, banks and businesses close.

WHAT'S ON WHEN

The following are just a few of California's myriad festivals and celebrations.

January *Tournament of Roses Parade*, Pasadena
Palm Springs International Film Festival

February *Chinese New Year Celebration*, San Francisco
Napa Valley Mustard Celebration, Napa

March *International Asian Film Festival*, San Francisco
Los Angeles Marathon
Mendocino Whale Festival

April *Toyota Grand Prix*, Long Beach
Cherry Blossom Festival, San Francisco
Palm Desert Springfest, Palm Desert
Cinco De Mayo Celebration, state-wide

May *San Francisco International Film Fest*
Muscle Car Show, Bakersfield
Sacramento Jazz Jubilee
San Francisco Bay to Breakers, a race where people run in costume

June *Scottish Highlands Games and Gathering of the Clans*, Modesto
Amador County Wine Festival, Plymouth
Sonoma Valley Shakespeare Festival, Sonoma

July *Festival of Arts and Pageant of the Masters*, Laguna Beach
California Rodeo, Salinas
Greek Festival, Santa Barbara
San Francisco Marathon

August *Mozart Festival*, San Luis Obispo
Sawdust Festival, Laguna Beach
San Francisco Mime Troupe

Summer Park Season
Old Spanish Days Fiesta, Santa Barbara
Japanese Cultural Bazaar, Sacramento
California State Fair, Sacramento
Children's Festival of the Arts, Hollywood

September *Greek Food Festival*, Sacramento
Oktoberfest, Huntington Beach
Danish Days, Solvang
Monterey Jazz Festival, Monterey
Armenian Food Festival, San Francisco
Bowlful of Blues Festival, Ojai
California International Air Show, Salinas

October *Jazz Festival*, San Francisco
Rose Show, Santa Barbara
San Francisco Fleet week
Halloween, San Francisco

November *West Coast Ragtime Festival*, in
various locations
Christmas Parade, Hollywood

December *America's Tallest Living Christmas Tree*,
Ferndale
Newport Harbor Christmas Boat Parade, Newport
Beach
Celebrity Cooks and Kitchens Tour, Mendocino
New Year's Eve Torchlight Parade, Big Bear Lake

Getting there

BY AIR

Los Angeles Airport

15 miles (24km) to city center

45–60 minutes

35 minutes

30 minutes

San Francisco Airport

16 miles (26km) to city center

N/A

30–60 minutes

30 minutes

International direct flights operate into Los Angeles (LAX ☎ 310/646-5252) – one of the world's busiest airports – and San Francisco (SFO ☎ 650/821-8211). San Diego Airport (SAN) also has international flights but most stop en route first. Charter flights also use these airports. For the Federal Aviation Authority's air safety hotline ☎ 800/322-7873.

BY CAR

Interstates 10, 15, 40 and 80 are the main routes into the state from the east. Interstate 5 is the principal route that runs from north to south. Route 101 is the smaller, more scenic route to drive while traveling along the coast. In some places it turns into Route 1. All gas stations have detailed maps.

BY RAIL AND BUS

There are Amtrak railroad stations in or near most of the major cities in California that connect from Las Vegas and other large places in the southwest. Many travelers find this a sensible way to see the state. Of particular interest is the scenic route that follows the coastline – the Coast Starlight – from Seattle to Los Angeles or on to San Diego via Oakland, Salinas, San Luis Obispo, Santa Barbara and the Malibu coast. For the most up-to-date information visit www.amtrak.com or ☎ 800/872-7245).

For information about Greyhound Lines long-distance buses (☎ 800/231-2222; www.greyhound.com).

Getting around

PUBLIC TRANSPORTATION

Internal flights Flying is the quickest way of getting around California and is not all that expensive if you take advantage of deals offered by airlines. The international airports of San Francisco, Oakland, Los Angeles and San Diego connect with a number of regional airports.

Trains Rail service is provided by America's National Railroad Corporation, Amtrak. Carriages are clean, comfortable and rarely crowded. A Far Western Region Rail Pass (available only outside the US) gives 45 days unlimited travel over the far western states.

Long-distance buses Buses are by far the cheapest way of getting around. Greyhound Lines operates an inter-city service and also links many smaller towns within California. The Ameripass (only available outside the US) gives 4, 5, 7, 15, 30 or 60 days' unlimited travel throughout the USA.

Ferries A ferry service links San Francisco with the Bay communities of Sausalito, Larkspur and Tiburon in scenic Marin County, and to Vallejo, Oakland and Alameda (departures from Pier 1, foot of Market Street). There is also a boat service from Long Beach and Newport Beach to Catalina Island.

Urban transportation Local communities and major cities are served by local bus services. In addition, San Francisco has cable-cars serving the downtown area and the BART train system covering the Bay areas. Los Angeles has its metrorail and San Diego has a trolley car service through the downtown area.

TAXIS

Cabs may be hailed on the street but few cruise outside tourist areas. If you are away from airports or major hotels it is best to phone for one (look under "cabs" in Yellow Pages). In most cities rates are high, except San Francisco because of its comparatively small size.

DRIVING

- Drive on the right.
- Seat belts must be worn in front seats at all times and in rear seats where fitted.
- Random breath-testing takes place. Never drive under the influence of alcohol.
- Fuel (gasoline or gas), leaded and unleaded, is sold in US gallons (3.8 liters). Most gas stations are self service. When removing the nozzle

from the pump you must lift or turn the lever to activate it. Fuel is more expensive in remote areas and you may also be charged more if paying by credit card.
- If you break down in a rented car, phone the emergency number on the dashboard. Summon help from emergency telephones located along freeways (every half mile) and remote highways (every 2 miles/3.2km), or sit tight and wait for the cruising highway patrol or state patrol to spot you (a raised hood should help).
- Speed limits are as follows:
  On rural interstate roads (motorways) 55–70mph (88–113kph)
  On many freeways (two-lane or more carriageways) 65mph (105kph)
  In residential and business districts and school zones 25mph (40kph) or as signposted

CAR RENTAL

If you are planning to rent a car, consider taking advantage of one of the fly/drive programs many airlines offer before you go. Otherwise most car rental companies have offices throughout the state. Charges depend on the size of car, locale and time of year. Pay by credit card to avoid a hefty cash deposit.

None of the major companies will rent to anyone under the age of 25. It may be possible to find a local company that will do so, but be prepared to pay a loaded insurance premium.

It is advisable to find out whether your own insurance would cover damage to a rented car, and what the details are of Collision Damage Waiver (CDW).

FARES AND CONCESSIONS

Students Upon production of ID proving student status, there are discounts available on travel, theater and museum tickets, plus at some nightspots. It is always worth asking at the outset.

Senior citizens For anyone over the age of 62 there is a tremendous variety of discounts on offer (upon proof of age). Both Amtrak (train) and Greyhound (bus), as well as many US airlines, offer (smallish) percentage reductions on fares. Museums, art galleries, attractions, cinemas, and even hotels offer small discounts, and as the definition of senior can drop to as low as 55, it is always worth enquiring.

Being there

TOURIST OFFICES

Anaheim/Orange County Visitor & Convention Bureau, 800 West Katella Avenue, Anaheim, CA 92802
☎ 714/765-8857

California Deserts Tourism Association, 37–115 Palm View Road, Rancho Mirage, CA 92270
☎ 760/328-9256

Los Angeles Convention &Visitors Bureau, 685 Figueroa Street, Los Angeles, CA 90017
☎ 213/689-8822

Monterey Peninsula Visitors & Convention Bureau, 150 Oliver Street, PO Box 1770, Monterey, CA 93940
☎ 831/649-1770

Palm Springs Tourism, 777 N Canyon Drive, Suite 201, Palm Springs, CA 92264
☎ 760/778-8415

Sacramento Convention & Visitors Bureau, 1608 "I" Street, Sacramento, CA 95814
☎ 916/264-7777

San Diego Convention & Visitors Bureau, 401 B Street, Suite 1400, San Diego, CA 92101
☎ 619/236-1212

San Francisco Convention & Visitors Bureau, 201 Third Street, Suite 900, San Francisco, CA 94103
☎ 415/974-6900

MONEY

The American monetary unit is the dollar ($), which is divided into 100 cents. There are coins of 1 cent (penny), 5 cents (nickel), 10 cents (dime), 25 cents (quarter), 50 cents (half dollar) and 1 dollar. Bills (notes) are available in denominations of 1, 2 (rarely seen), 5, 10, 20, 50 and 100 dollars.

POSTAL SERVICES

Post offices are plentiful in cities. Stamps are also sold from stamp machines in hotels and shops but have a 25 percent mark up. Main post offices in larger cities normally open 8–6 (noon Sat); closed Sun.
☎ 213/483-3745 (Los Angeles); ☎ 415/487-8981 (San Francisco).

TIPS/GRATUITIES

Yes ✓   No ✗

Restaurants	✓	15–20%
Cafeterias/fast-food outlets	✗	
Bars	✓	15–20%
Cabs	✓	15–20%
Porters	✓	$1 per bag
Chambermaids	✓	$1 per day
Toilet attendants	✗	

TELEPHONES

Telephones are located in hotel and motel lobbies, drugstores, restaurants, garages and in roadside kiosks. Exact change in 5-, 10- or 25-cent pieces is required to place a call. For internal calls dial 1 before the number when the area code is different from the one on the phone you are using. For the operator dial 0, for directory assistance dial 411.

International Dialing Codes
From the USA to:
UK: 011 44
Germany: 011 49
Netherlands: 011 31
Spain: 011 34

Emergency telephone numbers
Police 911
Fire 911
Ambulance 911

EMBASSIES AND CONSULATES

UK ☎ 310/481-0031 (LA)
Germany ☎ 323/930-2703 (LA),
☎ 415/775-1061 (SF)

Netherlands ☎ 310/268-1598 (LA)
Spain ☎ 323/938-0158 (LA),
☎ 415/922-2995 (SF)

HEALTH ADVICE

Sun advice California enjoys a lot of sunshine with more than 250 clear days a year. Along the coast mornings can be hazily overcast and sea breezes (especially in the north) can make it feel cooler than it is. Protect the skin at all times.

Drugs Quick-remedy medicines such as aspirin are readily available at any drugstore (pharmacy). For tablets containing acetaminophen read paracetamol. Also, many pain-killing pills available "over the counter" at home may need a prescription in the US.

Safe water It is quite safe to drink tap water. In hotels and restaurants a nice touch is that water, generally ice cold, is provided free with meals. Bottled water is also widely available but is not as popular as in Europe.

PERSONAL SAFETY

California is certainly not crime free and drugs are a problem, but exercise due caution, especially in downtown areas, and you should be safe. Away from these areas crime is quite low key. Some precautions:

● If confronted by a mugger, hand over your money.
● If driving do not stop the car in any unlit or deserted urban area.
Police assistance:  911 from any call box

ELECTRICITY

The power supply is 110–115 volts. Round 3-hole sockets taking plugs with 2 flat pins in a parallel position, with an upper, round, earth pin for earthed appliances. European visitors should bring a voltage transformer as well as an adaptor.

OPENING HOURS

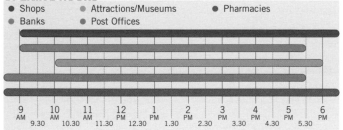

In addition to the times shown above, many shops, particularly department stores within shopping malls, are open evenings and during afternoons on Sunday. Some supermarkets and grocery shops open 24 hours. Banks open until 5:30pm Friday and some major banks open on Saturday. Banks in some major towns and tourist areas may have longer hours. Some pharmacies open from 7am to 9pm or even midnight, while some open 24 hours. Opening times of attractions and museums vary (see individual entries in the What to See section). Some post offices open Saturday 8am–1pm.

LANGUAGE

English is the official language of the USA. Californians, however, are a fascinating mix of cultures, most notably of Spanish or Mexican extraction. In fact, Spanish is heard throughout California. The five largest cities in California, Los Angeles, San Diego, San Francisco, San Jose and Sacramento, bear Spanish names. However, although English is the native language there are many differences between its British and American usage. Some of the more commonly encountered are listed below:

holiday	*vacation*	lift	*elevator*
fortnight	*two weeks*	eiderdown	*comforter*
ground floor	*first floor*	hotel porter	*bellhop*
first floor	*second floor*	chambermaid	*room maid*
flat	*apartment*	surname	*last name*
cheque	*check*	25 cent coin	*quarter*
traveller's cheque	*traveler's check*	banknote	*bill*
1 cent coin	*penny*	banknote (colloquial)	*greenback*
5 cent coin	*nickel*	dollar (colloquial)	*buck*
10 cent coin	*dime*	cashpoint	*automatic teller*
aubergine	*eggplant*	confectionery	*candy*
chips (potato)	*fries*	prawns	*shrimp*
crisps (potato)	*chips*	soft drink	*soda*
courgette	*zucchini*	spirit	*liquor*
car	*automobile*	motorway	*freeway*
bonnet (of car)	*hood*	main road	*highway*
boot (of car)	*trunk*	petrol	*gas*
caravan	*trailer*	tram	*streetcar*
lorry	*truck*	underground	*subway*
shop	*store*	trousers	*pants*
chemist (shop)	*drugstore*	nappy	*diaper*
cinema	*movie theater*	glasses	*eyeglasses*
pavement	*sidewalk*	post	*mail*
toilet	*lavatory*	post code	*zip code*

Best places to see

Balboa Park   26–27

Catalina Island   28–29

Disneyland® Park   30–31

Golden Gate Bridge and National
Recreation Area   32–33

Hearst Castle   34–35

Hollywood   36–37

Monterey Peninsula   38–39

Napa Valley   40–41

Redwood National Park   42–43

Yosemite National Park   44–45

1 Balboa Park

This immense expanse of parks and museums includes the world-renowned San Diego Zoo.

A 100-tone chime serenades from the 200ft (60m) California Tower, creating an exquisite backdrop for the historical buildings, museums and gardens of this 1,200-acre (486ha) park. Start your visit from the main thoroughfare, El Prado (The Promenade). Here you'll find original exhibit halls from the 1915 Panama–California International Exposition, most notably the Casa del Prado. The Timken Museum of Art, a few blocks south, has interesting Russian icons among its exhibits.

At the park's center are several small museums: San Diego History Museum, Museum of Photographic

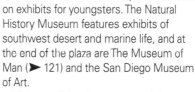

Arts, Model Railroad Museum and Hall of Champions (sports). The nearby Reuben H. Fleet Space Theater and Science Center provides hands-on exhibits for youngsters. The Natural History Museum features exhibits of southwest desert and marine life, and at the end of the plaza are The Museum of Man (➤ 121) and the San Diego Museum of Art.

Visit any of the three stages of the Globe Theatre to see contemporary or Shakespearean plays, or enjoy a summer musical at The Starlight Bowl.

Simply stated, the **San Diego Zoo** is among the finest zoos in the world. The 100 acres (40ha) simulate the natural habitats of the 800 species living here, and allows expansive roaming of its 4,000 animals, which include the only pair of pandas in the US. The Children's Zoo offers close-up views. There are guided bus tours, as well as an aerial tramway that rises 170ft (52m) over the zoo's grottoes and mesas, providing a fine overview of the park.

✚ 141 B8 ✉ 1 mile (1.61km) north of downtown San Diego ☎ 619/239-0512 🕐 Daily 9–4:30 (4 in winter) ✋ Moderate 🍴 Restaurants, stands ($$) 🚌 7, 7A or 7B from downtown ❓ Visitor Center sells multi-day passports to the park; free in-park tram

San Diego Zoo
☎ 619/234-3153; www.sandiegozoo.com 🕐 Daily 9–4; zoo grounds close at 6pm ✋ Inexpensive

2 Catalina Island

Known as "The Island of Romance," Catalina Island is a perfect blend of relaxed resort, pristine shoreline and untouched wilderness.

Discovered in 1542 by Juan Rodriguez Cabrillo, Santa Catalina (commonly called Catalina Island) is

roughly 26 miles (42km) from the mainland. One of the eight California Channel Islands, it is 21 miles (34km) long and 8 miles (13km) wide. No cars are allowed on the island, so use the public transportation or rent the electric golf carts and bicycles available.

In 1811, the indigenous Gabrileño Indians were forced to resettle on the mainland, leaving the island that later became the private property of the Wrigley family, the chewing gum heirs. Today, 86 percent of the island is owned by the non-profit Santa Catalina Island Conservancy, established in 1972 to preserve the island's natural beauty. The island provides a welcome retreat from mainland crowds, with its silent beaches, water sports, picturesque pier and deep-sea fishing.

The 1929 Avalon Casino is the most famous building on the island, best known for its art deco ballroom, which in its heyday was host to many of the world's most famous orchestras and big bands. The Catalina Island Museum, on the first floor of the Casino, exhibits the island's history. The Wrigley Mansion, with its botanical gardens, and the Avalon Pier, in the middle of Avalon Bay, provide fine views of the interior hills and the breathtaking shoreline.

✚ 141 D7 ✉ Visitors Center, Green Pier ☎ 310/510-1520; www.catalina.com ⏰ Daily 8–5 ✋ Travel moderate; exhibits inexpensive 🍴 Restaurants ($$$) 🚢 Catalina Express 310/519-1212 or 800/618-5533; 1 hour each way; hourly from San Pedro or Long Beach. Catalina Passenger Service 949/673-5245; 75 mins each way; departs from Balboa Pavilion 9, returns 4:30 🚁 Helicopter Service from Island Express 800/228-2566; 15 mins each way

3 Disneyland® Park

www.disneyland.com

Disneyland Park sets the standard for theme parks. This "happiest place on earth" attracts around 12 million visitors each year.

© 2007, Disney Enterprises Inc.

Children and adults alike are enchanted by the illusion and entertainment of "magic kingdom," opened in 1955. The 80-acre (32ha) park is divided into eight sections, offering such diverse attractions as fantasy rides, musical performances, parades, restaurants and shops.

A series of pastel-colored walkways lead from the central plaza at the end of Main Street, U.S.A. into the various themed areas, each with their own attractions. Mickey's Toontown brings out the kid in everyone; Adventureland offers a jungle boat ride and the charming "Tiki Room." New Orleans Square has a Mississippi steamwheeler, the "Pirates of the Caribbean" attraction and the "Haunted Mansion."

In Frontierland, you can career down Big Thunder Mountain Railroad on a runaway train or raft across to Tom Sawyer Island. Critter Country is the home of the "Splash Mountain" flume ride. Fantasyland begins when you cross the moat to Sleeping Beauty Castle, while Tomorrowland explores the future with attractions like "Space Mountain" and "Star Tours." For the courageous, the "Indiana Jones Adventure" takes you on a trek to the Temple of the Forbidden Eye. Disney characters roam the streets and pose for pictures. Disney's California Adventure Park, a celebration of the State's past and future, is next to Disneyland.

✚ 141 C6 ✉ 1313 Harbor Boulevard, Anaheim
☎ 714/781-4565 🕐 Summer Mon–Fri 9am–midnight (until 1am Sat; winter Mon–Fri 10–6 (until 9pm weekends, public hols). Hours can vary, check first 👖 Expensive ❓ Hours and prices subject to change; on busy days park at the Disneyland Hotel and ride the monorail to the park

4 Golden Gate Bridge and National Recreation Area

The Golden Gate Bridge is quite easily the most beautiful and easily recognized bridge in the world.

The rust-colored symbol of the West Coast stands as a beacon at the entrance of San Francisco Bay. Built in 1937, it is beautiful and impressive from any angle. Often cloaked in fog, the bridge is extraordinarily graceful and delicate in design even though its overall length is 8,981ft (2,737m), and the stolid towers reach 746ft (227m) high. Connecting San Francisco to Marin County and northern California, the suspension bridge withstands winds of up to 100mph (161kph) and swings as much as 27ft (8m). Enjoy the drive over, or walk across for a truly spectacular perspective.

Golden Gate Park, the largest urban national park in the US, covers 74,000 acres (29,959ha) from San Mateo County to Tomales Bay. The giant recreation area offers many attractions, including Fort Mason on San Francisco's waterfront. A former military embarkation point for soldiers during World War II, today the fort is the site of museums, theaters, galleries, restaurants and the last unaltered, operational liberty ship, the SS *Jeremiah O'Brien*.

The Golden Gate Promenade is a scenic bayshore hike stretching 3.5 miles (5.5km) from Hyde Street Pier to Fort Point and beyond, across the Golden Gate Bridge. Among other sights in this impressive area are The Presidio, Baker Beach, Cliff House, Ocean Beach and Fort Funston, most of which are accessible by San Francisco's MUNI system.

✚ 135 D7

Golden Gate Bridge ☎ MUNI 28; 415/554-6999 (hotline)

✋ Free northbound; southbound toll inexpensive

❓ Alcatraz tour info 415/981-7625

Recreation Area

✉ GGNRA, Building 201, Fort Mason, San Francisco

☎ 415/561-4700 (information line) 🕐 Mon–Fri 9:30–4:30

✋ Moderate 🍽 Cafés, stands ($)

5 Hearst Castle

www.hearstcastle.com

William Randolph Hearst's tribute to excess and grandiosity crowns a hillside above the village of San Simeon.

The history of this fabulous castle dates back to 1865, when George Hearst purchased 40,000 acres

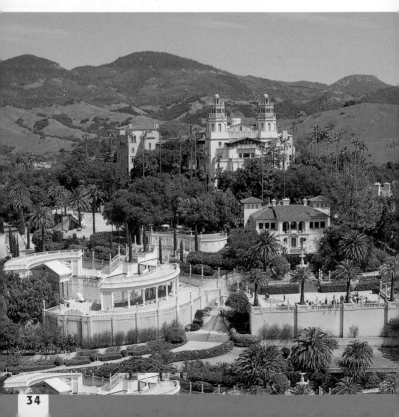

arst Castle©/CA State Parks

(16,194ha) of Mexican land
adjacent to San Simeon
Bay. His son, newspaper
magnate William Randolph
Hearst, began the castle
when he took possession of
the land in 1919, which now
covers 250,000 acres

(101,215ha). Steamers
and chain-driven trucks
were used to transport
materials to the remote
spot, but the palatial residence was not completed until 1947.

Casa Grande, as the mammoth mansion is called, boasts more than 100
rooms filled with priceless objects of art and antiques. It was donated to
the California Park Service in 1957.

Among the mansion's exquisite attributes are Gothic fireplaces,
Flemish tapestries, Renaissance paintings and ceilings ranging in style
from 16th-century Spanish to 18th-century Italian. In its prime, the doge's
suite was reserved for the most important guests: presidents, visiting
heads of state such as Winston Churchill, and Hollywood luminaries.
Marble colonnades and statuary flanking the indoor and outdoor pools
replicate figures of antiquity.

There are also five greenhouses with over 700,000 annuals providing
year-round color, tennis courts and a movie theater (in which Walt Disney
hosted the first screening of *Snow White* in 1938). There are also two
libraries, riding stables and the world's largest private zoo.

✚ 137 B7 ✉ 750 Hearst Castle Road, San Simeon ☎ 805/927-2020 or 800/444-4445
🕐 Daily 8:20–3:20 (Dec start times may vary). Five different tours offered daily
✋ Moderate ❓ 214 miles (345km) southeast of San Francisco; 242 miles (390km)
northwest of Los Angeles; parking just off Hwy 1 with shuttles buses to the castle.
Four tours, priced separately. Tour 1 is recommended for first-time visitors.
Reservations suggested

6 Hollywood

A one-time cow town, Hollywood is now the movie-making capital of the world and trend-setting center of glamour, glitter and excess.

Hollywood Boulevard is a relatively short street, but is one of the best known of all Los Angeles thoroughfares. Its wealth of art deco architecture has elevated it to the status of national historic district. From the 1920s to the 1950s, Hollywood boasted some of the country's largest movie palaces and exclusive department stores. As the movie industry expanded outward, Hollywood lost its luster, but the faded star is now staging a comeback.

The Hollywood Roosevelt Hotel, site of the first Academy Awards, has been renovated and displays historical film memorabilia throughout. An ambitious three-block redevelopment project around Sid Grauman's

1927 Chinese Theatre (now Mann's Chinese Theatre; ➤ 100–101) offers shops, restaurants, movie theaters and the Hollywood Studio Museum.

Hollywood abounds with guided bus tours of every sort. Walking tours of its bronze-starred Walk of Fame are extremely popular. Begun in 1960 with only eight stars, there are now close to 3,000 celebrity handprints. The 1920s Hollywood sign can best be viewed by venturing up Beachwood Canyon on the eastern edge of Hollywood or from Griffith Observatory, high atop Mount Hollywood.

Paramount Studio provides a peek into the world of film-making. Free tickets to several popular TV shows are readily available outside Mann's Theatre or through the major network studios.

Hawkers along Sunset and Hollywood boulevards offer surprisingly accurate maps to celebrity homes at a low price; you can drive yourself or take a bus tour.

✚ 141 D5 ✉ Hollywood Visitors Bureau, 333 South Hope Street ☎ 213/624-7300; 323/937-3661 (LA TOURS); 323/469-8311 (Hollywood Chamber of Commerce)
🍴 Numerous restaurants, some open 24 hours ($–$$$)

7 Monterey Peninsula

"This is the California men dreamed of years ago. The face of the earth as the Creator intended it to look." Henry Miller

For more than 300 years the Monterey Peninsula has enchanted everyone who has seen it. Formed by the Monterey and Carmel bays, the peninsula juts into the Pacific Ocean 120 miles (194km) south of San Francisco. Pristine beaches, craggy rock formations and wind- and wave-warped cypresses make the area among the most popular scenic spots in the world.

Nowhere in California is the state's Latin heritage more prevalent than in Monterey, where its exquisitely restored adobe buildings give testimony to the Spanish and Mexican periods of California history.

From art galleries in Carmel (➤ 84) to the grand estates in the dense woods of the Del Monte

Forest, the scenic 17-Mile Drive through the forest between Pacific Grove and Carmel is almost incomparable in beauty.

The legacy of famed California author John Steinbeck can be traced at The National Steinbeck Center in Salinas (➤ 86; open daily). You can also visit his preserved cottage in nearby Pacific Grove.

Carmel-by-the-Sea is an enchanting seaside village. Much of its architecture is reminiscent of rural European and early California styles.

Monterey's touristy Fisherman's Wharf has a magnificent promenade of fish markets, seafood restaurants, shops and theaters. For a different perspective, a sail can be arranged aboard the restored tall ship *Californian*.

Established at the turn of the 20th century by a group of writers and artists, Carmel was originally a planned resort. As its popularity soared, it took on the reputation of something completely different: an exclusive bohemian retreat. Resisting efforts for modernization, Carmel has preserved its idyllic setting. At Point Lobos State Reserve, 2 miles (3.5km) south of Carmel, harbor seals, gray whales and California sea lions frolic among a variety of sea birds and pelicans, a sight seen nowhere else in the world.

✚ 137 C6 ✉ 122 miles (197km) southeast of San Francisco; 334 miles (539km) northwest of LA
☎ 831/649-1770 (Visitors Bureau); 831/649-7118 (State Historical Park); 831/624-2522 (Carmel Business Association); 831/659-0333 (Steinbeck Country Tours)
🍴 Various ($–$$$) 🚌 Monterey–Salinas Transit

8 Napa Valley

Only 30 miles (48km) long and 3 miles (5km) across at its widest, this little valley boasts some 220 wineries.

Leader of the American wine industry, the Napa Valley boasts such well-known names as Robert Mondavi, Domaine Chandon, Beringer and Sterling. Although the greatest concentration of wineries is along State Route 29, north from Napa to Calistoga, knowledgeable travelers use the Silverado Trail, a scenic, vineyard-lined parallel road along the eastern edge of the valley.

The city of Napa is the largest, although each of the valley towns has its charms. In Calistoga there are spas and geysers, one of which shoots 60ft (18m) into the air every 40 minutes. St. Helena claims many of the region's best dining and lodging choices, as well as a wine library and the Silverado Museum. An ancient volcanic eruption from Washington's Mount St. Helens around 3 million years ago caused the giant redwoods of California to become instantly petrified. You'll find the Petrified Forest between Calistoga and Santa Rosa.

Outside of these towns lie more wineries, markets, inns, quiet picnic areas and historic parklands. Most visitors tour the vineyards, which offer a look at the wine-making process and feature wine-tastings, but there are also five different walking tours of the incredible architectural highlights of the valley (maps available at the information center). If possible, avoid the crowded summer weekends. Most vintners now charge a small fee for the tastings and a few require reservations.

✚ 135 C6 ✉ Visitor Information Center, 1310 Napa Town Center, Napa ☎ 707/226-7459 (Visitor Information Center), 707/253-2111; www.napavalley.com/visitorsinfo; 800/427-4124 (Napa Valley Wine Train) 🕙 Hours vary; some tours require reservations 🎟 Free–inexpensive 🍴 Restaurants in the towns ($$–$$$)

9 Redwood National Park

www.nps.gov/redw/

A vast forest of giant redwoods grows naturally nowhere else in the country except in this coastal region.

Before California's famous gold rush, and the resulting surge of new population, the world's tallest trees blanketed an area 30 miles (48km) wide and 450 miles (726km) long. The majority of today's redwood "stands" are along US 101, from Leggett north to Crescent City. It is about a five-hour drive from San Francisco to the southern edge of the Redwood Forest, via the scenic coastal highway.

A small segment of old growth redwoods and outstanding coastal scenery have been protected in the 106,000-acre (42,915ha) Redwood National Park. Eight miles (13km) of shoreline roads and more than 150 miles (242km) of trails afford close-up encounters with these trees and the abundant plant and animal life they nurture.

The three main state parks within the Park's boundaries are Prairie Creek, Del Norte Coast and Jedediah Smith. Campers favor Prairie Creek

because of its herds of native Roosevelt elk and expansive beach (Gold Bluffs Beach). Lady Bird Johnson Cove is especially beautiful. Don't miss the Libby Tree, the tallest known tree, which towers to over 368ft (112m).

A drive through Del Norte Coast park allows you to enjoy spectacular ocean views and the inland forest simultaneously. The giant redwoods grow closest to the shoreline at the Damnation Creek Trail. In the spring, this area is the best place to view the abundant growth of rhododendrons and azaleas.

At the north end of the park, the Jedediah Smith terrain gives you an elevated perspective.

✚ 134 E2 ✉ National Park Headquarters, 1111 Second Street, Crescent City ☎ 707/464-6101 (Redwood National Park Information Center) ✋ Moderate 🍴 Restaurants ($); picnic facilities

10 Yosemite National Park

www.nps.gov/yose/

By any standards, Yosemite is the most spectacular national park in the country. To call it awe-inspiring would be an understatement.

Nearly 70 percent of the annual visitors to Yosemite National Park arrive in the summer and stay within the compact but awesome Yosemite Valley. The main section of the park, just 7sq miles (18sq km) in area, boasts monumental granite walls and high-diving waterfalls, but there remains almost 1,200sq miles (3,076sq km) of splendor to explore. Beyond are such natural wonders as giant sequoias, alpine meadows, lakes and trout-filled streams, Glacier Point and majestic 13,000ft (3,963m) Sierra Nevada peaks. There are giant sequoias in the Mariposa Grove, near the park's south entrance, about 30 miles (48km) from Yosemite Valley. In this great forest, over 200 trees measure more than 10ft (3m) in diameter.

Some of the park's finest scenery is in the wild back country along the Tioga Road. There are rustic lodges and campgrounds (permit camping). In the main valley, 3,500ft (1,067m) El Capitan attracts climbers from around the world.

Off-season visits are also spectacular. In fall, leaves turn from green to crimson and gold

and nights are cool and pleasant. Spring offers magnificent waterfalls that create rainbows across the valley floor. For the ambitious, there's the 200-mile (322km) John Muir Trail that follows the naturalist's path through the wilderness. For many, the winter provides solitude and restores the raw grandeur of the park. The ski season at Badger Pass lasts from the end of November until mid-April.

✚ 138 E3 ✉ Yosemite Valley Visitors Center ☎ 209/ 372-0200 🕔 Apr–May daily 9–6; Jul–Aug daily 8–8; Sep–Oct daily 8–6; Nov–Mar daily 9–5 👏 Moderate 🍴 Restaurants ($)

Exploring

San Francisco	49–63
Northern California	64–81
Central Coast	82–89
Los Angeles	90–103
Southern California	104–129

Describing California and its people is like trying to describe a beautiful painting: most people will have a different perspective and feeling. The word that most readily comes to mind is extreme. Nowhere on earth can one find such *extreme* variances of scenic splendor or inhabitants. Within an 80-mile (129km) span are the highest and lowest elevations in the United States, each with its own unique beauty.

From the very first person to set foot in the state to its most recent émigré, the trait that has most greatly characterized the state's populace is a deep commitment to adventure. California seems to define the concept of diversity with both its geography and its inhabitants. With nearly every culture represented throughout the state, there are enough dining and entertainment selections to suit everyone's desire.

San Francisco

San Francisco

**The Gold Rush of the mid-19th
century brought a diverse ethnicity to
San Francisco. Areas like Chinatown and North Beach
have preserved their different native cultures.**

Out in the bay to the north is the infamous Alcatraz Island, the site
of the notorious former prison. It is easily seen from Coit Tower, on
top of Telegraph Hill. Russian Hill provides a panoramic look at the
Golden Gate Bridge and the bay. To the north and east of the city
lie the Napa Valley and Marin County, where wine-tasting is the
hobby of choice.

Few places in the world can boast, as San Francisco can, the
sophistication of a major metropolitan area while also being offset
by 42 hills and, at the same time, surrounded by the serenity of
lush vineyards.

ALCATRAZ

Of the 14 islands punctuating the massive San Francisco Bay, 12-acre (5ha) Alcatraz is the most famous. Rising 135ft (41m) out of the bay, it is easy to see why it is nicknamed "The Rock." Although wild flowers are abundant on the island and the views of the bay and the Golden Gate bridge are breathtaking, most visitors visit the island to tour the massive fortress that covers most of the grounds. Built in 1858 as a military post, it soon became a military prison and finally a federal penitentiary.

Because of the severe tides and undertow of the surrounding chilly waters, escape from the prison was reputed to be impossible. Three inmates dug their way out of their prison cells and disappeared in 1962. No one knows if they made it to the mainland, but their bodies were never found. The prison closed soon after the attempt, and a group of Native Americans claimed the island as their birthright. Some of the buildings were burned before the National Park Service took control and reopened Alcatraz as a tourist attraction in 1973.

Three prominent movies have been filmed on the island: *Escape from Alcatraz*, *The Birdman of Alcatraz* and *The Rock*. Tours include a close-up look at the cells with audio-cassette narration by former prisoners and guards and exterior trail walks led by park rangers. Dress warmly and wear comfortable shoes.

www.alcatrazcruises.com

✚ 142 A2 (off map) ☎ 415/981-7625 ⏰ Hours vary, advance reservations recommended 💰 Moderate 🚢 Ferry from Pier 41, Fisherman's Wharf

ASIAN ART MUSEUM

More than 40 Asian countries are represented in this museum, the largest of its kind outside the Asian continent. Exclusive to this museum are works of Asian art spanning 4,000 years of Chinese history. It also houses outstanding exhibits from India, Japan and Korea and more than 300 works from the estates of Chinese emperors.

www.asianart.org

✚ 142 F2 ✉ 200 Larkin Street, Civic Center ☎ 415/581-3500 ⏰ Tue–Sun 10–5, Thu 10–9 💰 Moderate, free 1st Tue of month

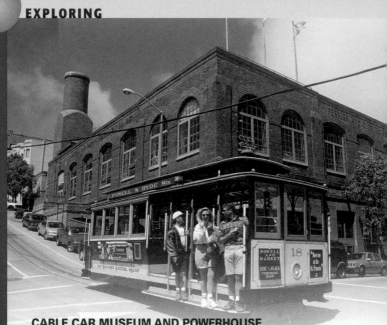

CABLE CAR MUSEUM AND POWERHOUSE VIEWING GALLERY

If you're fascinated by San Francisco's cable-cars, visit this working nerve center and museum. On exhibit are the first cable-cars, which went unchanged for almost 100 years. Their design was modernized in 1982. Also housed in the three-level, red-brick 1907 barn are photographs, artifacts and a model collection. From the viewing gallery you can watch craftsmen working on the cars.

✚ 142 D3 ✉ 1201 Mason Street ☎ 415/474-1887 ⏰ Daily 10–5 (extended hours in spring and summer) ✋ Free

CALIFORNIA ACADEMY OF SCIENCES

Dating back to the mid-19th century, this is considered one of the finest natural history museums in the world. It houses several galleries, an exhibit that allows visitors to "experience" an earthquake, and a hands-on Discovery Room for children. The Steinhart Aquarium has almost 14,000 salt-water species which include octopuses, sea-horses, dolphins and sharks. The ANTS exhibit showcases the nest-building and food-collecting behavior of six live ant colonies. The Howard Street location also has a nurturing place called the Nature Nest for young visitors. Note: The Academy has moved to temporary premises in Howard Street and is expected to return to Golden Gate Park in 2008.

✚ 142 F4 ✉ 875 Howard Street, between 4th and 5th streets ☎ 415/750-7145 ⏰ Daily 10–5 (extended hours in summer) ✋ Moderate; senior/children rates. Free 1st Wed of month

CALIFORNIA PALACE OF THE LEGION OF HONOR

Refurbished in 1995, this classical palace was inspired by the Hotel de Salm in Paris, the site where Napoleon established the Legion D'Honneur. The Palace houses an extraordinary collection of 75,000 prints and drawings from the Achenbach Foundation, and expansive European art dating from 2500BC through to the 20th century. Rodin's *The Thinker* is on display in the courtyard.

✚ 142 D1 (off map) ✉ 34th Avenue and Clement Street, Lincoln Park ☎ 415/750-3600 ⏰ Tue–Sun 9:30–5 ✋ Moderate; senior/children rates; free every Tue

CARTOON ART MUSEUM

This museum houses permanent and rotating exhibits of original
two- and three-dimensional art and cartoon artifacts. You can see
the original artwork and drawings used in the production of
cartoons. Some exhibits go back to the 18th century. Video
presentations are also part of the program.
www.cartoonart.org
✚ 142 E4 ✉ 655 Mission Street ☎ 415/227-8666 ⏰ Tue–Sun 11–5.
Closed public hols ♿ Moderate; senior/children rates

CHINESE HISTORICAL SOCIETY OF AMERICA

The largest collection of Chinese-American artifacts in the US is
housed here, including Chinese dragon heads, an 1880 Buddhist
altar and a concise history of the Chinese experience in America,
from 1840 to the present day.
✚ 142 D3 ✉ 965 Clay Street ☎ 415/391-1188 ⏰ Tue–Fri noon–5, Sat–Sun
noon–4 ♿ Inexpensive

CIVIC CENTER PLAZA

Dominated by the French Renaissance-inspired City Hall, the
complex dates back to the 1906 earthquake. On the west end is
the War Memorial and Performing Arts Center. The Center is home
to the Louise M. Davies Symphony Hall, the War Memorial Opera
House and the War Memorial Veterans Building. The latter contains
the San Francisco Museum of Modern Art and the Herbst Theatre,
where the United Nations charter was signed in 1945. Other
classically styled buildings in the plaza complex are the Civic
Auditorium, the San Francisco Public Library and the State Building.
✚ 142 F2 ✉ Van Ness Avenue/Polk Street at Grove and McAllister streets
☎ 415/557-4266 (information) ♿ Free

DE YOUNG MUSEUM

An extensive collection of American artwork is contained in this
22-gallery complex set in Golden Gate Park. The museum's

exhibits include paintings, sculpture, decorative arts, textiles and furniture. Some of the artwork dates to the mid-17th century. Also on display are classical and tribal works.

✚ 142 F1 (off map) ✉ 2501 Irving Street (at 26th Avenue) ☎ 415/750-3600
🕙 Tue–Sat 10–4:45 ✋ Free

FISHERMAN'S WHARF

Bustling Fisherman's Wharf is the center of San Francisco's thriving tourist trade. It has many shops, street stands, food emporia and the like. Originally, it was an active base for San Francisco Bay's once busy fishing industry, until the late 1940s. A small fleet still operates.

✚ 142 A2 ✉ North of North Beach 🍴 Cafés, stands ($)

a walk around Chinatown

This walk takes you through the largest Chinese community outside Asia.

Enter through the Chinatown Gate, at Bush Street and Grant Avenue.

Note the dragon-entwined lampposts and pagoda roofs as you are greeted by a cacophony of Chinese street merchants and the aromas of simmering noodles.

Walk north on Grant to the Dragon House Antiques (No 455).

Continue up Grant to St. Mary's Park where there's a 12ft (3.5m) sculpture of Sun Yat-sen.

Continue north to Clay, turn right to Kearny, then left to Portsmouth Square. Across Kearny is the Holiday Inn.

Pop inside to the Chinese Cultural Center.

Go north on Kearny, to Pacific, then left to the New Asia restaurant (No 772), a good choice for lunch. Continue west on Pacific to Grant, then go left two blocks to Washington. Turn right.

Admire the three-tiered pagoda-style Bank of Canton, then continue west to the Tien Hou Temple (in Waverly Place on Washington). Around the corner is The Great China Herb Co. (No 857), where sellers fill herbal prescriptions.

Continue west on Washington to Stockton, then turn left.

The Chinese Six Companies building (No 843) is an architectural wonder, with its curved roof tiles and elaborate cornices.

Walk south on Stockton to the Stockton Street Tunnel. A 15-minute walk through the tunnel brings you to downtown Union Square.

Distance 5 miles (8km)
Time 2–4 hours
Start point Chinatown Gate ✚ 142 D4
End point Union Square ✚ 142 E3
Lunch New Asia ($$) ✉ 772 Pacific Avenue ☎ 415/391-6666

GOLDEN GATE BRIDGE AND NATIONAL RECREATION AREA

Best places to see, pages 32–33.

GRACE CATHEDRAL

Taking over a half-century to build, this marvelous structure is a near-perfect replica of a Florentine cathedral. The singing of the Vespers each Thursday at 5:15pm is a truly spiritual experience.

➕ 142 D2 ✉ 1100 California Street
☎ 415/749-6300 🖐 Free, but donations accepted

HYDE STREET PIER AND HISTORICAL SHIPS

In the Fisherman's Wharf area, this pier is the permanent home of several historical ships. Here you will find the ferry boat *Eureka* (1890), once the world's largest ferry boat, and the *Balclutha*, a square-rigged sailing ship from Scotland (1886), famed for rounding Cape Horn several times. Before leaving the area, drop into the National Maritime Museum at nearby Aquatic Park.

➕ 142 A1 ☎ 415/561-7100 🕐 Daily 10–5
💰 Inexpensive. National Park Golden Eagle Pass free

LOMBARD STREET

Located in the Russian Hill district, this is San Francisco's famous "crookedest" street. Traffic zigzags down it at 5mph (8kph), moving around colorful gardens which were established in the 1920s.

➕ 142 B1–B4 ✉ Between Hyde and Leavenworth streets

MISSION SAN FRANCISCO DE ASIS

Founded in 1776 and moved to its present site in 1782, the
mission is thought to be the oldest standing structure in the city.
Adjoining is the Mission Dolores Basilica, the least changed of
all California's existing missions. The architecture of Mission
Dolores is a combination of Moorish, Mission and Corinthian
styles, and the garden cemetery is filled with the burial sites of
San Francisco pioneers.

➕ 142 F2 (off map) ✉ 16th and Dolores streets ☎ 415/621-8203 🕐 Daily
9–4:30 (until 4 in fall and winter) ♿ Inexpensive

NORTH BEACH

This thriving, trendy neighborhood, on the northeastern tip of San
Francisco, is bound by Chinatown, the Financial District and
Russian Hill. North Beach has a distinctly Italian atmosphere, and is
central to most attractions, shops and restaurants in the area. Its
heyday in the 1950s saw Jack Kerouac and other Beat Generation

poets frequenting the cafés and bookstores, which remain important cultural meeting places. At the center of the neighborhood is **Coit Tower**, an impressive 210ft (64m) landmark, built in 1934, reached on foot via the Filbert Steps by Darnell Place.

✚ 142 B3

Coit Tower

☎ 415/362 0808 ⊙ Daily 10–6:30 ✋ Inexpensive (to go to top of tower)

PALACE OF FINE ARTS

This Bernard Maybeck Greco-Romanesque rotunda is one of the most photographed buildings in San Francisco. Levelled by the great earthquake of 1906, it was completely rebuilt in 1915 and today presents continuing cultural events. Inside the complex is the Exploratorium, a wonderful hands-on science museum, ideal for families, with toys disguised as science education.

✚ 142 B1 (off map) ✉ 3601 Lyon Street ☎ 415/561-0360 ⊙ Tue–Sun 10–5; open on Mon hols ✋ Moderate, free 1st Wed of month

ST MARY'S CATHEDRAL OF THE ASSUMPTION

The radical architecture by Pietro Belluschi and Pier Luigi Nervi caused great debate during construction. Rising on concrete pylons to a height of 190ft (58m), the exterior resembles a washing machine agitator. Inside, however, the soaring cruciform is nothing short of breathtaking. The majestic pipe organ, itself, is worth seeing.

✚ 142 E1 ✉ 1111 Gough Street ☎ 415/567-2020 ⊙ Mon–Fri 7–5, Sun 7–6:30 ✋ Free, but donations accepted

SAN FRANCISCO MUSEUM OF MODERN ART

Devoted solely to modern art and occupying a quarter million square feet, this is the main structure in the Yerba Buena Arts Center (SoMo district). Exhibits include a world-renowned collection of photography, and 20th-century works from such artists as Dali, O'Keeffe and Jasper Johns. A current feature exhibit is "From Matisse to Diebenkorn: Works from the Permanent Collection."

✚ 142 E4 ✉ 151 Third Street ☎ 415/357-4000
🕐 Mon, Tue, Fri–Sun 11–5:45; Thu 11–8:45
✋ Moderate, senior/student rates, free 1st Tue of month

TRANSAMERICA PYRAMID

Depending on who you ask, this structure is either a landmark or an eyesore. Completed in 1972, the pyramid skyscraper juts 853ft (260m) skyward, making it the tallest building in San Francisco.

✚ 142 D4 ✉ 600 Montgomery Street
🕐 Mon–Fri 8–4

UNION STREET

Union Street runs east–west from Montgomery Street in North Beach to the Presidio. It is one of the city's most fashionable areas in which to live and shop, with its many beautifully restored Victorian mansions that have been converted into boutiques, art galleries and cafés. Scattered among the bustling retail spots are several landmarks. The **Octagon House** (just off Union Street) is a pale-blue, eight-sided structure that features antique furniture from the 18th and 19th centuries. Also of interest is an exhibit containing the signatures of 54 of the 56 original signatories of the Declaration of Independence.

➕ 142 C2–B4

Octagon House

✉ 2645 Gough Street ☎ 415/441-7512 🕐 2nd and 4th Thu and 2nd Sun of each month (except Jan), noon–3. Closed public hols ✋ Contributions

WELLS FARGO HISTORY MUSEUM

The Wells Fargo History Museum connects the Wells Fargo Bank's history to the Gold Rush, historic San Francisco and stage coach travel in early California. Henry Wells and William Fargo started Wells Fargo & Co in 1852, providing express and banking services to the '49ers. Visitors can see an original stage coach and rare gold coins and nuggets, work a telegraph, and learn about the people who built the West.

➕ 142 D4 ✉ 420 Montgomery Street ☎ 415/396-2619 🕐 Mon–Fri 9–5. Closed public hols ✋ Free

Northern California

Some of California's most beautiful areas can be found in the north of the state. The Monterey Peninsula and Big Sur coastlines are possibly the most scenic in the country, and San Francisco, with its rich cultural diversity, one of the most fascinating.

Yosemite National Park, Lake Tahoe and the Wine Country all share qualities of untouched beauty. The northern coastline is the least

populated and is a perfect contrast to the busy beach areas to the south. Nowhere can you find natural beauty like that of the Redwood National Forest, which is said to contain the world's tallest tree.

Silicon Valley, south of San Francisco, is the center of the country's computer and electronics industries, and Sacramento is the state capital and center of government.

EUREKA

Eureka is the largest town on California's northernmost coast. Set along Humboldt Bay, it is home to an impressive fishing fleet. Its name, from the Greek word for "I have found it," refers to the cries from many gold miners (called '49ers) in the 19th century. The Old Town section is worth a visit for its elegantly refurbished Victorian homes.

The old 1912 building, once the town's main bank, now houses the **Clarke Memorial Museum.** It houses an excellent collection of California Native American historic artifacts.

Blue Ox Millworks is a working mill that includes a blacksmith shop and a re-creation of a logging camp. **Sequoia Park,** a beautiful grove of virgin redwoods in 52 acres (21ha), has a formal flower garden, duck pond, and deer and elk paddocks.

✚ 134 E3

Clarke Memorial Museum

✉ 240 E Street ☎ 707/443-947 🕐 Tue–Sat 11–4 ✋ Free

Blue Ox Millworks

✉ Foot of X Street ☎ 707/444-3437 🕐 Mon–Fri 9–5, Sat by appointment ✋ Inexpensive

Sequoia Park

✉ 3414 W Street ☎ 707/442-6552 🕐 Daily 10–5 ✋ Inexpensive 🍴 Picnic facilities

GOLD COUNTRY TOWNS

Also known as the Mother Lode Country, this scenic area extends 300 miles (484km) along Highway 49, through the western Sierra

Nevada foothills. Once the thriving Old West, it is now mostly ghost towns, several of which are open to tourists.

Angel's Camp Museum, in Angel's Camp (➤ 68), was the center for gravel and quartz mining in 1849. You can see photographs, relics and 3 acres (1.21ha) of old mining equipment from the old days.

Marshall Gold Discovery State Historic Park is where James Marshall discovered gold. The drive-through park features a replica of Sutter's Mill and memorial statue and grave site of James Marshall.

The Empire Mine State Historic Park (➤ 69), 2 miles (3.5km) east of Grass Valley, is the Gold Country's best preserved quartz mining operation. During the boom years, the 367 miles (592km) of mine shafts produced six million ounces of gold.

Mercer Caverns, 1 mile (1.6km) north of Murphys, via Main Street, were discovered in 1885 by Walter Mercer, a gold prospector. The 45-minute tour gives the opportunity to view the enormous stalagmites and stalactites close up.

✚ 135 A7

Angel's Camp Museum

✉ 753 South Main Street ☎ 209/736-2963 🕐 Mar–end Dec daily 10–3; Jan–end Feb Sat, Sun 10–3 👋 Inexpensive

Marshall Gold Discovery State Historic Park

✉ South fork of the American River and Highway 49, Coloma ☎ 530/622-3470 🕐 Museum daily 10–3; park 8–sunset 👋 Inexpensive

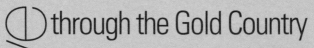 # through the Gold Country

This drive will take you through Gold Country along historic Highway 49.

Begin in Mariposa, where SR 49 meets SR 140.

Here you can visit the California State Mining and Mineral Museum and the Mariposa County Museum.

Proceed north on SR 49 to Chinese Camp and the State Historic Park. A few miles north is Jamestown.

Jamestown served as a backdrop for the film *High Noon* and the television series *Little House on the Prairie*.

Follow 49 north, stopping in Tuttletown.

You can view a replica of Mark Twain's cabin on Jackass Hill (Tuttletown was originally called Jackass Gulch).

Continue to Columbia.

Here you can try your hand at panning for gold, or ride an authentic stagecoach.

Continue north on 49 to Angel's Camp.

This is where Mark Twain first heard the "jumping frog" story from bartender Ben Coon. If you are here in May, don't miss the frog jumping contest. The foundation of Angel's Mine is across from the Catholic Church.

Continue north to Jackson and Placerville.

Jackson was once home of the Mohawk Indians, and

Placerville was formerly known as "Hangtown." Gold Bug Mine is worth a visit.

Farther north are Coloma, Auburn and Grass Valley.

The latter is home to Empire Mine State Historic Park (➤ 67) and North Star Mine Museum, both offering tours.

The drive ends in Nevada City.

Distance Approximately 100 miles (162km)
Time 8 hours
Start point Mariposa ✚ 13/ A5 (off map)
End point Nevada City ✚ 135 B5
Lunch National Hotel Restaurant ($) ✉ 18183 Main Street, Jamestown ☎ 209/984-3446

LAKE TAHOE

Lying on the California–Nevada stateline, Lake Tahoe is one of the most popular resort communities in the state. Although this beautiful lake is 6,228ft (1,899m) above sea level, it never freezes because of its depth. You will find top-notch ski facilities here, and in summer, water sports include lake cruises, water skiing and sailing.

For a spectacular aerial view of the entire area, including the site of the 1960 Winter Olympic Games, ride the gondola to the top of the Squaw Valley Ski Area.

✚ 135 A5

Squaw Valley Cable Car

✉ 1960 Squaw Valley Road, Olympic Valley ☎ 530/583-6985 🕐 Call to check. Closed mid-Oct to Dec 1
✋ Moderate

LASSEN VOLCANIC NATIONAL PARK

Lassen Park stretches over 100,000 acres (40,486ha) in the northeastern corner of California, where the Cascade and Sierra Nevada mountains meet. Highlights are Lassen Peak, Cinder Cone, Prospect Peak and Mount Harkness, the latter two volcanoes topped by cinder cones.

Lassen's numerous volcanic eruptions subsided in 1921 and have been replaced by hot springs and lakes, lava flows and mudpots, all linked together by hiking trails that lead to the summit and back.

➕ 134 B3 ✉ 9 miles (15km) east of Mineral, via SR 36 ☎ 530/595-4444 🕓 Year-round

MAMMOTH LAKES RECREATION AREA

This giant popular resort area in the Inyo National Forest has world-class skiing, and in summertime it's a mountain biking mecca. There is also good camping, fishing and horseback riding here. Hike to the 101ft (31m) Rainbow Falls, or visit the Devil's Postpile National Monument, 60ft (18m) multisided columns that are by-products of former volcanic activity.

➕ 138 E3 🍽 Restaurants ($$) ℹ Chamber of Commerce, PO Box 48, Mammoth Lakes, 93546 ☎ 760/934-2712 🕓 Mon–Fri 9–5

MENDOCINO

Mendocino, off scenic US 1, is perhaps the most charming small town in California. It is noted for its Cape Cod and Victorian-style architecture and its active, artistic community. The entire town is on the National Register of Historic Places. Film buffs will recognize it from such films as *The Summer of '42*, *East of Eden* and television's *Murder She Wrote*. The **Art Center** is the epicenter of the many art museums in the community, and includes galleries, live theater and arts and craft fairs.

www.mendocinocoast.com

✚ 135 E5

Mendocino Art Center

✉ 45200 Little Lake Street ☎ 707/937-5818 or 800/653-3328 ◷ Call for times ✋ Moderate

ℹ Mendocino Chamber of Commerce ✉ 332 North Main Street
☎ 707/961-6300 ◷ Daily 10–4

MODESTO

This quintessential California town was made famous by George Lucas's film *American Graffiti*. Near the center of the state, it is the home of the Blue Diamond Almonds company.

The **McHenry Museum** re-creates a 19th-century school, blacksmith shop, kitchen, country store and others with changing exhibits. The **McHenry Mansion,** a block away, exhibits antique furnishings and artwork in a restored Victorian home.

✚ 135 B8

McHenry Museum & Mansion

✉ 1402 "I" Street ☎ 209/577-5366 (museum); 209/577-5341 (mansion)
◷ Tue–Sun noon–4. Closed major holidays ✋ Free, donations requested
❓ Tours of mansion offered Sun–Thu 1–4, Fri noon–3

MOUNT SHASTA

Spiritual-minded Californians flock to this mountain because it is said to be a "vortex of spiritual energy." For the more earthbound there is hiking, climbing, and skiing in winter. Several surrounding lakes offer waterside camping, fishing and watersports, including skating in winter. The **Mount Shasta State Fish Hatchery,** in the center of the area, produces 5 to 10 million trout annually to stock Northern California lakes.

✚ 134 C2

Mount Shasta State Fish Hatchery

☎ 530/926-2215 🕓 Daily 7am–dusk ✋ Free

ℹ Chamber of Commerce Visitors Bureau ✉ 300 Pine Street ☎ 800/926-4865; www.mtshastachamber.com 🕓 Daily 9:30–5:30

NAPA VALLEY

Best places to see, pages 40–41.

NATURAL BRIDGES STATE BEACH

Set in 65 acres (26ha), this beach, just before Santa Cruz, is a
wonderful place to observe the migration of the colorful Monarch
butterfly between mid-October and February. There are also tide
pools to explore, as well as ecological and wildlife exhibits in the
visitor center.

➕ 137 C5 ✉ West Cliff Drive ☎ 831/423-4609 ⏱ Beach daily 8–dusk;
visitor center 10–4 ✋ Inexpensive

OAKLAND

Linked to San Francisco by the Bay Bridge, Oakland has long
suffered from its close proximity to the city across the bay. In

reality, it is a culturally rich and diversified town and has counted among its famous citizens Jack London and Gertrude Stein. **Oakland Museum** has an extensive collection of historical and contemporary art housed in the Gallery of California Art. The museum is one of the best in the state for studying the diverse cultural make-up and subsequent historical progress.

Lake Merritt, created in the late 19th century by the damming of a section of the Oakland estuary, was one of the first natural wildlife preserves established in the US.

🞤 135 C7

Oakland Museum

✉ 10th and Oak Street ☎ 510/238-2200 🕓 Wed–Sat 10- 5, Sun noon–5
✋ Inexpensive

PETALUMA

Petaluma is another one of the quintessential small California towns. Situated on the Petaluma River, it has retained most of its 19th-century architecture and, like Modesto (➤ 72), has become a favorite for filming television series and movies. *American Graffiti* and *Peggy Sue Got Married* were both filmed here.

Philanthropist Andrew Carnegie endowed $12,500 toward the construction of the **Historical Museum/Library** in 1903. It houses permanent and rotating exhibits of early 19th-century Petaluma.

🞤 135 D7

Petaluma Historical Museum/Library

✉ 20 4th Street ☎ 707/778-4398 🕓 Wed–Sat 10–4, Sun noon–3
✋ Inexpensive

REDWOOD NATIONAL PARK

Best places to see, pages 42–43.

SACRAMENTO

Sacramento was once a major supply center for the California '49ers (gold seekers); now it is the state capital. The names of 5,822 Californians killed in the Vietnam War are engraved on the 22 black granite panels of the California Vietnam Veterans Memorial, near the State Capitol Park.

The exquisite **Governor's Mansion** dates from the 1800s and is now a museum of Victoriana. Items from former governors include a 1902 Steinway piano and Persian carpets.

The Historic Paddlewheeler *Spirit of Sacramento* is available for a Sacramento River cruise or special events. The boat's murder-mystery trips are especially popular.

A million-dollar gold collection, ethnic photos and a historic print shop are just some of the items in the five separate areas of the **Discovery Museum. The California State Railroad Museum** has three entire floors devoted to railroad-related exhibits, including train cars and 21 locomotives.

Noted for its 210ft (64m) dome, the **State Capitol** building is nearly 150 years old, and is open daily for tours. Adobe-style **Sutter's Fort** was the first European outpost in California and contains some interesting period relics.

Sacramento Zoo has a large reptile display and 350 species of wild animals.

The Towe Ford Museum and Six Flags Waterworld are also worth visiting.

✚ 135 B6

Governor's Mansion State Historic Park

✉ 16th and "H" streets ☎ 916/323-3047 🕐 Daily 10–4 ✋ Inexpensive

Spirit of Sacramento

✉ Old Sacramento's "L" Street Landing ☎ 916/552-2933 🕐 Cruises: lunch, brunch, happy hour, dinner, sunset and sightseeing ✋ Moderate 🍴 Dinner, brunch and happy hour cruises available

Discovery Museum

✉ 101 "I" Street ☎ 916/264-7057 🕐 Summer daily 10–5; winter Tue–Sun 10–5 ✋ Inexpensive

California State Railroad Museum

✉ Second and "I" streets ☎ 916/445-6645; www.californiastaterailroadmuseum.org 🕐 Daily 10–5 ✋ Moderate

State Capitol

✉ Between 10th, 15th, "L" and "N" streets ☎ 916/324-0333 🕐 Tours daily 9–4 ✋ Free

Sutter's Fort

✉ 27th and "L" streets ☎ 916/445-4422 🕐 Daily 10–5 ✋ Inexpensive

Sacramento Zoo

✉ 3930 Westland Park Drive ☎ 916/264-5885; www.saczoo.com 🕐 Daily 9–4 (10–4 Nov–Jan) ✋ Moderate

SAN JOSE

San Jose is the 11th largest city in the US. It was founded in the last quarter of the 18th century as El Pueblo de San Jose, and is the oldest Spanish civilian settlement. From 1849 to 1851 it served as the state's capital.

Kelley Park, apart from being a popular city park with such attractions as Happy Hollow family play area and zoo, also contains the Japanese Friendship Garden and Teahouse and the San Jose Historical Museum.

Babylonian, Sumerian and Assyrian artifacts, mummies, sculptures and more can be found at the **Rosicrucian Egyptian**

Museum and Planetarium. There is also a contemporary art gallery.

The **Winchester Mystery House,** a Victorian mansion and home of eccentric firearms heiress Sarah Winchester, was designed to confuse evil spirits. The layout of the house is so complex, with blind closets, secret passageways, 13 bathrooms and 40 staircases, that even Sarah herself needed a map to find her way around. Over looking the Santa Clara Valley from the 4,209ft (1,283m) summit of Mount Hamilton is the **Lick Observatory.**

✛ 135 C8

Kelley Park

✉ Senter and Story roads ⏱ Daily 8am to 30 mins before dusk 🍴 Picnic facilities ✋ Inexpensive

Rosicrucian Egyptian Museum and Planetarium

✉ 1342 Naglee Avenue ☎ 408/947-3636 ⏱ Mon–Fri 10–5, Sat–Sun 11–6 ✋ Moderate; senior/student rates

Winchester Mystery House

✉ 525 S Winchester Boulevard ☎ 408/247-2101 ⏱ Daily from 9am, closing times vary with time of year ✋ Expensive

Lick Observatory

✉ Mount Hamilton Road ☎ 408/274-5061 ⏱ Mon–Fri 12:30–5, Sat–Sun 10–5 ✋ Free 🍴 No nearby food or auto services

SAUSALITO

This is the first small town in Marin County after crossing the Golden Gate Bridge. Once a fishing town, it has unfortunately been overrun with tacky tourist shops and no longer has the great charm of years past.

✛ 135 D8 ✉ 5 miles (8km) north of San Francisco ⛴ Ferry from Ferry Building or Fisherman's Wharf

THE WINE COUNTRY

North of San Francisco lie some of the most lush valleys in all of California, the best known of which are the **Napa** (➤ 40–41) and **Sonoma Valleys**. It is here that California's vintners tend their grape vines and produce the many varied wines known and enjoyed worldwide. Whether you are driving, bicycling, taking the Wine Train or flying over the area in one of the many hot air balloons that offer spectacular views of the verdant, rolling, wine lands, you will never forget your excursion to the Wine Country.

The estates of the wineries are incredible to see. Take one of the guided tours of the processing facilities with their informative, enticing tastings. While the large wineries are the most popular, don't pass up the small, family-owned ones, of which there are many. Most have wines that rival the greats, with more convivial atmospheres.

The **Napa Valley Wine Train** provides daily excursions through the Napa Valley. The 1917 Pullman Dining Car relives the gracious era of elegant rail travel and distinguished service and makes you feel as if you're riding the Orient Express as the three-hour, 36-mile (58km) trip between Napa and St. Helena allows for a leisurely brunch, lunch or dinner. Many concerns are aired by residents that the wineries are a bit too commercial for the area, but there are rarely complaints from the visitors.

To the west, the Sonoma Valley runs for 15 miles (24km) and is a bit less populated than the Napa Valley. As a rule, the 30 or so wineries here offer more personalized tours, with free tastings and a more relaxed atmosphere. The town of Sonoma itself is a good place to start if you wish to visit the valley. The other center of activity is Santa Rosa, to the north of the region.

The Sonoma Valley is particularly rich in Spanish and Mexican history, so be sure to take note of the area's beautiful architecture.

If you're looking for souvenirs of your visit to California, the on-site gift shops have unique offerings and superb wines they will ship anywhere in the world. The wineries listed are just some of the ones you'll want to explore. *Spotlight's Wine Guide* is a complete guide to the area (☎ 415/898-7908).

✚ 135 D6

Napa Valley Visitors Bureau

✉ 1310 Napa Town Center, Napa ☎ 707/226-7459; www.napavalley.com
🕐 Hours vary; some tours require reservations

Sonoma Valley Visitors Bureau

✉ 453 1st Street, E Sonoma ☎ 707/996-1090; www.sonomavalley.com
🕐 Daily 9–5

Napa Valley Wine Train

✉ 1275 McKinstry Street, Napa ☎ 707/253-2111 or 800/427-4124
🕐 Year-round 💷 Expensive, reservations and deposit required

Beringer Vineyards

Beringer was one of the very first wineries to open its cellar doors to visitors. The staff here are especially attentive and knowledgeable in discussing the process of wine-making and its history. There are regular tours throughout the day.

✉ Just north of downtown St. Helena, 2000 Main Street ☎ 707/963-7115; www.beringer.com 🕐 Hours and tours vary, phone for information

Buena Vista Winery

As the site of the first vineyard in the valley, Buena Vista, 2 miles (3km) northeast of Sonoma, has become a historical landmark. Hungarian Count Agoston Haraszthy planted the first vines, and the wine cellars, built in 1857, are the oldest stone cellars in the state. The Tasting Room offers selection of award-winning wines and there is a gift shop, a picnic area, an artists' gallery, self-guided tours and historical presentations.

✉ 18000 Old Winery Road, Sonoma ☎ 707/938-1266; www.buenavistacarneros.com 🕓 Daily 10–5

Kenwood Vineyards

Operating on Jack London's former ranch since 1970, this Sonoma country winery produces Cabernet Sauvignon, Zinfandel, Sauvignon Blanc, Chardonnay, Gewürztraminer, Merlot and Pinot Noir on the estate which is about an hour's drive north of San Francisco. Visitors are welcome to sample up to four wines, which are produced from grapes grown on site and sourced from local vineyards, and can hike and take bicycle rides around the property.

✉ 9592 Sonoma Highway (Highway 12), Kenwood ☎ 707/833-4134; www.kenwoodvineyards.com 🕓 Daily 10–5

YOSEMITE NATIONAL PARK

Best places to see, pages 44–45.

Central Coast

The central coast is the least crowded. Here, rolling hills meet the quiet beach areas, and there are plenty of parks in which to explore hiking and biking trails. Hearst Castle, which sits high above the shoreline, is an extraordinary architectural link to the California of another era. Morro Bay's beach area is perfect for a slower, more relaxed vacation.

Oxnard

The diversity of the Central Coast is marked by the Danish-influenced town of Solvang. You can see thatched huts and real working windmills and enjoy any number of Scandinavian-style restaurants and shops. Further inland, the Santa Ynez valley boasts several wineries to rival any in the world.

Santa Barbara, Cambria and Montecito are all special in their own way, and should be on the itinerary of any visitor to California.

CARMEL

Carmel was established in the late 19th century and has since gained a reputation as a bohemian retreat. It has some of the most picturesque coastal residences in the state, many in Spanish-Mission style. **Mission San Carlos Borromeo del Rio Carmelo** (1769) was moved to its riverside site here in Carmel in 1771. Father Junípero Serra is buried in the church.

✚ 137 C6

Mission San Carlos Borromeo del Rio Carmelo

✉ 3080 Rio Road ☎ 831/624-1271 🕐 Mon–Fri 9:30–4:30, Sat, Sun 10:30–4:30 💰 Inexpensive

HEARST CASTLE

Best places to see, pages 34–35.

MONTEREY PENINSULA

Best places to see, pages 38–39.

MORRO BAY

Morro Rock, the conical, volcano-shaped rock that towers 578ft (176m) out of the Pacific Ocean, sits guarding the entrance to Morro Bay, which is known primarily for its commercial fishing and oyster farming. Although the town has a modest tourist trade, the locals are mostly concerned with the daily business of fishing. Beneath the rock stretches a 5-mile (8km) long beach with

85ft-high (26m) white sand dunes that serve as a habitat for bird and plant life.

The Morro Bay Arts Festival takes place each weekend in October, and the **Museum of Natural History** exhibits marine life native to the central coast, including the Bay's entertaining sea lions. **Tiger's Folly Cruises** offers harbor cruises.

The State Park, south of Morro Bay, is beautiful and a must for those who enjoy camping and hiking. The campgrounds are at the southern end of the park, surrounded by cypress and eucalyptus. The Galley Restaurant serves delicious seafood dishes.

✚ 137 B8 ✉ 845 Embarcadero Road, Suite D ☎ 805/772-4467 ⏰ Mon–Fri 8:30–5, Sat 10–4 💲 Free

Museum of Natural History

✉ Morro Bay State Park ☎ 805/772-2694 ⏰ Daily 10–5 💲 Inexpensive

Tiger's Folly Cruises

✉ 1205 Embarcadero ☎ 805/772-2257 ⏰ Call for times 💲 Inexpensive

OXNARD

Oxnard is a harbor town located on the Ventura–Los Angeles county line, and is home to an annual Strawberry Festival each May. Surpisingly overlooked by visitors are the 7 miles (11km) of beautiful beaches lining the town.

The **Carnegie Art Museum** has a permanent collection of 20th-century California painters, while changing exhibits feature photography and sculpture, with some shows spotlighting local artists. The **Ventura County Gull Wings Children's Museum's** hands-on exhibits of fossils and minerals, including a puppet theater and make-believe campground, will entertain the kids.

✚ 141 E5

Carnegie Art Museum

✉ 424 S "C" Street ☎ 805/385-8157 ⏰ Thu–Sat 10–5, Sun 1–5 💲 Inexpensive

Ventura County Gull Wings Children's Museum

✉ 418 W 4th Street ☎ 805/483-3005 ⏰ Tue–Sat 10–5 💲 Inexpensive

SALINAS

John Steinbeck was born in this working-class town 17 miles (27km) inland from Monterey, now home to the **National Steinbeck Center.** While it's sometimes overlooked in favor of its more affluent neighbors, Salinas is charming. For those visiting in August, there is the Steinbeck Festival. Many rodeo fans visit the town in July to catch one of the major stops on the professional rodeo circuit.

The *Hat In Three Stages of Landing* is a unique giant sculpture by Claes Oldenberg, which captures a trio of bright yellow hats, each weighing 3,500lb (1,590kg). The sculpture graces the lawn of the Community Center, where there are art exhibits and musical/theatrical performances.

🔁 137 C6

National Steinbeck Center

✉ 1 Main Street ☎ 831/796-3833; www.steinbeck.org ⏰ Daily 10–5, closed major holidays 💵 Moderate

SANTA BARBARA

A pleasant and affordable day trip from Los Angeles by train (moderate cost) taking you along the Pacific coast in the morning, gives you time to explore the historic adobes and museums. Lunch on Stearns Wharf, explore the specialty shops there, then stroll the white-sand beach, or play a short round of golf before returning in late afternoon.

The County Courthouse, on Anacapa Street, is one of the best examples of Spanish-Moorish architecture in the US.

El Presidio de Santa Barbara State Historic Park, on the site of a late-1700 Spanish outpost, includes historical buildings such as El Cuartel, the second-oldest surviving edifice in California.

Mission Santa Barbara is the best preserved of the 21 California missions, and the church is filled with Mexican art from the 18th and 19th centuries. A Moorish fountain from 1808 graces the front and the mission is the site of The Little Fiesta each August.

The **Santa Barbara Museum of Art** has a wide variety of American, Asian and 19th-century French, Greek and Roman antiquities, including a major photographic collection.

Visit the Zoological Gardens which are natural habitats for 600 animals, and feature over 80 exhibits.

✚ 141 E5

El Presidio de Santa Barbara State Historic Park
✉ 122–129 E Canon Perdido Street ☎ 805/965-0093
🕐 Daily 10:30–4:30 ✋ Free

Mission Santa Barbara
✉ E Los Olivos and Laguna Street ☎ 805/682-4149 🕐 Daily 9–5; closed major holidays ✋ Inexpensive, under 16 free

Santa Barbara Museum of Art
✉ 1130 State Street ☎ 805/963-4364 🕐 Tue–Sun 10–4 ✋ Moderate. Free Sun

SOLVANG

Denmark in California might best describe Solvang, with its Danish architecture, windmills, gaslights and cobblestone walks. A tour of Solvang is possible in a horse-drawn Danish streetcar, and the town hosts several remarkable festivals annually. Contrasting the Scandinavian motif is the 1804 **Old Mission Santa Ines.**

✚ 141 F5

Old Mission Santa Ines
✉ 1760 Mission Drive ☎ 805/688-4815 🕐 Summer 9–6, Oct–May 9–5:30; closed major holidays ✋ Inexpensive 🍴 Scandinavian restaurants or cafés ($–$$$)

ℹ Chamber of Commerce, 1693 Mission Drive ☎ 805/688-0701

VENTURA

This small beach town between Los Angeles and Santa Barbara is worth a brief visit.

San Buenaventura Mission was founded in 1782 by Father Junipero Serra and was reputed to be his favorite mission. The church is restored and the museum exhibits Native American artifacts from the Chumash tribes.

Next to the Mission is the Albinger Archaeological Museum. It displays over 3,500 years of remains, all from areas around the Mission, while Ventura County Museum of History and Art has Native American, Hispanic and pioneer exhibits.

✚ 141 E5

San Buenaventura Mission

✉ 211 East Main Street ☎ 805/643-4318 🕐 Mon–Fri 10–5, Sat 9–5, Sun 10–4; closed major holidays 🖐 Inexpensive

Los Angeles

Los Angeles

Whether you come for the beaches, mountains, museums or movie stars, Los Angeles teems with activity. Bring your sunglasses and your tanning lotion because here in California there is plenty of sunshine. For dedicated sun-seekers, beautiful beaches stretch along the western edge of this seemingly endless metropolis. Zuma Beach is one of the best for enjoying the pastime made famous by the music of The Beach Boys – surfing.

At Venice Beach you can either stroll barefoot along the beach or join the hustle along the Boardwalk, where vendors hawk their souvenirs. This is home to some of the nation's most colorful characters: musicians, magicians and mime artists, as well as Muscle Beach body builders.

BEVERLY HILLS

The City of Stars is the place where shopping and the entertainment industry each vie for their place as the number one attraction (➤ 94–95). Here you will find some of the most expensive real estate in the country. The city's most recognizable zip code (90210) receives more than 14 million visitors a year, making it the most popular destination in Los Angeles.

Beverly Hills has several main thoroughfares, all running east to west. Sunset Boulevard, at the north end, roughly splits the commercial and residential areas. Wilshire Boulevard is the main thoroughfare to the business and commercial centers. At the south end, Pico Boulevard marks the Beverly Hills border.

www.lovebeverlyhills.org

➕ 141 D5

ℹ Visitors Bureau, 239 S Beverly Drive, Beverly Hills 90212

☎ 310/248-1015 ⏰ Mon–Fri 8:30–5

CHINATOWN

The cultural center of this unique community is home to about 5 percent of LA's 200,000 Chinese residents. Chinatown encompasses 16 square blocks, and its downtown area is filled with Asian architecture, good restaurants and import shops. The Kong Chow Temple is exquisite.

➕ 143 C4 ✉ 900 block of Broadway

CITY HALL

This was the first skyscraper to be built in Los Angeles and served as The Daily Planet Building in the *Superman* television series of the 1950s. Guided

tours are free (weekdays 10–1) and last 45 minutes.
There's an observation deck on the 27th floor.

✚ 143 E3 ✉ 200 N Spring Street ☎ 213/978-0721 🕐 Mon–Fri
9–4 ✋ Free

DESCANSO GARDENS

These glorious gardens cover 65 acres (26ha), including a
30-acre (12ha) California live oak forest. Over 100,000
camellias from around the world flourish here, as do
many roses, lilacs and other blossoms. The Japanese
Garden has a serene teahouse, worth a visit.

✚ 141 D5 ✉ 1418 Descanso Drive, La Cañada Flintridge
☎ 818/949-4200 🕐 Daily 9–5. Closed Christmas Day
✋ Moderate, special discounts

EL PUEBLO DE LOS ANGELES STATE
HISTORICAL PARK

Here, on 44 acres (18ha) near downtown, you can visit
the Avila Adobe (the oldest adobe house), Masonic Hall,
Old Plaza Church and Sepulveda House. Founded in
1781, the main attraction for most visitors is Olvera
Street, an open-air Mexican-style market place lined
with specialty shops, vendors, cafés and restaurants.

✚ 143 D4 ✉ Betweeen Alameda, Arcadia, Spring and
Macy streets ☎ 213/628-1274 🕐 Hours vary call for times
✋ Free

a walk around Beverly Hills

This walk begins on one of the most expensive shopping streets in the world.

Walk north from Wilshire on Rodeo Drive.

Do a spot of window-shopping in Tiffany's, Saks and other high end boutiques.

Proceed north several blocks to Little Santa Monica, then go east (right) a couple of blocks to Crescent.

On the corner of Crescent you'll see the historic former Beverly Hills Post Office and the magnificent Beverly Hills Municipal Building. The latter houses City Hall and the Beverly Hills library and police station.

Take a left on Crescent and proceed north across Santa Monica Boulevard and through the Beverly Hills "flatlands."

The homes along here are absolutely gorgeous.

At Sunset Boulevard, walk across to the newly restored Beverly Hills Hotel.

Take a few minutes to stroll through the splendid lobby.

Proceed east on Sunset to the West Hollywood business district.

Here you will pass the famous Roxy theater, Spago restaurant and The Whiskey A Go-Go.

Continue east, stopping for lunch at the chic Sunset Plaza, then on to Sunset. Turn right on Crescent Heights Road and go south to Melrose Avenue. Turn left on to Melrose and walk several blocks to Fairfax Avenue.

At this corner is the sprawling CBS Television City. Here you can get free tickets to live tapings of television shows.

South of CBS is the Farmers' Market and the Grove, where your tour ends.

Distance 4 miles (6.5km)
Time 3–4 hours, depending on time spent at attractions
Start point Beverly Hills, corner of Wilshire and Rodeo
End point Farmers' Market and the Grove complex of shops, restaurants and movie theaters
Lunch Chin Chin ($) ✉ 8618 Sunset Boulevard ☎ 310/652-1818

EXPOSITION PARK

The Los Angeles Memorial Coliseum was host to the Olympics in 1932 and 1984. Several museums are contained within, including the **California Museum of Science and Industry,** with interactive exhibits, Aerospace Complex and the surround-vision IMAX theater, featuring a five-story-high screen. Other museums include the **California Afro-American Museum** and the **Los Angeles County Museum of Natural History,** with three floors of dinosaur, fossil and cultural exhibits.

✚ 143 E1 (off map)

California Museum of Science and Industry

✉ Exposition Boulevard at Figueroa ☎ 213/744-7400; www.californiasciencecenter.org ⏲ Daily 10–5 ✋ Free, charge for IMAX

California Afro-American Museum

✉ 600 State Drive, Exposition Park ☎ 213/744-7432 ⏲ Wed–Sat 10–4 ✋ Free ($6 parking fee)

LA County Museum of Natural History

✉ 900 Exposition Boulevard, Exposition Park ☎ 213/763-3466 ⏲ Mon–Fri 9:30–5, Sat, Sun 10–5 ✋ Moderate, free first Tue of month

FOREST LAWN MEMORIAL PARK

A cemetery may seem like an unusual attraction, but there are 300 lush acres (121ha) of grounds here, with reproductions of such works as da Vinci's *Last Supper*, and the world's largest religious painting on canvas, Jan Styke's *The Crucifixion*. Also not to be missed are the ornate tombstones of celebrities and the beautiful gardens. Forest Lawn cemetery is the final resting place of such Hollywood film legends as Humphrey Bogart, Errol Flynn,

STAN LAUREL
1890 – 1965
A MASTER OF COMEDY
HIS GENIUS IN THE ART OF
HUMOR BROUGHT GLADNESS
TO THE WORLD HE LOVED.

Spencer Tracy, Stan Laurel, Jean Harlow, Carole Lombard, W C Fields and Cary Grant.

➕ 141 D5 ✉ 1712 South Glendale Avenue, Glendale ☎ 818/241-4151 ⏰ Daily 10–5 ✋ Free

GETTY CENTER

This billion-dollar arts complex sits high on a hill off the 405 San Diego freeway to the north of the city. Although still in its infancy, it seems destined to become one of LA's main attractions. With everything from Greek sculptures to paintings by European masters and modern photography, the museum is surrounded by ponds, beautiful landscaping and a fine herb garden.

➕ 141 D6 ✉ 1200 Getty Center Drive ☎ 310/440-7300 ⏰ Tue–Thu, Sun 10–6, Fri, Sat 10–9 ✋ Free ($7 fee for parking)

GRIFFITH PARK

Here, in the Santa Monica Mountains, Griffith Park contains the LA Zoo, Griffith Observatory and Planetarium, as well as Travel Town, an outdoor transportation museum. The Observatory is the perfect spot to view the Hollywood sign and the entire city, while the Planetarium has incredible laserium shows. There are horseback riding and children's attractions, and plenty of picnic areas.

🔳 141 D5 ✉ Mount Hollywood ☎ 323/664-1191 (Observatory/Planetarium); 323/666-4650 (Zoo); 323/913-4688 (tourist information) 🕔 Hours vary so call for information ✋ The park is free; some attractions have moderate fees

HOLLYWOOD

Best places to see, pages 36–37.

HOLLYWOOD WAX MUSEUM

Over 220 of Hollywood's greatest stars, political leaders and sports greats – all made of wax, but very lifelike – are on show at the Hollywood Wax Museum. Also included are displays on television, motion pictures and religion. Exhibits rotate every six months or so. The Chamber of Horrors is a favorite, as well as the recent additions of current stars.

🔳 141 D5 (Hollywood) ✉ 6767 Hollywood Boulevard ☎ 323/462-8860 🕔 Sun–Thu 10–midnight, Fri–Sat to 1am ✋ Moderate

HUNTINGTON LIBRARY, ART GALLERY AND GARDENS

The historical library contains over four million items, including art treasures and an extraordinary treasury of rare and precious manuscripts. After taking in the Huntington's art and books, take a

walk through the immaculate botanical gardens, the best in the state. Here, 15 separate garden areas contain around 14,000 different types of plants and trees. Arrive early because the grounds fill up fast.

➕ 141 C5 ✉ 1151 Oxford Road, San Marino ☎ 626/405-2141 🕐 Tue–Fri 12–4:30, Sat–Sun 10:30–4:30 ✋ Moderate

LITTLE TOKYO

The city's Japanese quarter features the 40-shop Japanese Village Plaza, which resembles a rural village. Also here are Noguchi Plaza, with its fan-shaped Japan America Theater, the Japanese American National Museum, and quiet Japanese gardens. Some great sushi bars can also be found here.

➕ 143 F3 ✉ First Street and Central Avenue

LONG BEACH

Long Beach is now California's fifth largest city. Its Shoreline Village and Wilmore Park surround the Convention and Entertainment Center, a popular corporate convention spot. Boats to Catalina Island depart from Golden Shore Boulevard. Of special interest is the *Queen Mary*, which came to rest in Long Beach in 1967. With 12 decks and weighing in at 50,000 tons, it is the largest passenger ship ever built, the *crème de la crème* of 1932 art deco luxury. There are lots of shops and eateries on board.

✚ 141 D6 ✉ Pier J, Long Beach Harbor ☎ 562/435-3511 ◷ Daily 10–5
✋ Free; moderate-priced guided tours

LOS ANGELES STATE AND COUNTY ARBORETUM

The trees and shrubs in the Los Angeles Arboretum are arranged according to the continent they originate from. Also featured are greenhouses, a bird sanctuary and historic buildings like the Queen Anne Cottage, home of the estate's former owner, Elia Jackson Baldwin. Picnic areas and tours available.

✚ 141 C5 ✉ 301 N Baldwin Avenue, Arcadia ☎ 626/821-3222 ◷ Daily 9–4:30 ✋ Inexpensive; various discounts

MANN'S CHINESE THEATRE

Originally Grauman's Chinese Theatre, Mann's, a prime Hollywood tourist attraction, is a good starting point for a tour of Los Angeles.

The theater was opened in 1927 by showman Sid Grauman, and whenever a film was premiered here, stars left their hand- or footprints.

✚ 141 D5 (Hollywood) ✉ 6925 Hollywood Boulevard ☎ 323/464-8111

MUSEUM OF CONTEMPORARY ART (MOCA)

This seven-tiered museum (much of it below street level) has 11 giant pyramidal skylights and a 53ft (16m) barrel-vaulted entrance. It is dedicated to works of art since the 1940s and features traveling exhibitions. Also at Geffen Contemporary and Pacific Design Center.

✚ 143 E2 ✉ 250 S Grand Avenue ☎ 213/621-2766 🕐 Mon, Fri 11–5, Thu 11–8, Sat, Sun 11–6 ✋ Moderate; free Thu

PETERSEN AUTOMOTIVE MUSEUM

If you are an automotive fan, the Petersen Museum, with one of the largest auto collections in the world, is a must. It explores automotive history and culture from the earliest jalopies. Highlights are the 1957 Ferrari 250 Testa Rossa, and customized cars from Dean Jeffries and George Barris.

✚ 143 C1 (off map) ✉ 6060 Wilshire Boulevard ☎ 323/930-CARS 🕐 Tue–Sun 10–6 ✋ Moderate

SOUTHWEST MUSEUM

This mission-revival style building, high above downtown LA, focuses on Native American art, including jewelry, basketwork and weaving. The founder, Charles Lummis, director of the Los Angeles Library in 1907, also donated rare books to the museum.

✚ 143 B4 (off map) ✉ 234 Museum Drive ☎ 323/221-2164 🕐 Tue–Sun 10–5 ✋ Moderate

UNIVERSAL STUDIOS HOLLYWOOD AND CITYWALK

For a fascinating behind-the-scenes look at movie-making, plan to spend the better part of a day at Universal Studios, the world's biggest and busiest motion picture and television studio-cum-theme park. Citywalk features outdoor dining and a wide variety of shops that are a cut above what you might expect. There are huge outdoor screens that show music videos and movie previews and a theater complex shows all the latest movies.

The upper and lower sections are connected by a long escalator, making the 420-acre (170ha) park easy to navigate. Some of the more interesting sets still standing are from such films as *The Sting*, *Animal House* and *Home Alone*. There are theme rides based on other successful films such as *Revenge of the Mummy* and *Jurassic Park*.

www.universalstudioshollywood.com; **www.**citywalk.com

✚ 141 D5 (Hollywood) ✉ 100 Universal City Plaza, Universal City ☎ 800-UNIVERSAL 🕐 Daily from 9 or 10am; closing hours vary ✋ Expensive

VENICE BEACH

Just south along the beach from Santa Monica is Venice Beach. Although it appears to be a throwback to the 1960s, it is really a thriving enclave for modern bohemians. The neighborhood was founded in 1905 by Abbot Kinney, who hoped to create a haven for artistic types. Gondolas were imported from Italy and, for a time, the canals were eerily similar to those in Europe. Try a free self-guided tour. The most popular today is the Ocean Front Walk, teeming with visitors, street performers and souvenir stands. You can also rent a bicycle or rollerblades.

✚ 141 D6 ✉ 15 miles (24km) from downtown Los Angeles, access via Lincoln Boulevard

WATTS TOWERS AND ARTS CENTER

Italian immigrant Simon Rodia took 30 years to build these extraordinary towers by himself, using scraps of whatever materials he could find. The Arts Center, next to the towers, contains rotating exhibits of African American art.

✚ 141 D6 ✉ 1765 E 107th Street ☎ 213/847-4646 🕐 Tower Tours: Fri–Sun 11–4 ✋ Inexpensive

Arts Center

✉ 1727 107th Street 🕐 Tue–Sat 10–4, Sun 12–4 ✋ Inexpensive

Southern California

The commercial center of the state, Southern California is the most densely populated area. The vast metropolitan areas of Los Angeles and San Diego are surrounded by largely empty deserts.

San Diego

Southern California is also the center of the entertainment and aerospace industries. Hollywood, Disneyland and the many beaches that stretch south to Mexico are the favorites of most people who visit the area. There is a distinct Spanish influence in the architecture, and most of the missions are located along the coast between San Diego and Los Angeles.

ANAHEIM

Anaheim was originally founded as the center of a wine-producing colony by German immigrants in 1857. The vineyards were replaced by orange groves late in the 19th century, after a brutal drought. Oranges thrived until the 1950s, when commercial interests and the rapid growth of the Los Angeles metropolitan area took over. The two main attractions in the area are Disneyland Park (➤ 30–31) and Knott's Berry Farm (➤ 112).

✚ 141 C1 ✉ 46 miles (74km) from Los Angeles via I–5; directly across from Disneyland

BAKERSFIELD

Bakersfield is California's main oil-producing center. Many consider it a less-than-desirable part of California, its furnace-like, 100°F-plus (38°C) summers a major drawback. However, the downtown area is a mix of restored buildings and newer offices. Of note are a genuine schoolhouse, church and a fully restored 1868 log cabin.

The **California Living Museum** focuses on the state's wildlife and native plants, many of which are rare or endangered.

Kern County Museum has exhibits representing both the human and the natural history of the area.

✚ 140 E3
California Living Museum
✉ 10500 Alfred Harrell Highway ☎ 661/872-2256 🕐 Daily 9–5 🍴 Picnic
facilities 🖐 Inexpensive
Kern County Museum
✉ 3801 Chester Avenue ☎ 661/852-5000 🕐 Mon–Sat 10–5, Sun noon–5
🖐 Inexpensive

BARSTOW

Barstow is the halfway point between Los Angeles and Las Vegas.
It was settled in the early 19th century when silver mines
flourished in the surrounding areas. The town of **Calico** boomed in
the late 1800s, and its mines produced $15 million worth of ore.
When the price of silver dropped, the town went bust. Today, you
can visit the "ghost town" of Calico to pan for gold, ride the steam
railway or see a show at the Calikage Playhouse.

North of Barstow is **Rainbow Basin National Natural
Landmark.** Fossils, the forces of nature and an abundance of
minerals give it its dramatic shapes and colors.
✚ 140 B4
Calico Ghost Town
✉ 11 miles (18km) northeast of Barstow via I-15 ☎ 760/254-2122 🕐 Daily
9–5 🍴 Restaurants ($$) 🖐 Inexpensive
Rainbow Basin National Natural Landmark
✉ Fossil Bed Road, 8 miles (13km) north of Barstow via SR 58

BIG BEAR LAKE

One of California's largest recreation areas, the Big Bear Lake
region has two distinct sections; Big Bear Lake and Big Bear City,
on the eastern end of the lake. Big Bear Village, centered around
the lake, is popular for lodging, dining and shopping. Camping,
hiking and riding are available in summer and skiing in winter.
✚ 141 B5 ✉ Big Bear Chamber of Commerce, 630 Bartlett Road
☎ 909/866-4607; www.bigbearchamber.com 🍴 Many restaurants ($–$$$)

CATALINA ISLAND
Best places to see, pages 28–29.

DEATH VALLEY NATIONAL PARK

Three million years ago, inner-earth forces tormented, twisted and shook the land in what is now Death Valley, creating snowcapped mountains and superheated valleys. Lakes, formed during the Ice Age, evaporated, leaving alternating layers of mud and salt deposits.

More than three million acres in size, Death Valley ranges in elevation from 282ft (86m) below sea level to slightly over 11,000 (3,354m) above. Temperatures reach well over 100°F (38°C) in summer, making it one of the hottest regions in the world. **Scotty's Castle,** on the northern boundary of the park, is a Spanish/Moorish construction built by Chicago insurance tycoon Albert Johnson for Walter E. Scott, alias "Death Valley Scotty."

✚ 140 B2 ✉ Furnace Creek Visitors Center ☎ 760/786-3244 ⏲ Daily 8–5 ✋ Inexpensive ❓ Camping facilities

Scotty's Castle
☎ 760/786 2392 ⏲ Daily 8–5 ✋ Moderate

FRESNO

Fresno lies in the heart of the San Joaquin Valley. One of the foremost agricultural areas in the country, it is also the gateway to the Sierra Nevada's three national parks.

The town's fine **Metropolitan Museum of Art, History and Science** features an extensive collection of Asian art, as well as American still-life paintings. Wild Water Adventure Park, on E Shaw

Avenue, contains over 20 water rides, pools and a small fishing lake.

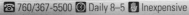

✚ 140 E1

Metropolitan Museum of Art, History and Science
✉ 1555 Van Ness Avenue ☎ 559/441-1444 ◷ Tue–Sun 11–5
✋ Inexpensive

JOSHUA TREE NATIONAL MONUMENT

Known for its distinctive Joshua trees (a desert tree of the yucca species), and its uniquely shaped rock formations, the park connects the "high" and "low" deserts. In the park is Key's View, a high elevation with incredible views on a clear day. Not to be missed is the Cholla Cactus Garden, about 10 miles (16km) south of the Oasis Visitors Center.

✚ 141 A6 ✉ Oasis Vistors Center. National Monument Drive, 29 Palms
☎ 760/367-5500 ◷ Daily 8–5 ✋ Inexpensive

LAKE ARROWHEAD

Known locally as a sophisticated mountain getaway, this is where LA's wealthy spend leisurely weekends in luxury homes. Restrictive development laws help preserve the area's natural beauty. Swimming and boating are popular activities in summer, and skiing in winter. Children will enjoy the **Lake Arrowhead Children's Museum,** which contains historical information on the area and anthropological exhibitions.

www.lakearrowhead.net

➕ 141 B5

ℹ Chamber of Commerce, Lake Arrowhead Village ☎ 909/337-3715

🕓 Mon–Fri 9–5, Sat 10–3

Lake Arrowhead Children's Museum

✉ Lake Arrowhead Village ☎ 909/336-3093 🕓 Daily 10–5, 10–6 in summer

♿ Inexpensive

ORANGE COUNTY

Known by Californians as the "conservative" enclave of the state, Orange County is a sprawling expanse of humanity between Los Angeles and San Diego, with its own unique charms.

Disneyland Park

Best places to see, pages 30–31.

Festival of the Arts/Pageant of the Masters

A state-of-the-art art exhibit in the scenic wooded Laguna Canyon, this is a landmark event, the former featuring an exhibit of 150 Laguna artists of all kinds. The most interesting aspect of this seven-week event, however, is the Pageant of the Masters, in which human models stand perfectly still for three minutes in re-creations of famous paintings and sculptures, with a musical accompaniment.

✚ 141 C6 ✉ Laguna Canyon Road, Laguna Beach ☎ 949/494-1145 🕐 Jul–Aug 10am–11pm ✋ Expensive

Huntington Art Center

Though small, the Huntington Art Center is concerned with local contemporary art and architecture in a big way. It has been renovated and is a favorite with many local artists. Films are shown the first and third Friday of each month.

✚ 141 C6 ✉ 538 Main Street E, Huntington Beach ☎ 714/374-1650 🕐 Wed–Sun noon–6, Sun noon–4 ✋ Free

International Surfing Museum

Huntington Beach calls itself "Surf City," with good reason, and is a mecca for surfing enthusiasts. Exhibits tell the sport's history, and the store sells surf gear, all, of course, to the music of the Beach Boys.

✚ 141 C6 ✉ Olive Street, block off Main, Huntington Beach ☎ 714/960-3483 🕐 Summer daily noon–5; winter Thu–Mon noon–5 ✋ Inexpensive

Knott's Berry Farm

One of California's original theme parks, Knott's has grown from a true berry farm to a modern 150-acre (61ha) attraction with more than 165 rides. The Western theme areas include Ghost Town and Gold Mine Ride. Other attractions include Camp Snoopy, Wild Water Wilderness, Mystery Lodge, Reflection Lake, California Marketplace and Kingdom of the Dinosaurs. The adventurous can try the four awesome rollercoasters, the Boomerang, Montezooma's Revenge, the Jaguar and the Silver Bullet. Finally, Knott's still serves its original, delicious, world-famous boysenberry pie.

✚ 141 C6 ✉ 8039 Beach Boulevard, Buena Park ☎ 714/220-5200
🕓 Subject to change; call for current times ✋ Expensive

Laguna Art Museum

The Laguna Art Museum was founded in 1918 and is the showcase venue for the Laguna Art Association. It usually features several visiting exhibits of paintings and sculpture by California artists. On permanent display are historical California landscapes and vintage photographs of the region.

✚ 141 C6 ✉ Pacific Coast Highway and Cliff Drive, Laguna Beach
☎ 949/494-8971 🕓 Daily 11–5 ✋ Moderate

Mission San Juan Capistrano

Founded in 1776, this is one of California's most beautiful missions, and the only building still standing where Father Junípero Serra said Mass. On 19 March each year, the Feast of St. Joseph celebrates the legendary "return of the swallows."

➕ 141 C6 ✉ Corner of Ortega Highway/Camino Capistrano ☎ 949/234-1300 🕐 Daily 8:30–5

Richard Nixon Presidential Library and Birthplace

The Richard Nixon Library in Yorba Linda, has galleries, theaters and gardens, and personal memorabilia of this former US president. The grounds feature the small house where he was born, his post-presidency private study and a re-creation of the White House's Lincoln Sitting Room.

➕ 141 C6 ✉ 18001 Yorba Linda Boulevard ☎ 714/993-3393; www.nixonlibrary.org 🕐 Mon–Sat 10–5, Sun 11–5 ✋ Moderate

Sherman Library and Gardens

The unique gardens here are filled with orchids and koi ponds, while the library itself is a large building, taking up a whole city block. It functions as a center of historical research for the region. There is an extensive collection of historical Orange County documents and photographs.

➕ 141 C6 ✉ 2647 E Coast Highway, Newport Beach ☎ 949/673-2261 🕐 Gardens daily 10:30–4 ✋ Inexpensive

PALM SPRINGS

Rising out of the desert like an oasis, Palm Springs is one of the most famous resort towns in the world. It has become a favorite of wealthy retirees with a penchant for good golf and bad driving habits, and an ever-increasing number of young people are looking here for a brief spring retreat from their studies. The summers are insufferably hot, however, and the population dwindles from June through early September.

Anza-Borrego Desert State Park offers spectacular desert scenery. Set in 600,000 acres (242,915ha), the main flora includes lupin, poppy, dune primrose, desert sunflower and desert lily. A variety of short trails and camp-grounds can be found here.

Five miles (8km) south of Palm Springs is **Agua Caliente Indian Reservation.** The Tribal Council here has opened part of the reservation for hiking and picnics.

An awesome view of the San Jacinto Mountains awaits if you ride the **Palm Springs Aerial Tramway,** almost 5,000ft (1,524m) straight up. The perfect way to escape the debilitating summer heat, you ride up to the wooded trails and campgrounds at the top, where refreshments are available.

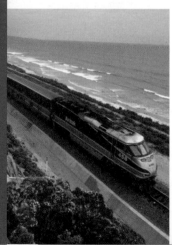

✚ 141 B6

Anza-Borrego Desert State Park
✉ Visitors Center, 2 miles (3.2km) west of Borrego Springs Township
☎ 760/767-4205;
www.anzaborregostatepark.org ◷ Call for hours and more information
✋ Inexpensive

Agua Caliente Indian Reservation
☎ 760/323-0151 ◷ Wed–Sat 10–5, Sun noon–5 (shorter hours in summer)
✋ Inexpensive

Palm Springs Aerial Tramway

✉ Tramway Road, 3 miles (5km) southwest of SR 111
☎ 760/325-1391 ⏰ Mon–Fri 10–8, Sat–Sun 8–8.
Closed 2 weeks in Aug ✋ Expensive

PALOMAR MOUNTAIN

Palomar Observatory houses the world-famous 200in (513cm) Hale telescope. High above the distracting, bright city lights, the observatory also has several smaller telescopes, used to monitor the planet's movement. The small Greenway Museum contains photographs of the observatory's celestial sightings.

✚ 141 B7 ✉ 40 miles (65km) northeast of San Diego on SR 6 ☎ 626/395-4033 ⏰ Daily 9–4 ✋ Free

RIVERSIDE

Because the region has the ideal climate and soil for growing navel oranges, this was the wealthiest US city per capita and the metropolitan center of Southern California at the turn of the 20th century. Several buildings remain from around this time: the Italian Renaissance-style City Hall, the Classic Revival municipal museum, and many exquisite Victorian homes. In addition, mission architecture and adobe residences still reflect the early wealth and prestige.

California Citrus State Historic Park has a grove of 80 different varieties of citrus tree. The visitor center is located in a Victorian house. The Riverside Municipal Museum, at 3720 Orange Street, traces the history of citrus-growing in the region.

✚ 141 C6

California Citrus State Historic Park

✉ Van Buren Boulevard at Dufferin Avenue ☎ 951/780-6222 ⏰ Daily 8–5 (until 7 Apr–Sep); visitor center Wed, Sat, Sun 10–4 ✋ Free 🍴 Picnic facilities

SAN DIEGO

San Diego rarely gets rain, never freezes, has an average annual daytime temperature between 58 and 70°F (14 and 21°C), and more than 70 miles (113km) of sandy beaches. California's second largest city, it retains a small-town ambience. Ralph Waldo Emerson must have visited San Diego when he said "California has better days and more of them."

✚ 141 B8

Balboa Park

Best places to see, pages 26–27.

The Beaches

The most popular of the city's beaches is Pacific Beach (known as "PB" by the locals), which features The Tourmaline Surfing Park, a surfer's paradise. Mission Beach has a 3-mile (5km) walk of shops and skateboard, rollerblade and bicycle rental stands. Ocean Beach is one of the liveliest in San Diego, and a good place to fish. Point Loma is an upscale beach, with spectacular views of the naval ships' comings and goings.

Cabrillo National Monument

A 144-acre (58ha) park along steep cliffs, Cabrillo rewards with great views of San Diego Bay, and it's an especially good place to spot gray whales migrating to Mexico between mid-December and mid-March. The Old Point Loma Lighthouse, dating from 1855, is 25 miles (43km) out to sea, but visible from here on a clear day.

✉ 10 miles (16km) west of I-8 on Catalina Boulevard ☎ 619/557-5450
🕐 Daily 9–5:15 ✋ Inexpensive

Coronado Island

A combination of wealthy enclave and naval base, Coronado sits just across the bay from downtown San Diego. The easiest way to reach it is on the Bay Ferry. Leaving from Broadway Pier downtown, the ferry arrives at Old Ferry Landing in Coronado in 15 minutes. You can also reach the island via the towering San Diego–Coronado Bay Bridge (toll). The main attraction on the island is Hotel Del Coronado. A testament to the beauty of Victorian architecture, the "Del" was opened in 1888, and film buffs might remember it as one of the main locations in Marilyn Monroe's film *Some Like It Hot*.

✉ Visitor Center at 1100 Orange Avenue ☎ 619/236-1212 ☎ 619/437-8788 (Visitor Center), 619/234-4111 (Bay Ferry information) ✋ Inexpensive

Gaslamp Quarter
The reclamation of San Diego's 19th-century Gaslamp Quarter
is one of urban America's great success stories. Slated for
demolition, many of its Victorian-era cast-iron and other buildings
were restored and converted into stores, restaurants and
nightclubs, and the area is now the center of San Diego's
vibrant nightlife.
www.gaslamp.org

House of Pacific Relations

The culture and art of 31 nations is housed in the museum's 15 California/Spanish-style cottages located in the Pan American Plaza. Other Plaza attractions are the Aerospace Museum, San Diego Automotive Museum and the open-air Starlight Bowl.

✉ 2125 Park Boulevard, Balboa Park ☎ 619/234-0739 🕐 Sun, 2nd and 4th Tue of month 🖐 Free; donations welcome

La Jolla

Pronounced *La Hoya* (Spanish for "The Jewel"), this picturesque cove, just north of San Diego, is one of the prettiest places in the whole state. This unspoiled piece of coastline offers expensive restaurants and boutiques on its two main thoroughfares: Prospect Street and Girard Avenue. Just north of La Jolla are the equally scenic towns of Del Mar and Solana Beach. Relatively undiscovered by tourists, these beaches epitomize the beauty and tranquillity of Southern California.

✉ 10 miles (16km) north of San Diego via I 805 or Highway 1

Maritime Museum of San Diego

Just three ships are moored on the Embarcadero but oh, what legendary ships they are! The pick of the bunch is the 1863 *Star of India*, a fully equipped three-mast sailing ship, the oldest iron-hulled ship in America still afloat. San Francisco's *Berkeley* was the ferry used to evacuate victims of the 1906 earthquake. The 1904 steam-powered yacht *Medea* occasionally sails around the Bay.

✉ 1492 North Harbor Drive ☎ 619/234-9153 ⏰ Daily 9–8 (closes 9pm in summer) 👍 Moderate

Mission Bay Park

There are miles of cycling paths throughout this huge aquatic park, and a bicycle rental stand can be found just off East Mission Bay Drive. Kite flying and volleyball are popular pastimes here, and watersports, as well as golf, picnicking and camping, can be found. The park is also the home of Sea World (► 125). Next to the park is Fiesta Island, popular for jet skiing and "over the line" baseball.

⏰ Daily 👍 Free

ℹ 2688 E Mission Bay Drive ☎ 619/276-8200

Museum of Man

The San Diego Museum of Man, located below the California Tower (► 26), offers eclectic, ever-changing exhibits from Californians and Hopi tribes, ancient Egypt and mummies, to the Maya and early man.

✉ 1350 El Prado Drive ☎ 619/239-2001 ⏰ Daily 10–4:30 ✋ Inexpensive

Old Town San Diego State Historic Park

The remains of the first European settlement in California, Old Town is preserved with National Park status. The most important area is the Mission San Diego de Alcala, California's first mission, founded in 1769 by Father Junípero Serra. Restored and still used for services, it has beautiful gardens and adobe structures and houses the Museum de Luis Jayme. One of the oldest buildings, Casa de Estudillo, has survived several hundred years.

Old Town Plaza was a general meeting place and center for festivals, religious celebrations and even bullfights in the mid-1800s. Here you'll find the visitors' center, where you can sign up for free tours of the grounds.

✉ San Diego Avenue, at Twiggs Street ☎ 619/220-5422 ⏰ Daily 10–5, closed Jan 1, Thanksgiving, Christmas Day ✋ Free

Presidio Park

Formerly the fort here protected Mission San Diego de Alcala. The park is up the hill from the center of Old Town. As you sit on the benches scattered among the trees of this 50-acre (20ha) park you will have wonderful views of the Old Town expanse. San Diego's landmark museum, the Junipero Serra, sits high atop the hill where California's first mission and presidio were founded. Spanish, Mexican and Native American aspects of San Diego's history are recalled with exhibits of furniture, clothing, household items and other artifacts of the past 200 years.

✉ 2727 Presidio Drive ☎ 619/297-3258 ⏰ Park daily; Junipero Serra Museum daily 10–4:30 ✋ Inexpensive

a walk around San Diego

**Starting at the Old Town visitors'
center, you pass historic
buildings, museums and sites that
encompass the oldest and most
beautiful part of San Diego.**

*From the visitors' center, walk
southward and turn east on San Diego
Avenue, continuing to the Machado-
Silvas Adobe house.*

This is one of the more famous buildings
built in the mid-19th century, and houses
the Courthouse and the Colorado
House/Wells Fargo Museum.

*After touring the house, continue a
short distance north to Mason Street.*

Here you will see the Mason Street
School. Built in 1865, this one-room
building was San Diego's first publicly
owned school.

*Go north on Mason to San Diego
Avenue, then turn east to Dodson's
Corner.*

Dodson's Corner is a group of false-front
shops where merchants sometimes
dress in period costume. Across San
Diego Avenue is the San Diego Union
Museum, home of the state's longest
running newspaper.

From here go north on Twiggs Street to Calhoun Street.

At Calhoun you will see the Steely Stables, and Blackhawk Smith and Stable, both worth a look.

Walk west on Calhoun to the Alvarado House and Johnson House, two beautiful and historic structures. Retrace your steps back to Mason Street, then head south to visit the Casa De Estudillo. After touring the Casa, step across the street back into Old Town Plaza to end your tour.

To complement your stroll through Old Town, you could visit the nearby Gaslamp Quarter, bound by Broadway, 4th, 6th and Harbor streets, which gives a comprehensive history of San Diego's architecture.

Distance 3.5 miles (5.5km)
Time 3 hours
Start point Visitors' Center, Old Town State Historic Park
End point Old Town Plaza
Lunch Old Town Mexican Cafe ($)
✉ 2489 San Diego Avenue
☎ 619/297-4330 🕐 Breakfast, lunch, dinner

San Diego Wild Animal Park

The park, 30 miles (48km) northeast of San Diego, is known for its authentic re-creation of African and Asian terrain. Almost 2,500 endangered animals are presented here by the Zoological Society of San Diego. This 2,100-acre (850ha) preserve features monorail tour, Nairobi Village animal shows, hiking trails and botanical exhibits.

www.wildanimalpark.org

✉ Via Rancho Pkwy exit off I–15 ☎ 619/234-6541 🕐 Daily 9–4

🎟 Expensive (combination pass with San Diego Zoo)

Scripps Oceanography and Birch Aquarium

Part of the University of California at San Diego, Birch Aquarium and the Memorial Pier are landmarks of the La Jolla coast. Marine scientists have been working here since the turn of the century. The Institute displays the aquatic world in indoor tanks, an on-shore tidepool and through additional oceanographic exhibits showing the latest advances in oceanography.

✉ 2300 Expedition Way ☎ 858/534-3474 🕐 Daily 9–5 👆 Moderate

SeaWorld

Perhaps one of, if not *the* finest marine biology park in the world, SeaWorld is impressive, and you can and should plan on spending the better part of a day here. Comfortably spread out over 150 acres (61ha), it features continuous killer whale and dolphin shows, and highly informative marine life exhibits. Between shows, you can touch or view live animals in the petting pools. Also not to miss are the nautical theme playground, marina and state-of-the-art research laboratories.

SeaWorld is home to killer whales Shamu and Baby Shamu, the real stars of the park, as well as seals, sea lions and walruses. The Rocky Point Preserve is a habitat for dolphins and sea otters, while "Penguin Encounter" has over 300 penguins. Other exhibits include "Pets Rule!" and "Fools with Tools." A family-oriented theme park is packed with interactive games and adventures. Guided tours are available, and in the summer there are evening aquatic shows. Owing to the park's popularity, you can expect long waits for some shows and exhibits, especially during the summer. Don't forget the re-entry stamp should you decide to leave the park and return later. Ticket sales stop 90 minutes before closing, which is around sunset most of the year, but as late as 11pm in the summer.

www.seaworld.com; **www.**4adventure.com

✉ SeaWorld Drive off the I–5, Mission Bay Park ☎ 619/226-3901 🕐 Daily from 10am, closing times vary with season 👆 Expensive

a walk in Sequoia National Park

This walk takes you through the forest of Sequoia National Park. Even if you visit during the heat of the summer, you will find the temperatures comfortably cool because of the towering foliage.

Begin at the General Sherman Tree, 2 miles (3.2km) east of Giant Forest Village.

The General Sherman tree (named for the Civil War general) is 275ft (84m) high. It is estimated to be more than 2,500 years old and contains enough wood to build 40 houses.

Walk down the self-guided, paved Congress Trail. Cross Sherman Creek on the quaint wooden bridge.

Experience the awesome giant sequoias, like the character-laden Leaning Tree and some lightning-struck and fire-scarred trees as well.

About a mile (1.6km) further, you will meet the junction with the Alta Trail and a grove known as The Senate. A little further along the fern-filled trail is The House Grove.

These two stands are named after the two governing bodies of the United States government. The path also visits the McKinley Tree (named for the US president). After World War II, the practice of naming big trees after politicos was abandoned.

Continue a half-mile (0.8km) back, and return to the trail head. For a longer hike (about six miles/10km), follow the Congress Trail to the junction of The Trail of the Sequoias. Take this path for a half-mile (0.8km) to the hike's high point, then gradually descend one and a half miles (2.5km) into Long Meadow.

Lunch before, or after, your hike at Giant Forest Village.

Distance 5 miles (8km)
Time 2–4 hours
Start point General Sherman Tree
End point General Sherman or Long Meadow
Lunch Grant Grove Restaurant ($$) ✉ Grant Grove Visitors Center
☎ 559/335-5500, ext 306

SANTA ANA

A typical thriving small city in Orange County, Santa Ana centers around the South Coast Plaza, a European-styled mall with shops, restaurants and cinemas. The **Bowers Museum of Cultural Art,** a mission-style museum, is the largest in Orange County. It focuses on American, Pacific and African art, with an impressive permanent collection and quarterly visiting exhibits.

✚ 141 C6

Bowers Museum of Cultural Art

✉ 2002 N Main Street ☎ 714/567-3600 ⊕ Tue–Sun 10–4 ✋ Inexpensive

SIMI VALLEY

The main reason for visiting Simi Valley is to see the **Ronald Reagan Presidential Library,** set in a beautiful, Spanish mission-style, hilltop mansion. Among the exhibits are photographs and memorabilia of the former US president's life, a full-scale replica of the Oval Office and a large portion of the Berlin Wall.

✚ 141 D5

Ronald Reagan Presidential Library

✉ 40 Presidential Drive ☎ 800/410-8354 ⊕ Daily 10–5; closed major holidays ✋ Inexpensive

SOLEDAD

Soledad, the oldest settlement in the Salinas Valley, was established in 1791 with the founding of **Mission Nuestra Señora de la Soledad,** 3 miles (5km) west on US 101. The ruins of this adobe mission, along with a restored chapel and museum, can be seen to the east of town.

✚ 137 B6

Mission Nuestra Senora de la Soledad

✉ Fort Romie Road ☎ 831/678-2586 ⊕ Daily 10–4 ✋ Donations

Index

17–Mile Drive 39

Agua Caliente Indian
  Reservation 114
air travel and airport services
  16, 17
Alcatraz 50–51
Anaheim 106
Angel's Camp 67, 68
Anza Borrego Desert State Park
  114
Asian Art Museum, SF 51
Avalon Casino, Catalina Island
  29

Bakersfield 106–107
Balboa Park, San Diego 26–27
banks 22
Barstow 107
Beringer Vineyards 80
Beverly Hills, LA 92, 94–95
Big Bear Lake 107
Big Sur 65
Blue Ox Millworks, Eureka 66
Bowers Museum of Cultural
  Art, Santa Ana 128
Buena Vista Winery 81
buses 16, 17

Cable Car Museum and
  Powerhouse Viewing Gallery,
  SF 52
Cabrillo National Monument 116
Calico 107
California Academy of Sciences,
  SF 52–53
California Citrus State Historic
  Park 115
California Living Museum,
  Bakersfield 106
California Museum of Science
  and Industry, LA 96
California Palace of the Legion
  of Honor, SF 53
California State Mining and
  Mineral Museum, Mariposa
  68
California State Railroad
  Museum, Sacramento 76, 77
Calistoga 40, 41
car rental 18–19
Carmel 38, 39, 84
Cartoon Art Museum, SF 54
Catalina Island 28–29
Catalina Island Museum 29

Central Coast 83–89
Chinatown, LA 92
Chinatown, SF 56–57
Chinese Historical Society of
  America, SF 54
City Hall, LA 92–93
Civic Center Plaza, SF 54
climate 12
Coit Tower, SF 61
Columbia 68
concessions 19
consulates 21
Coronado Island 116–117

Death Valley National Park 108
De Young Museum, SF 54–55
Descanso Gardens, LA 93
Devil's Postpile National
  Monument 71
Discovery Museum,
  Sacramento 76, 77
Disneyland® Park 30–31
drinking water 22
drive
  Gold Country 68–69
driving 16, 18

El Pueblo de Los Angeles State
  Historical Park 93
electricity 22
emergency numbers 21
Empire Mine State Historic
  Park 67, 69
Eureka 66
Exploratorium, SF 61
Exposition Park, LA 96

Festival of the Arts/Pageant of
  the Masters, Laguna Beach
  111
festivals and events 14–15
Fisherman's Wharf, Monterey
  39
Fisherman's Wharf, SF 55
Forest Lawn Memorial Park, LA
  96–97
Fort Mason Center, SF 32
Fresno 108–109

Gaslamp Quarter, San Diego
  118, 123
Getty Center, LA 97
Gold Country 66–67
Golden Gate Bridge/ National
  Recreation Area, SF 32–33

Governor's mansion,
  Sacramento 76, 77
Grace Cathedral, SF 58
Griffith Park, LA 98

health 13, 21
Hearst Castle 34–35, 83
historic ships 59, 120
Hollywood, LA 36–37
Hollywood Roosevelt Hotel 36
Hollywood Wax Museum, LA
  98
House of Pacific Relations,
  San Diego 119
Huntington Art Center,
  Huntington Beach 111
Huntington Library, Art Gallery
  and Botanical Gardens 98–99
Hyde Street Pier, SF 59

insurance 12, 13
International Surfing Museum,
  Huntington Beach 111

Jackson 68
Jamestown 68
Jeremiah O'Brien, SS 32
John Muir Trail 45
Joshua Tree National
  Monument 109

Kelley Park, San Jose 77
Kenwood Vineyards 81
Kern County Museum,
  Bakersfield 106
Knott's Berry Farm 112
La Jolla 119
Lady Bird Johnson Cove 43
Laguna Art Museum, Laguna
  Beach 112
Lake Arrowhead 110
Lake Merritt 75
Lake Tahoe 70
language 23
Lassen Volcanic National Park
  70–71
Lick Observatory, San Jose 78
Little Tokyo, LA 99
Lombard Street, SF 59
Long Beach, LA 100
Los Angeles 91–103
Los Angeles County Museum
  of Natural History 96
Los Angeles State and County
  Arboretum 100

Mammoth Lakes 71
Mann's Chinese Theatre, Los
    Angeles 36–37, 100–101
Mariposa 68
Mariposa Grove 44
Maritime Museum of San
    Diego 120
Marshall Gold Discovery State
    Historic Park 67
McHenry Museum and
    Mansion, Modesto 72
Mendocino 72
Mercer Caverns 67
Metropolitan Museum of Art,
    History and Science, Fresno
    108
Mission Bay Park, San Diego
    120
Mission San Francisco de Asis,
    SF 60
Mission San Juan Capistrano
    112–113
Modesto 72
money 20
Monterey Peninsula 38–39
Morro Bay 84–85
Mount Shasta 72–73
Museum of Contemporary Art
    (MOCA), LA 101
Museum of Man, San Diego
    121

Napa Valley 40–41, 79
national holidays 14
National Steinbeck Center,
    Salinas 39, 86
Natural Bridges State Beach 74
North Beach, SF 60–61
North Star Mine Museum,
    Grass Valley 69
Northern California 65–81

Oakland 74–75
Ocean Beach, San Diego 63
Octagon House, SF 63
Old Town San Diego State
    Historical Park 121
opening hours 22
Orange County 111–113
Oxnard 85

Palace of Fine Arts, SF 61
Palm Springs 114–115
Palomar Mountain 115
Paramount Studio 37

passports and visas 12
Petaluma 75
Petersen Automotive Museum,
    LA 101
Petrified Forest 41
Point Lobos State Reserve 39
police 21, 22
postal services 20, 22
Presidio Park, San Diego 121
public transportation 17

Queen Mary 100

Rainbow Basin National Natural
    Landmark 107
Redwood National Park 42–43
Richard Nixon Presidential
    Library and Birthplace 113
Riverside 115
Ronald Reagan Presidential
    Library, Simi Valley 128
Rosicrucian Egyptian Museum
    and Planetarium, San Jose
    77 -78

Sacramento 76–77
Sacramento Zoo 76
St. Helena 41
St. Mary's Cathedral of the
    Assumption, SF 61
Salinas 39, 86
San Buenaventura Mission,
    Ventura 89
San Diego 26–27, 116- 125
San Diego Wild Animal Park 124
San Diego Zoo 26, 27
San Francisco 49–63
San Francisco Museum of
    Modern Art 62
San Jose 77–78
Santa Ana 128
Santa Barbara 86–88
Santa Rosa 79
Santa Ynez 83
Sausalito 78
Scotty's Castle 108
Scripps Oceanography and
    Birch Aquarium, San Diego
    125
SeaWorld, San Diego 125
senior citizens 19
Sequoia Park 96
Sequoia National Park 126–127
Sherman Library and Gardens,
    Newport Beach 113

Silverado Museum, St. Helena
    41
Silverado Trail 40
Simi Valley 128
Soledad 128
Solvang 83, 88
Sonoma Valley 79–80
South Coast Plaza 62
Southern California 105–129
Southwest Museum, LA 102
Spirit of Sacramento 76, 77
Squaw Valley Ski Area 70
State Capitol, Sacramento 76
Steinbeck, John 39, 86
students 19
Sutter's Fort, Sacramento 76

taxis 17
telephones 21
time differences 13
tipping 21
tourist offices 13, 20
trains 16, 17
Transamerica Pyramid, SF 62
Twain, Mark 68

Union Street, SF 63
Universal Studios Hollywood
    and CityWalk 102

Venice Beach 91, 103
Ventura 89

Walk of Fame, Hollywood 37
walks
    Beverly Hills, LA 94–95
    Chinatown, SF 56–57
    San Diego 122–123
    Sequoia National Park
        126–127
Watts Towers and Arts Center,
    LA 103
websites 13
Wells Fargo History Museum,
    SF 63
Winchester Mystery House,
    San Jose 78
Wine Country 79–81
Wrigley Mansion, Catalina
    Island 29

Yosemite National Park 44–45

Zuma Beach 91

Acknowledgements

The Automobile Association wishes to thank the following photographers, companies and picture libraries for their assistance in the preparation of this book.

Abbreviations for the picture credits are as follows – (t) top; (b) bottom; (l) left; (r) right; (c) centre; (AA) AA World Travel Library.

4l I-5 Freeway, AA/M Jourdan; **4c** Monterey Bay, AA/R Ireland; **4r** Russian Hill, San Francisco, AA/K Paterson; **5l** Gaslamp Quarter, San Diego, AA/M Jourdan; **5c** Road leading to Hollywood sign, AA/C Sawyer; **6** Lombard Street, San Francisco, AA/C Sawyer; **7** Walk of Fame pavement, Los Angeles, AA/M Jourdan; **8** Bel Air Mansion, AA/C Sawyer; **9** Yosemite Falls, Yosemite National Park, AA/R Ireland; **10/11** I-5 Freeway, AA/M Jourdan; **12** Inline Skater, Venice Beach, AA/C Sawyer; **14/15** Memorial Day Parade, San Diego, AA/M Jourdan; **16/17** Portal Railway Museum, AA/R Ireland; **18** Tour Thru Tree, AA/R Ireland; **19** Policeman, AA/R Ireland; **24/25** Monterey Bay, AA/R Ireland; **26** Balboa Park after dark, Balboa Park; **26/27** California Building in Copley Park. Balboa Park; **28** Catalina Island, Courtesy of Anaheim/Orange Country Visitor and Convention Bureau; **30/31** Disneyland® Park, © 2007 Disney Enterprises, Inc; **32** Golden Gate Bridge, AA/K Paterson; **33** Golden Gate Bridge, AA/K Paterson; **34** Hearst Castle from the air, Hearst Castle; **35** Hearst Castle, main library, Hearst Castle; **36** Hollywood Walk of Fame, AA/C Sawyer; **37** Hollywood sign, AA/P Wilson; **38** Monterey Bay Aquarium, AA/R Ireland; **38/39** Monterey Bay, AA/R Ireland; **40/41** Vineyard in Napa Valley, AA/R Ireland; **41** Villa Sattui winery, Napa Valley, AA/H Harris; **42** Big Basin Redwoods State Park, AA/K Paterson; **42/43** Big Basin Redwoods State Park, AA/K Paterson; **44** Yosemite Falls, AA/R Ireland; **44/45** El Capitan Cathedral Rocks, AA/R Ireland; **46/47** Russian Hill, San Francisco, AA/K Paterson; **49** San Francisco Museum of Modern Art, AA/K Paterson; **50t** Cell in Alcatraz, AA/H Harris; **50b** Ferry, San Francisco, AA/K Paterson; **51** Asian Art Museum, exhibits, AA/K Paterson; **52/53** Cable Car Museum, San Francisco, AA/K Paterson; **53** Palace of the Legion of Honor, San Francisco, AA/K Paterson; **54/55** Fisherman's Wharf, San Francisco, AA/K Paterson; **56** Chinatown, San Francisco, AA/K Paterson; **57** Lantern, Chinatown, San Francisco, AA/K Paterson; **58** Grace Cathedral, San Francisco, AA/K Paterson; **58/59** Hyde Street Pier, San Francisco, AA/K Paterson; **59** Lombard Street, San Francisco, AA/B Smith; **60/61** Stained Glass window, Mission Dolores, San Francisco, AA/K Paterson; **61** Palace of Fine Arts, San Francisco, AA/K Paterson; **62** San Francisco Museum of Modern Art, AA/K Paterson; **62/63** Transamerica Pyramid, San Francisco, AA/K Paterson; **63** Wells Fargo Museum, gold exhibit, AA/K Paterson; **64** Lassen Volcanic Park, AA/R Ireland; **65** Pine Ridge Winery, Napa Valley, AA/H Harris; **66/67** Winter Sequoia National Park, Brand X Pictures; **69** Exhibit, Wells Fargo Museum, AA/K Paterson; **70** Lake Tahoe, AA/R Ireland; **70/71** Lassen Volcanic Park, AA/R Ireland; **72/73** Black Butte, Mount Shasta range, AA/R Ireland; **74/75t** Treasure Island Marina, AA/B Smith; **74/75b** View towards Treasure Island, AA/K Paterson; **76/77** Sacramento, AA/K Paterson; **77** Rosicrucian Egyptian Museum, San Jose, AA/K Paterson; **78/79** Rosicrucian Egyptian Museum, San Jose, AA/K Paterson; **79** Rhine House, Napa Valley, AA/K Paterson; **80/81** Grapes, Napa Valley, AA/H Harris; **82** Cypress Tree, Carmel, AA/R Ireland; **83** Santa Barbara, AA/C Sawyer; **84/85** Carmel Beach, AA/R Ireland; **86** Santa Barbara, Paseo Nuevo Center, AA/C Sawyer; **87** Santa Barbara, AA/C Sawyer; **88/89** Solvang, Alamy (© David Muscroft); **90** Rollerblading, Santa Monica, AA/M Jourdan; **91** Chinatown Shops, Los Angeles, AA/M Jourdan; **92** Sunset Boulevard Sign, AA/M Jourdan; **92/93** Stretch limo, Beverley Hills, Los Angeles, AA/M Jourdan; **93** City Hall, Old Pasadena, AA/P Wilson; **94t** Beverly Hills Hotel sign, AA; **94b** Vermont and Sunset Metro station, Los Angeles, AA/M Jourdan; **95** Rodeo Drive, Los Angeles, AA/C Sawyer; **96** Natural History Museum, Los Angeles, AA/M Jourdan; **96/97** Getty Center, Central Garden, AA/M Jourdan; **97** Stan Laurel memorial, Forest Lawn Memorial Park, AA/P Wilson; **98** James Dean Statue, Griffith Park Observatory, Los Angeles, AA/M Jourdan; **98/99t** Japanese Garden, Huntington Library, Los Angeles, AA/P Wilson; **98/99b** Little Tokyo, Los Angeles, AA/M Jourdan; **100** Long Beach Shoreline Village, AA/C Sawyer; **101** Mann's Chinese Theatre, Los Angeles, AA/M Jourdan; **102/103** Lifeguard station, Venice Beach, Los Angeles, AA/M Jourdan; **104** Surfer, AA/N Hicks; **105** Death Valley National Monument, Imagestate; **106/107t** Angel Stadium, Anaheim, Courtesy of AOCVCB/Lovero Group; **106/107b** Anaheim Ducks Sculpture, Honda Center, Anaheim, Courtesy of Anaheim/Orange Country Visitor and Convention Bureau; **108/109t** Death Valley National Monument, Brand X Pictures; **108/109b** Joshua Tree National Park, Imagestate; **110** Orange County Sunset, Courtesy of Anaheim/Orange Country Visitor and Convention Bureau; **112** Snoopy at Knotts Berry Farm, Courtesy of AOCVCB/Knotts Berry Farm; **112/113** Mission San Juan Capistrano, AA/K Paterson; **114** Amtrak Train, Courtesy of Anaheim/Orange Country Visitor and Convention Bureau; **114/115** Antique Shop in the Olde Towne Orange, Courtesy of AOCVCB/Ellen Clark; **116/117** Surfer, Malibu, AA/M Jourdan; **118/119** International Aerospace Hall of Fame, San Diego, AA/M Jourdan; **120** Star of India, Maritime Museum, San Diego, AA/M Jourdan; **122/123** Gaslamp Quarter, San Diego, AA/M Jourdan; **124/125** San Diego Zoo, Courtesy of Anaheim/Orange Country Visitor and Convention Bureau; **126** Sequoia National Park, Brand X Pictures; **127** Sequoia National Park, Brand X Pictures; **128** Discovery Science Center at night, Santa Ana, Courtesy of Anaheim/Orange Country Visitor and Convention Bureau; **129** Death Valley National Monument, Brand X Pictures

Every effort has been made to trace the copyright holders, and we apologise in advance for any unintentional omissions or errors. We would be pleased to apply any corrections in any following edition of this publication.

Maps

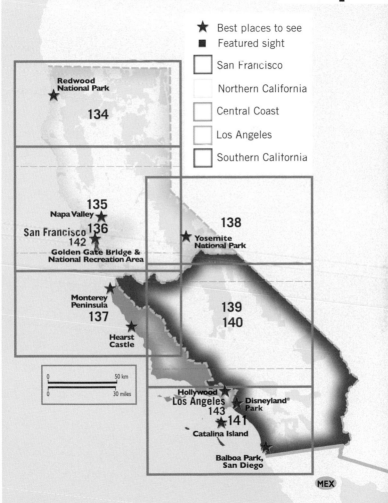

★ Best places to see
■ Featured sight
☐ San Francisco
☐ Northern California
☐ Central Coast
☐ Los Angeles
☐ Southern California

Redwood National Park
★
134

135
Napa Valley ★
San Francisco ★ 136
142 ★
Golden Gate Bridge & National Recreation Area

138
★ **Yosemite National Park**

Monterey Peninsula ★
137

Hearst Castle ★

139
140

0 ___ 50 km
0 ___ 30 miles

Hollywood ★ ★ **Disneyland® Park**
Los Angeles
143 ★ 141
★
Catalina Island

★
Balboa Park, San Diego

MEX

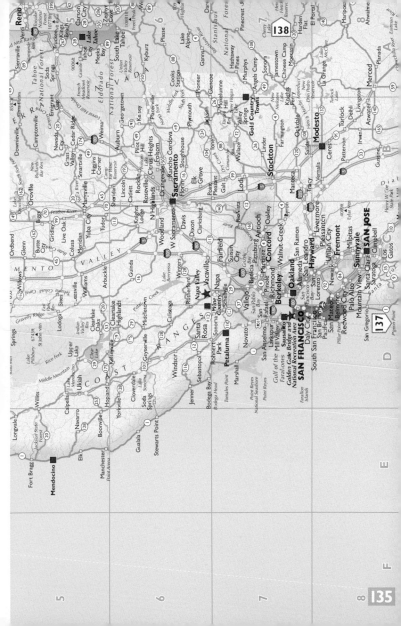

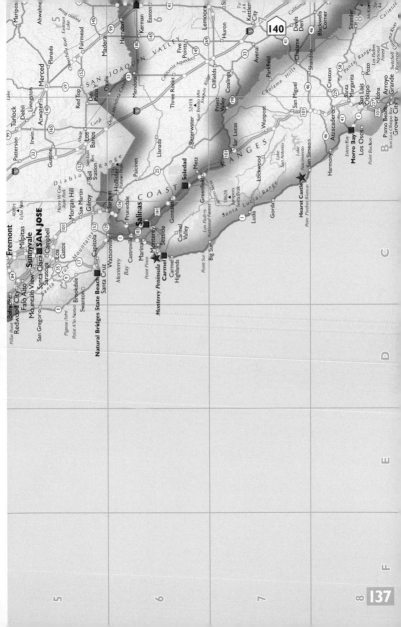

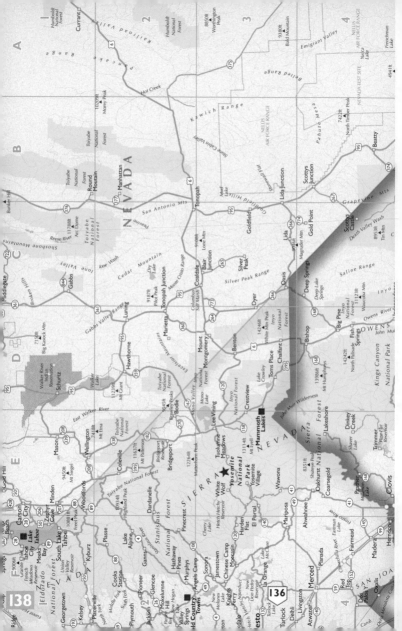

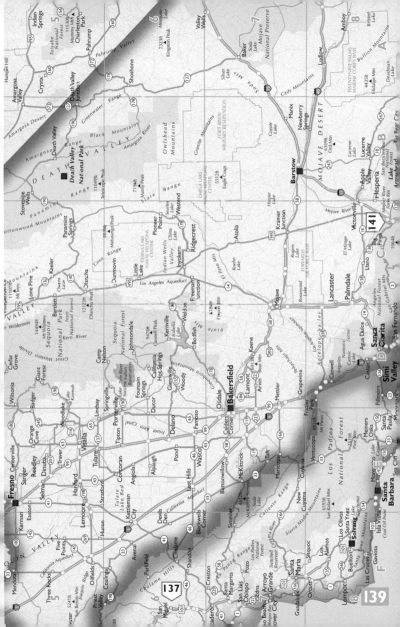

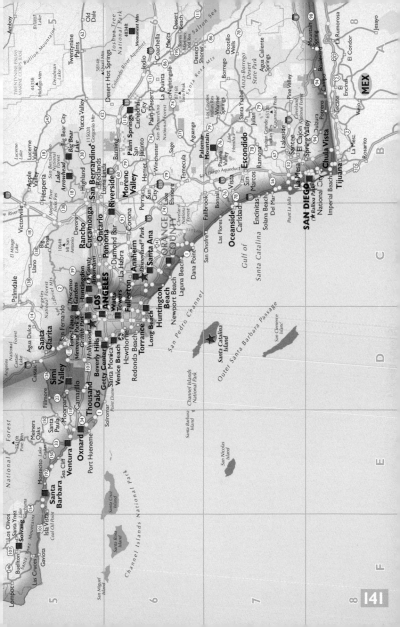

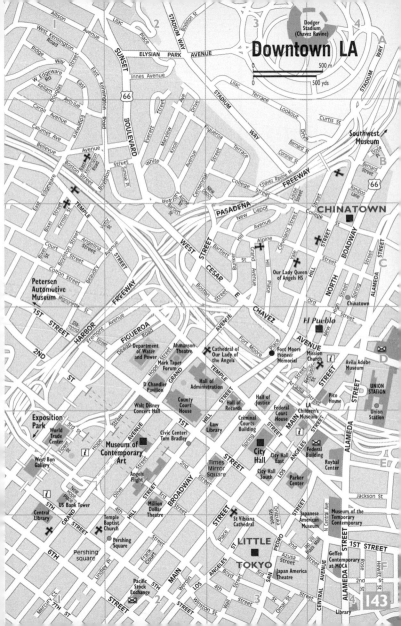

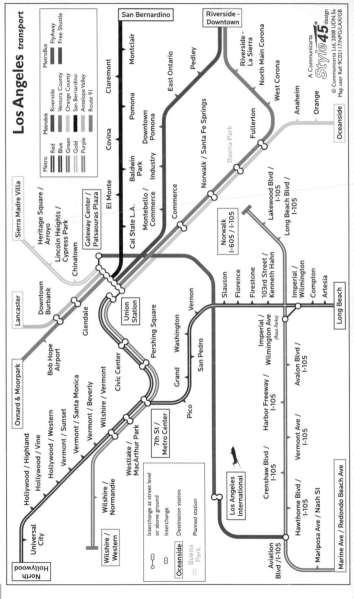

Los Angeles *transport*

San Bernardino

Riverside - Downtown

Metro
- Red
- Blue
- Green
- Gold
- Purple

Metrolink
- Riverside
- Ventura County
- Orange County
- San Bernardino
- Antelope Valley
- Route 91

MetroBus
- FlyAway
- Free Shuttle

Montclair

Pedley

East Ontario

Riverside - La Sierra

North Main Corona

West Corona

Claremont

Pomona

Downtown Pomona

Fullerton

Anaheim

Orange

Covina

Baldwin Park

Industry

Norwalk / Santa Fe Springs

Buena Park

Oceanside

El Monte

Cal State L.A.

Montebello / Commerce

Commerce

Sierra Madre Villa

Heritage Square / Arroyo

Lincoln Heights / Cypress Park

Chinatown

Gateway Center / Patsaouras Plaza

Lancaster

Downtown Burbank

Glendale

Union Station

Pershing Square

Civic Center

Bob Hope Airport

Oxnard & Moorpark

Hollywood / Highland

Hollywood / Vine

Hollywood / Western

Vermont / Sunset

Vermont / Santa Monica

Vermont / Beverly

Wilshire / Vermont

Wilshire / Normandie

Wilshire / Western

Universal City

North Hollywood

Westlake / MacArthur Park

7th St / Metro Center

Washington

Grand

San Pedro

Pico

Vernon

Slauson

Florence

Firestone

103rd Street / Kenneth Hahn

Imperial / Wilmington Ave
(Rosa Parks)

Imperial / Wilmington

Compton

Artesia

Long Beach

Norwalk
I-605 / I-105

Lakewood Blvd / I-105

Long Beach Blvd / I-105

Harbor Freeway / I-105

Avalon Blvd / I-105

Vermont Ave / I-105

Crenshaw Blvd / I-105

Hawthorne Blvd / I-105

Aviation Blvd / I-105

Mariposa Ave / Nash St

Marine Ave / Redondo Beach Ave

Los Angeles International

Interchange at street level or above ground

Interchange

Destination station

Planned station

Oceanside

Buena Park

144